AF541433

HOSTILITY

HOSTILITY

A DIPLOMAT'S DIARY ON PAKISTAN-INDIA RELATIONS

ABDUL BASIT

HarperCollins *Publishers* India

First published in Pakistan in 2021 by
Lightstone Publishers (Pvt) Ltd,
Plot no. B-113, Sector 6/F, Mehran Town, Korangi Industrial Area
Karachi 74900, Pakistan

First published in India in 2021 by
HarperCollins *Publishers*
A-75, Sector 57, Noida, Uttar Pradesh 201301, India
www.harpercollins.co.in

2 4 6 8 10 9 7 5 3 1

Copyright © Abdul Basit 2021

P-ISBN: 978-93-5422-645-8
E-ISBN: 978-93-5422-697-7

The views and opinions expressed in this book are
the author's own and the facts are as reported by him,
and the publishers are not in any way liable for the same.

Abdul Basit asserts the moral right
to be identified as the author of this work.

All rights reserved. No part of this publication may be reproduced,
stored in a retrieval system, or transmitted, in any form or by any means,
electronic, mechanical, photocopying, recording or otherwise,
without the prior permission of the publishers.

Printed and bound at
Thomson Press (India) Ltd

This book is produced from independently certified FSC™ paper
to ensure responsible forest management.

In memory of my parents
Hakeem Abdul Hafeez Nadvi
and
Begum Zia Tabassum

Dedicated to the valiant people
of Jammu & Kashmir

Contents

Acronyms 7
Acknowledgements 9
Introduction 11

Chapters
1. From Berlin to New Delhi, Not Islamabad 27
2. 2014 39
3. 2015 95
4. 2016 143
5. 2017 200
6. Back in Pakistan 238
7. Fine Words Butter No Parsnips 249
8. Epilogue 281

Annexures
Annex I - Fax message of 25 October 2014 signed by Foreign Secretary Jilani 309
Annex II - Sharm el Sheikh Joint Statement of 16 July 2009 310
Annex III - Joint Statement of 6 January 2004 311
Annex IV - Ufa Joint Statement of 10 July 2015 312
Annex V - Joint Statement of 9 December 2015 313
Annex VI - Agreement on consular access between Pakistan-India on 21 May 2008 314
Annex VII - UNCIP Resolution of 13 August 1948 316
Annex VIII - UNSC Resolution of 23 December 1952 319
Annex IX - Pak-China Boundary Agreement of March 1963 321
Annex X - UNSC Resolution of 6 June 1998 325

Suggested Bibliography 328
About the Author 331

Acronyms

AFSPA	Armed Forces Special Powers Act
BCCI	Board of Control for Cricket in India
BJP	Bharatiya Janata Party
CBMs	Confidence Building Measures
COAS	Chief of Army Staff
CPEC	China-Pakistan Economic Corridor
FICCI	Federation of Indian Chambers of Commerce and Industry
FIR	First Information Report
FoDP	Friends of Democratic Pakistan
FSA	Foreign Service Academy
GB	Gilgit-Baltistan
HoA	Heart of Asia Conference on Afghanistan
HuM	Hizbul Mujahideen
ICJ	International Court of Justice
IPRI	Islamabad Policy and Research Institute
ISI	Inter-Services Intelligence of Pakistan
IWT	Indus Waters Treaty
JeM	Jaishe-e-Mohammad
JuD	Jamat ud Dawah
KP	Khyber Pakhtunkhwa
LeT	Lashkar-e-Taiba
MEA	Ministry of External Affairs of India; and Minister for External Affairs

MFN	Most-Favored Nation
MoFA	Ministry of Foreign Affairs of Pakistan
MRM	Muslim Rashtriya Manch
NAM	Non-Aligned Movement
NDMA	Non-Discriminatory Market Access
NIA	National Investigation Agency of India
NOC	No Objection Certificate
NPT	Nuclear Non-Proliferation Treaty
NSA	National Security Advisor
NSG	Nuclear Suppliers Group
OIC	Organization of Islamic Cooperation
PAK	Pakistan Administered Kashmir
PCB	Pakistan Cricket Board
PDP	People's Democratic Party
PTI	Pakistan Tehreek-i-Insaf
R&AW	Research and Analysis Wing of India
RSS	Rashtriya Swayamsevak Sangh
SAARC	South Asian Association for Regional Cooperation
SAPM	Special Assistant to Prime Minister
SCO	Shanghai Cooperation Organization
SIT	Special Investigation Team
SOM	Senior Officials Meeting
UNHRC	United Nations Human Rights Council

Acknowledgements

I had first thought of writing a book on my diplomatic experiences when I was appointed spokesperson of the Ministry of Foreign Affairs (MoFA) in January 2009. From there, I was posted to Berlin as Pakistan ambassador in early 2012. Though I still wanted to start the book project as soon as possible, lethargy never let me embark on this seemingly difficult journey.

It was my posting to New Delhi in 2014 under almost sui generis circumstances, and then the fairly eventful stint and the equally peculiar circumstances under which I had to leave New Delhi that I was kind of pushed towards rethinking the project. However, as soon I returned from India, I took over the reins of the Islamabad Policy Research Institute (IPRI) and also started a TV talk show. Then some domestic chores, including the construction of my house and back-to-back weddings of my son Ammar and daughter Umamah had driven me almost crazy. With both official and domestic work pressures, writing a book became a forgotten proposition.

It was on 12 April 2020 that I was talking to Mr Murtaza Shibli, a well-known Kashmiri writer and columnist, with whom I had shared my plans to write a book when I first met him in India. When he asked me about the proposed book, I felt somewhat ashamed that I had not even prepared an outline. He was so emphatic in his encouragement that I got convinced especially when time was aplenty due to the COVID-19 pandemic. I started writing on 13 April and completed and sent the manuscript to the publishers by August.

I am grateful to many for their advice and support, especially my wife, Summiya, without whose support this work would have not been possible. As my life partner, she has been with me through my ups and downs. The time spent in India was indeed very exciting, but there also were enormous pressures to cope with. We kept up the appearances together.

My children also kept pushing me lest I abandon the project halfway through. They know the down sides of their father quite well. My father-in law, Dr Abdul Haseeb had also, perhaps unknowingly, maintained the pressure on me by assiduously asking me about its progress.

Of my former colleagues, I may express my gratitude to Foreign Secretary Shamshad Ahmad Khan, Ambassador Sher Afgan, Ambassador Burhanul Islam and my coursemate and alter-ego, Khalid Mahmood, presently Chairman, Sindh Board of Revenue, for their words of encouragement.

I am also beholden to Ms Ameena Saiyid OBE, S.I., Chairperson and Managing Director of Lightstone Publishers who readily and very kindly agreed to publish the book.

Last but not the least, I am indebted to Nadia Ghani for her careful editing.

It was a pleasure working with the team at HarperCollins for publication of the Indian edition of this book. I am particularly grateful to Swati Chopra, executive editor, for her diligent work in completing the project in the shortest possible time.

This book may engender a few controversies. The responsibility of whatever it contains is fully and only mine.

Introduction

Hostility is not a memoir. Nor does it trace the history of Pakistan-India relations. It is, in large measure, about my tenure in India as Pakistan high commissioner from March 2014 to August 2017. It is my account of Pakistan-India relations during that period; the ups and downs that generated hopes and created stalemates; how the two sides dealt with them; why and how the bilateral relationship reached the present troublesome phase; whether there is any realistic possibility that the two countries would ever be able to become normal neighbors. In short, *Hostility* is not only about hostility between Pakistan and India but will also divulge how non-professionalism and personal grudges leave the art of diplomacy in disarray and, in turn, hurt state interests.

As the top Pakistan diplomat in New Delhi at the time when both Prime Minister Nawaz Sharif and Prime Minister Narendra Modi had made a very encouraging start with their first meeting in New Delhi on 27 May 2014, I do share some, if not total responsibility for the later developments on the diplomatic front.

Some in Pakistan and many in India continue to hold me responsible for not being able to build on the Modi-Sharif meeting. In fact, I am blamed, especially in India, for deliberately undermining the significant opportunities that had arisen. To them, I was uncompromisingly hawkish toward my host country and, perhaps, the most bellicose Pakistan high commissioner in India ever. Instead of contributing to building bridges, I was a source of exacerbating bilateral tensions, making sure that the initiatives taken to break deadlocks led to more deadlocks. In short, it was primarily because of me that Pakistan and India had not been able to take advantage of the bonhomie that the two prime ministers were able to generate and tried their utmost to retain even in the most difficult of circumstances.

Some even suggested that I was working at the behest of the Pakistan establishment and worked in close coordination with them rather than pursuing the peaceful aspirations of the civilian leadership. Had I not been the Pakistan high commissioner during that time period, things might have been relatively better. I somewhat crossed my mandate by displaying excessive zeal on Kashmir. Whenever relations were looking to take a positive turn, I would throw in a monkey wrench. For instance, I should have avoided meeting the Kashmiri leadership which led to the cancellation of India's foreign secretary's scheduled visit to Pakistan in August 2014. Similarly, there was no point in my speaking in New Delhi about the issues related to the Pathankot incident which had created avoidable additional difficulties in the bilateral relationship. In a nutshell, I failed to serve the cause of normalizing Pakistan-India relations.

This book is not an attempt to clarify my position or put the entire onus of recurring setbacks on others and cast aspersions. Throughout my stay in India, I did what I thought was in the best interests of Pakistan and in sync with the strategic framework of Pakistan's India policy. Even now, with the advantage of hindsight, I can say, with complete honesty and conviction, that I would not have conducted myself differently.

Diplomats, like other human beings, do come under pressure and, at times, do take decisions that may appear unintelligent and even undiplomatic. But how decisions are made is not always clear to outsiders. Thus, it is not uncommon to find analysts and experts forming and presenting their opinions driven by their own predilections and national prejudices.

At the public level, opinions are usually formed with half-truths and on the basis of what is shared or not shared by governments. Many developments taking place off-stage are made public to the extent possible, and rightly so, as diplomacy is not any other profession. Here, one is sometimes dealing with sensitive inter-state issues which require confidentiality even long after decisions have been made. Accordingly, I will still not be able to share many facets of our India policy and diplomacy as Pakistan's interests take precedence over everything else. But *Hostility* will still reveal many inside details hitherto unknown to the people on both sides of the border.

People who are in the business of diplomacy know full well that there are multiple dependent and independent variables that shove and shape inter-state relations. When relations are deeply rooted in hostility and mistrust, the space for diplomatic maneuverability is discouragingly limited. Positions on issues are profoundly entrenched, and showing flexibility even at the tactical level, becomes hugely problematic and controversial. Both Pakistan and India have been facing the same dilemma almost from the very outset of their independence.

Over the decades, instead of resolving the Jammu & Kashmir dispute through a United Nations-supervised plebiscite, as pledged by the two countries, we created more issues and more cleavages. Resultantly, we fought wars, went nuclear and tried to undermine each other at all levels with the implacable mutual hostility continuing to be the major impediment in fostering regional cooperation.

South Asia remains the least integrated region in the world with intra-regional trade barely touching 5 percent of its total trade. Like other regions in the world, South Asia is also facing massive common challenges, ranging from terrorism to climate change to a worsening water crisis. But regional cooperation cannot be established and fostered in a vacuum. There is so much unpredictability in bilateral relations that the South Asian Association for Regional Cooperation (SAARC), formed in 1985, is finding it harder and harder to realize its potential. So much so that it has now become hostage to confrontational Pakistan-India relations and is literally dysfunctional.

India is the biggest country in the region but it is not difficult to explain why it has not been up to the task. Though it claims to be the world's largest democracy, the country's internal situation and its external policies leave much to be desired in this context. Minorities in India, particularly Muslims, are going through a very rough patch. The recently introduced National Register of Citizens may leave close to 2 million Muslims stateless in the state of Assam alone. Earlier, we had seen how the historical Babri Mosque in Ayodhya, built in the first half of the 16th century, was razed to the ground by Hindu extremists on 6 December 1992; and the Gujarat inter-communal riots of 2002 in which close to 2,000 Muslims were massacred on Modi's watch. He was then the chief minister of Gujarat.

Even over 200 million Dalits are facing the wrath of the Indian right-wing extremists. The anachronistic caste system is intrinsically antithetical to liberal democratic norms and practices. But there is no possibility of India getting rid of this antediluvian system for aeons to come.

Recent judgments allowing the building of Ram Mandir at the site of Babri Mosque in Ayodhya and using dilatory tactics on hearing in cases against the revocation of Articles 370 and 35A related to Jammu & Kashmir have caused concern. Hindutva is gradually pushing India towards a binary that is not only retrogressive in its essence but also detrimental to India's long-term stability.

It is the Hindutva votary versus the rest who must accept Hinduism as the sole cultural basis of India. Those who do not would find their loyalties to India questioned. Thus, undue privileges given to them under the garb of secularism, such as Muslim personal laws, should be dispensed with to build a truly Hindu Rashtra (polity) with its native socio-politico economic systems. To Hindutva, anything that is not Hindu in its origin is exogenous and must be extirpated, even violently, if necessary.

On the external front, India has not even spared the landlocked, peaceful Hindu-majority Nepal; it was punished with an economic blockade for months when it refused to accept India's dictation on amendments to the Nepalese constitution in 2015 while the country was still struggling to recover from the devastation caused by the massive earthquake earlier that year. Its relations with other neighbors including Sri Lanka and the Maldives had also witnessed many a crises. And Bhutan, in any case, is literally treated as an extension of India, its Union Territory, with no jurisdiction over its foreign and defense policies.

On the other hand, skirmishes with China along the Line of Actual Control (LoAC) have now become almost commonplace—the deadliest taking place in the Ladakh region in May-June 2020. So, India may well claim to be seeking peace within and without but it cannot absolve itself of the responsibility for the mess its hubristic and self-serving policies have created in the region. No doubt, all states do pursue their interests and try to increase their regional and global clout commensurate with their respective potential. However, a country is highly unlikely to attain much, no matter how big it is, if it lacks the vision and capacity to be flexible and accommodative in its own backyard.

Not that everything is hunky dory in Pakistan. It has its own serious problems which ineluctably play out in its foreign relations. Minorities in Pakistan, though minuscule, do feel threatened at times and there have been unfortunate and reprehensible incidents of destroying their places of worship. There are also issues related to the abuse of the Blasphemy Law to settle personal scores as well as the problem of forced conversion of minor Hindu girls. But these are local issues and do not happen often. Nevertheless, federal and provincial governments have been taking measures to stop these abuses and violations. At least there is no official complicity in these matters. Pakistan is fully cognizant of its obligations under several international human rights conventions and has been taking all possible steps to plug the gaps in its system at all levels. There is definitely some improvement on the ground which is also acknowledged by the *Universal Periodic Review* at the Geneva-based United Nations Human Rights Council.

Also, civil-military relations are a perennial problem and it manifests itself in different ways in both internal and external policy matters. Indians would always argue that engaging with the civilian leadership of Pakistan is meaningless as the shots are called by the military establishment. It is also a widely held view in India that it is the Pakistan Army and the ISI (Inter-Services Intelligence) that do not let India-Pakistan relations improve and normalize as that would take away the very raison d'etre of maintaining such huge armed forces which, given Pakistan's serious economic constraints, cannot be justified.

There is no gainsaying that Pakistan has not been able to establish strong democratic traditions and systems for a raft of reasons. The subject is vast and beyond the purview of this book. Suffice it to say that democracy is not only about holding elections after every four or five years but also, in my view, more about social attitudes and the national mindset that help determine whether a particular state is indeed democratic. These democratic attitudes evolve overtime. Transformation is a process and not an event; there are no shortcuts. Pakistan is moving slowly but surely towards improving and consolidating the democratic gains it has made during the last 12 years or so. Aberrations still exist but Pakistan, as a whole, is moving in the right direction.

The free electronic and print media and now also the social media are integral to democracy. The fact that the media engages in no-holds-barred criticism of the government on all issues day in and day out is a good omen for the country. The media itself is yet to come of age. Lack of professionalism and non-adherence to the journalistic code of ethics do create problems occasionally, but I genuinely believe that the genie is now out of the bottle and no government in Pakistan can take the risk of muzzling the media. The world has changed and the tools available to people to express themselves and put across their views freely cannot be taken away from them, even if any future government wants to get into such a futile and regressive adventure. Pakistan is no longer the country of the 1980s.

Coming back to *Hostility*, readers should know from the very beginning that it is not a research work written by following a well-established and universally accepted research methodology. This book is based on my own extensive notes which I started taking when I took over as MoFA spokesperson in January 2009. Moreover, human beings, no matter how hard they try, cannot be absolutely objective. But I can assure readers that this book is not written with the purpose of maligning anyone or bragging about myself. The sole purpose for me was to straighten the record on several issues and clear the miasma that still surrounds them.

However, to maintain some sanity in terms of methodology, I have structured this book in chronological order as far as possible. As inter-state relations cannot be strictly compartmentalized by year, I do at times switch back and forth so that the reader gets a full picture of an issue under discussion. On some complex issues I have dilated in more detail with historical background to remove ambiguities to the extent as is possible. Despite this, I would still refrain from calling this book totally free from my personal and national subjectivities. But I can at least claim that this work is an honest effort that tries to capture the essence of Pakistan-India relations during the period I served in New Delhi.

This book also covers the period from August 2017 to August 2020 when many bilateral issues kept resurfacing as I used to caution Islamabad from New Delhi. Moreover, there are also some important post-retirement stories to share with readers and my assessment on what the future holds for Pakistan in the growingly complex world. At the end, I also give a couple of suggestions towards reorganizing the MoFA as, without the appropriate organizational set-up and wherewithal, policies remain mostly non-implementable and desirable objectives ever more elusive.

I could have written this book in the form of a memoir covering my entire diplomatic career. From Moscow to New Delhi, this has been an exciting and wonderful journey. I was witness to many critical phases in our foreign policy. Even when I was posted in Moscow as Third Secretary in 1985, there was so much happening between the erstwhile Soviet Union and Pakistan in the context of Afghanistan. There are countless stories to tell including about the first-ever visit by a Pakistani diplomat to Dagestan, its capital Makhachkala and the historical city of Narin. The report I submitted on the visit was also seen by the then President General Mohammad Zia ul-Haq, who had, through the foreign office, sent me a letter of appreciation.

From Islamabad I wanted to be posted to Pakistan Permanent Mission to the United Nations in New York but, for some odd reason, I landed at the Pakistan Consulate General in the Big Apple in 1991. Though initially I was somewhat unhappy, as I started working there, I found how lucky I was to have been given the opportunity to serve Pakistanis. It was a very enriching experience. Our Consul General, Iqbal Ahmad Khan, was the finest boss one could wish for. I would always cherish the way we worked hand-in-hand with Pakistani-Americans to promote Pakistan's interests in the United States. Organizing the annual Pakistan Day parade in Manhattan on 14 August was a great experience in its own right especially in view of petty intra-Pakistan community differences. We had also organized an open concert in the Central Park where the late maestro, Nusrat Fateh Ali Khan, entertained the huge audience for over three hours.

From New York I was transferred to Sana'a, Yemen, in 1994. That was quite a journey as I am sure readers would imagine but that is how diplomats are trained to adapt. At the end, Sana'a also became a very satisfying stint because I was able to contribute effectively towards enhancing Pakistan's imports into Yemen significantly within two years. Sana'a is known as the Chicago of West Asia for its centuries-old multi-storied buildings, which are truly architectural marvels. Once the Arabia Felix (Happy Arabia) and the land of Queen Sheba, it is once again in the throes of a gory civil war with no end in sight. Millions of Yemenis have become homeless facing hunger, disease and death. I pray for Yemen to become Happy Arabia again. In August 1997, I was posted back to Islamabad.

Then, as Director (Disarmament) in the foreign office during the time of the nuclear tests in 1998, I was part of the internal discussions in the foreign office. Former Foreign Secretary, Shamshad Ahmad Khan, had played an important role in ensuring that Pakistan did not dither. The date 28 May 1998 was a proud day for all Pakistanis. We must keep paying tributes to Dr Abdul Qadeer Khan for leading Pakistan's nuclear program and delivering despite heavy odds. During those 17 days after India had conducted its nuclear tests on 11 May 1998, Pakistan was under immense US pressure to not respond in kind. There used to be daily meetings in MoFA that would also be attended by Dr Khan.

The last time I met this hero of Pakistan was on 25 May 2018 at his Islamabad residence. He was very kind to receive me and share his experiences, especially about how the then leadership was double-minded about conducting nuclear tests and how he eventually managed to prevail upon them. Despite what he subsequently went through, he has not become bitter in any way. He is a true son of the soil. His columns on different subjects that appear regularly in Pakistan's largest newspapers are invariably worth reading.

From Islamabad, I was transferred to Geneva in 2001; represented Pakistan at the 65-member Conference on Disarmament, participated in protracted negotiations on several arms control issues related to Biological Weapons

Convention; Certain Conventional Weapons Convention; and above all, fought hard against commencing negotiations for a fissile material cut-off treaty that would not take into account the existing stockpiles of fissile material.

From Geneva, I was posted to London in 2003 and stayed there for almost five years, first as minister (political), and then as deputy high commissioner. I thoroughly enjoyed my work on many fronts, including restoring Pakistan's Commonwealth membership which was suspended following the 1999 military coup. Dr Maleeha Lodhi was the high commissioner and we worked hard with the Pakistani community to promote our interests in the United Kingdom. I remember, in particular, how we worked day and night to raise funds for the 2005 earthquake victims in Pakistan Administered Kashmir. It was also during those years and under the leadership of Dr Lodhi that we were able to get the two separate Parliamentary Groups on Pakistan and Kashmir established. The bilateral trade also increased substantially in Pakistan's favor. In the UK, opportunities for Pakistan abound. It is important to post the right persons as Pakistan high commissioner rather than obliging cronies who do little beyond keeping their masters happy.

And then, back in the foreign office from 2009–2012, we dealt with many a difficult situation including the US clandestine action against Osama bin Laden in Abbottabad; the Raymond Davis case; and the US attack on the Salalah check-post, all happening in 2011. In May 2012, I was posted to Berlin on my first ambassadorial assignment.

On the foreign policy front, whereas we can count many successes, there have also been some serious failures. This reminds me of a decision that I can now share only to highlight how sometimes the right decisions are taken after due process in MoFA, but then changed whimsically to cater to individual proclivities.

After India and Pakistan became de facto nuclear powers in May 1998, both countries were invited to attend a conference in New York under the aegis of the Nuclear Supplier's Group (NSG) in November 1998. There were in-depth discussions in MoFA whether Pakistan should attend. My Director General, the late Shahbaz (a great patriot and a man of uncompromising dignity and honor), and I were of the view that Pakistan should attend. Now that it had become a nuclear power, it should conduct itself accordingly. The NSG had invited Pakistan despite the fact it was not a party to the Nuclear Non-Proliferation Treaty (NPT). We firmly believed there was no reason for Pakistan to stay away from the conference, as engaging with the NSG was now in our strategic and long-term interest. When the dust of nuclear tests was settled, Pakistan should be working to join the NSG, and the New York conference was the opportune moment for Pakistan to take the first step in that direction.

As recommended by the Disarmament Division, Foreign Secretary Shamshad Ahmad Khan approved my name as Director (Disarmament) to attend the conference.

Just a day before I was to leave for New York, our then permanent representative in Geneva, Ambassador Munir Akram, sent a message strongly opposing Pakistan's participation on the ground that it would compromise our principled position vis-à-vis the discriminatory NPT and the NSG. To cut the long story short, Pakistan did not attend the NSG-sponsored conference. Now, looking back with the benefit of the hindsight, it is clear how ill-considered it was not to attend. There was nothing for Pakistan to lose but it could have gained an informal recognition as a nuclear weapons state. I can narrate many such foreign policy matters where decisions were made viscerally and not necessarily in consonance with Pakistan's long-term interests. Maybe I will have to write a separate book titled: *Pakistan's Foreign Policy and a Litany of Faux Pas*.

I am never hesitant of admitting where I err and do try to learn from my mistakes and not repeat them. Our weaknesses, our fallibilities are relative to our fellow human beings and the circumstances we live in. They are also judged by the impact they leave. Mistakes made in state matters affect millions and cannot be easily ignored or forgotten. Pakistan's bureaucracy is particularly adept at finding escape goats. It is our juniors who are always wrong. There is simply no worthwhile accountability, even though elaborate rules and procedures do exist. On the contrary, we shower praise on mediocrity and even end up rewarding those who knowingly play havoc with state interests. Whoever blows the whistle also has to suffer.

This reminds me of one of my ambassadors who favored one of his staff members so blatantly that I could not swallow it. I reported the matter to Islamabad but also endorsed a copy of my letter to the ambassador so that he would know I was not doing anything behind his back. To my utter shock, instead of reprimanding the ambassador, MoFA issued orders of my transfer back to the headquarters. I was obviously disturbed but that transfer became a blessing in disguise as my career took a turn for the better. I still hear stories of junior officers being punished for no wrongs but for their courage to stand up to the turpitudes of their seniors.

When the wheel of a ship is in weak and wrong hands for too long, a shipwreck becomes difficult to avoid. Whereas I do not see positive changes taking place any time soon, one hopes that the elaborate structural reforms being worked out by the

Imran Khan government, if implemented, will help rejuvenate the Pakistan bureaucracy and jolt it out of its protracted dormancy.

The Pakistan foreign office, in particular, has been in the tight grip of a few who would not let this otherwise great institution step up to the plate. Calling it a great institution may appear to readers as non sequitur. They may interpret it as my biases in favor of an organization with which I have worked for over 35 years. It is not always easy or possible to overcome such propensities.

But this does not mean I have lost the capacity to be critical of the foreign office and the way it works and pursues foreign policy objectives. It is, however, true that whenever I am critical, it is personally painful. The foreign office, like many other institutions in the country, is fast losing its prestige and reputation. Nepotism is the biggest curse for any organization; the foreign office has, unfortunately, seen more of this in the last fifteen years or so. It goes without saying that, until the foreign office reorganizes itself wholly and in an integrated manner, Pakistan's diplomacy will remain in doldrums and in the mode of fire-fighting.

MoFA is not just any institution. It is our first line of national defense but, alas, in the tight grip of self-proclaimed highly skillful professionals who build their reputation through sycophancy and by getting postings to important missions abroad. MoFA needs a major surgery; not a Panadol. There are officers who always get postings to "A" category stations like New York, Geneva, Washington DC and London. The principle of rotation must be followed and all officers must be given equal opportunities. It is only then can one judge where officers stand in terms of their professional skills in all aspects. Also, they should all be exposed to every facet of diplomacy in both bilateral and multilateral contexts. Every officer should also be put through the rigors of consular, protocol and administrative work so that, when they become ambassador, they do not become hostage to lack of experience in these vital areas.

Do Pakistan-India relations have a future that would be free of mutual hostility? Diplomats are usually cautious and hedge their bets. However, now I am retired and have the freedom to express my views freely. I am afraid I do not see any silver lining in the dark clouds that continue to envelop this vexed relationship. I sincerely hope I am off the mark because, at the end of the day, peace is in our mutual interest. Continuing hostility is a recipe for more crises, with increasing hazards of unprecedented consequences. A panacea may be around if only we were to comprehend the necessity of flexibility and hone our abilities in the art of the possible.

Let me now first take you to Berlin and tell you how I ended up becoming the Pakistan high commissioner in New Delhi instead of the foreign secretary of Pakistan.

1

From Berlin to New Delhi, Not Islamabad

I was into the second year of my tenure in Berlin. As Pakistan ambassador, I had been working reasonably well to inject more substance into our relations with Germany, the economic power house of the European Union. It was somewhat discouraging that Chancellor Angela Merkel had still not been to Pakistan despite being in the office since November 2005, whereas every Pakistani leader during this period had made it a point to pay an official visit to Germany. Taking her to Pakistan was one of my top priorities. However, I could not succeed for my stint in Germany came to an unexpectedly abrupt end.

It was the second week of October 2013 that I received a call from Syed Tariq Fatemi, Special Assistant to the Prime Minister on Foreign Affairs (SAPM), directing me to reach Islamabad immediately as the prime minister wanted to see me. Fatemi, despite my insistence, didn't share the purpose but laconically said, "Don't worry, it is something good." As soon as we hung up, I called Foreign Secretary Jalil Abbas

Jilani if he could let me know as to why I was being called for a meeting with the prime minister. I was surprised to know that he was not even aware that I had been asked to come to Islamabad. He said he would check with Fatemi and let me know. He never called me back.

As instructed, I took a flight from Frankfurt on 9 October arriving in Islamabad the same day. While I still had no official word, my hunch was that I was being posted to Beijing. However, my gut feeling was off the mark.

The next day, Fatemi took me to see the prime minister. Now it was clear that the prime minister had decided to appoint me as foreign secretary, since Jilani was being sent to Washington DC to replace Ms. Sherry Rahman who succeeded Hussain Haqqani. The latter had to step down in November 2011 following the "Memogate" scandal that revolved around a memorandum ostensibly written to seek help of the Obama administration to avert a military takeover in Pakistan which the then President Asif Ali Zardari had perhaps thought was imminent.

My call on Prime Minister Nawaz Sharif in the presence of Fatemi lasted for about twenty minutes. The prime minister conveyed to me that he had decided to appoint me as foreign secretary and that I should return to Islamabad as soon as possible. On my part, thanking him for the confidence he reposed in me, I assured the prime minister that I would spare no effort to promote and protect Pakistan's interests under his guidance.

The news of my appointment as the next foreign secretary was now public. Back in the foreign office, I called on Sartaj Aziz, Advisor to Prime Minister on Foreign Affairs and National Security. He congratulated me and expressed the hope that I would be able to contribute effectively. I also met the foreign secretary and some additional foreign secretaries including

Aizaz Ahmad Chaudhry, Ibne Abbas, Tasnim Aslam, Burhanul Islam and Mohammad Aqil Nadeem. The latter two and I were class-fellows at Islamabad's Quaid-e-Azam University, and our long friendship was well-known in the ministry. We celebrated the happy news of my elevation together over a dinner that night. We also discussed a slew of urgent organizational steps that were needed to restore the ministry's waning reputation and efficiency. In short, I also started identifying officers for different positions in the ministry shelving my personal likes and dislikes.

I have always believed that when one becomes a team leader, he or she should be fair, transparent and must have the confidence to delegate powers. Colleagues who have served with me in Berlin and New Delhi, or even at the headquarters when I was spokesperson/additional secretary, would hopefully vouch for what I am claiming. Doubtless, I have my own deficiencies and am cognizant of them but I would never intentionally harm anyone, nor would I ever engage in hatching conspiracies against my own colleagues. I strongly believe in the unchallengeable power of destiny.

I returned to Berlin after spending a week in Islamabad and my hometown, Peshawar, the capital of the Khyber-Pakhtunkhwa province.

Back in Berlin, I started winding up and had also informed my hosts that I would be leaving Germany by November end (as I had verbally discussed with Foreign Secretary Jilani), requesting them to arrange my farewell calls. All the while, I kept insisting to Jilani to put in writing what we had discussed in Islamabad including the dates of his departure for Washington DC and my arrival in Islamabad. I was fully aware of the weaknesses in our system, as well as of possible intrigues to undo the prime minister's decision.

Jilani had planned to relinquish charge on 1 December 2013. In a fax message of 25 October 2013 (Annexure I), he asked me to plan my arrival in Islamabad accordingly. He also informed me that, "I have moved a summary to formalize your appointment as Foreign Secretary."

It was painful to see subsequently off-the-record queries by Ms Mariana Babar of *The News*, being responded to with denial that Basit was ever asked to come to Islamabad. Ms Babar also called me for her story that was published on 10 December 2013, but I did not share much. I did not even mention the written instructions as then I had thought it was for the ministry to clarify that.

Germans are known for their highest standards of professionalism. They were generous and forthcoming. I was hosted over lunch by State Secretary Emily Haber. Special Representative for Afghanistan and Pakistan, Michael Koch, also hosted a dinner for me at his beautiful apartment. The Pakistani community in Germany also arranged events to bid me farewell. Me and my wife, Summiya, were overwhelmed by their genuine affection. Pakistanis in Germany had always been a great source of strength. They would always respond enthusiastically to national causes. I was looking forward to leaving Germany with fond memories.

My farewell call on President Joachim Gauk was on 28 October at 11:30 am. The same day, the Chief Minister of the Punjab, Mian Shahbaz Sharif, arrived in Berlin on a week-long visit. His younger son, Salman Shahbaz, was also part of the delegation. In an address to members of the Pakistani community at the embassy, Chief Minister Sharif, among other things, also felicitated me on being designated as foreign secretary.

My wife and I attended several farewell parties in Berlin, Frankfurt and other major cities of Germany. Now it was our turn to throw a party to reciprocate and say farewell to our German and Pakistani friends. We decided to host a reception on 28 November, that is, a day before our departure for Islamabad. As we were welcoming and entertaining our guests, Jilani called me to say that I should defer my departure date by a fortnight. He would, however, not share the reason. He asked me to wait for the ministry's further instructions.

I was obviously left shell-shocked but did not allow my guests to notice what I was going through. I delivered my farewell speech and then, from there, went straight to an international conference on Afghanistan. I was accompanied by my deputy Dr Mazhar Javed. On the way to the conference venue, I told Mazhar about the call I received from Jilani. I told him that I was smelling a rat knowing full well that there were many in our ministry who never wanted me to become foreign secretary. Mazhar, a thorough gentleman, however, consoled me; he was still hopeful that the prime minister's decision would be honored.

Throughout my career, I tried to deliver to the best of my abilities. I never believed in resorting to nepotism or patrons to climb the career ladder. I had seen some of my colleagues in utter disbelief when I was appointed as spokesperson of the foreign office in January 2009 after my return from London.

Ambassador Noor M. Jadmani, Director General in the Foreign Minister's Office and Ambassador Mohammad Sadiq, my predecessor as spokesperson, were both instrumental in my appointment. When Foreign Minister Shah Mahmood Qureshi visited London in 2008, he had informed me of his decision. Sadiq was under transfer to Kabul as Pakistan Ambassador.

The then foreign secretary, Salman Bashir, as I learnt later, was not in favor of appointing me as spokesperson. His preference was Ms Tehmina Janjua, who was to return from Geneva soon. Hence, I was not surprised (but definitely felt insulted) that, as soon Foreign Minister Qureshi resigned over the Raymond Davis issue, I was sacked by the foreign secretary and replaced by Janjua as spokesperson. This was done within a day so as to avoid any possible objection to the change by Ms Hina Rabbani Khar, who was to take over in a day or two as the new foreign minister.

I may be wrong, but Ms Khar was apparently not very happy with Janjua's work. Nevertheless, she was reluctant to remove her from the post as she was to leave on her first ambassadorial assignment in Rome later that year. As soon as she left for Italy, Ms Khar reappointed me as spokesperson, I am sure again to the chagrin of Salman Bashir. I also retained the charge of additional foreign secretary for Europe.

I found Ms Khar a very hard-working person, always willing to listen to logical arguments and appreciating quality work. I remember she got upset with me once as the briefing material that was prepared by the Europe Division for her official visit to London in May 2012 was not up to the usual standard. I was then under transfer to Berlin but took full responsibility as being in charge additional foreign secretary. As human beings we cannot always be at our best. However, she was extremely happy with her three-day official visit to Germany in September 2012 and I, as Pakistan ambassador in Berlin, ensured the visit went seamlessly and according to her priorities. She greatly impressed her German interlocutors by her clarity of vision and seriousness of purpose. In short, she was on top of everything and the way she conducted herself made us all proud as Pakistanis.

Earlier, Foreign Minister Qureshi had also appointed me as coordinator for "Friends of Democratic Pakistan" (FoDP) that was established in September 2008 to help Pakistan in economic development and institution building. The first and last summit-level meeting of the FoDP was held in New York in September 2009 which was co-chaired by President Zardari, US President Barack Obama and British Prime Minister Gordon Brown. The FoDP also held ministerial meetings in Istanbul, Dubai and Brussels. I attended all these meetings. The FoDP was consigned to history with the change of government in Islamabad after the general elections in 2013.

Foreign Secretary Bashir, after retirement, was sent to New Delhi though he wanted to go to Washington DC or New York. An officer working with him in New Delhi confided to me that Bashir was visibly unhappy over my appointment as foreign secretary. He knew that, if I were to become foreign secretary, it might be somewhat difficult for Janjua and then Sohail Mahmood, both of whom worked in his office as directors general, to be elevated to the coveted post, especially in the case of Janjua who would be retiring a year after my superannuation. I was not part of Salman Bashir's inner circle.

Aizaz Chaudhry, who was suffering from cancer, was preparing to leave for Brussels on his next ambassadorial assignment. As Fatemi told me, Aizaz himself opted for Brussels primarily to get better medical treatment. My appointment as foreign secretary must have forced him to think again. I was two years junior to him. It would be well-nigh impossible for him to become foreign secretary after three or so years. This was perhaps his last chance. On the other hand, Ambassador Sadiq was clearly the favorite of Sartaj Aziz who, in any case, had already been nominated for the post of Secretary in the newly created National Security Division.

As Aizaz was working with Jilani as additional foreign secretary, and was senior to me as well, I could not be the latter's first choice. An incumbent usually wants to be succeeded by someone who is beholden to him so that he can take care of his interests. Jilani going to Washington DC would have felt more comfortable with Aizaz as foreign secretary compared to Basit. Perhaps, Fatemi also acquiesced once Aizaz changed his mind. And the best way to undo my nomination was to block my promotion.

As it was known to Jilani that Prime Minister Nawaz Sharif had already decided to appoint me as foreign secretary, it was incumbent upon him to have ensured that I was promoted to Grade-22 (the highest grade in the civil services of Pakistan) at the promotion board to be held in November or early December. In fact, as he had informed me earlier in writing, my promotion case was being processed separately through a summary to the prime minister. And this was permissible under the rules. I could only conjecture as to what had finally happened to that summary or in the promotion board itself. I am still not aware of the details and, honestly speaking, never bothered to ascertain as that would have made no difference now that the decision was taken in favor of Aizaz to replace Jilani.

My only gripe was that the ministry should not have created an unnecessary bitter situation for me. Fatemi should have done his homework before calling me from Berlin. And when the prime minister had taken the decision to appoint me as the next foreign secretary, the procedural requirements should have been completed and a notification issued accordingly. That was not done; my promotion as I could assess was deliberately delayed by even promoting those officers, though senior to me, who had earlier been superseded. In the absence of sufficient seats, my name for promotion was put aside. Aizaz got the promotion and thus made foreign secretary on 18 December 2013. (I was promoted to Grade-22 in September 2014.)

Interestingly, when I went to see Aizaz in his office on 9 October, he himself told me that he was planning to leave for Brussels by end December.

He was to replace my very dear friend Ambassador Munawar Saeed Bhatti who, like Aizaz, was also suffering from cancer. He had requested the ministry for extending his stay there for a year after his retirement on 2 September 2013 with the view to completing his medical treatment. He was, however, given only three months, that is, until 31 December and that too because the European parliament was scheduled to vote on granting the Generalized System of Preferences (GSP) Plus facility to Pakistan in the second week of December. Bhatti, despite his critical illness, worked strenuously to get Pakistan the GSP Plus status. His commitment to Pakistan was simply incomparable.

Bhatti was allowed to stay in Brussels for three additional months but that happened only when Aizaz's designation to Brussels became redundant after his appointment as foreign secretary. Bhatti tried for a further extension but Aizaz, now foreign secretary, would argue that if he himself could be treated for cancer in Pakistan, there was no justification for others to seek an extension on health grounds. In fact, his successor was sent to Brussels and was asked to stay in the Pakistan House while Bhatti was still in the process of packing. Bhatti returned to Islamabad in April 2014. To the grief of many, this wonderful, lively and bright man left us for his heavenly abode in June 2015.

From my perspective, the entire foreign-secretary episode was quite disquieting and, as I said earlier, avoidable. Though feeling betrayed and humiliated, I nonetheless never lost my resolute faith in Allah. I was confident that I would be compensated by the Almighty in ways difficult to anticipate though it was now increasingly clear that I had missed the opportunity to ever serve my country as foreign secretary.

Be that as it may, I had made up my mind to not continue in Berlin. I spoke to Fatemi and also Shahbaz Sharif requesting them to get me transferred from Berlin. I was willing to go anywhere but preferably London as my children were studying/working there. This was also in some deference to my wife. Being a sensitive person, she took the entire episode to heart and was finding it difficult to reconcile to it. Considering her situation, I was of the view that it would be better if she were with her children. Moreover, as I had already served in London for close to five years, I thought I could contribute meaningfully to Pakistan-UK relations.

Additional Secretary Abbas had already been designated for New Delhi and he was all set to leave Islamabad soon. It never occurred to me that New Delhi could be my next possible destination. However, destiny has its own ways of disposing of things and it is better to readily and happily submit to it rather than continue whining in the wilderness. I have always believed that one should work hard and make all possible efforts to realize his/her aspirations but we should not become hostage to our ambitions. One must move on positively under all circumstances and leave the results to the Almighty.

I was informed about my posting to New Delhi by Fatemi. I was surprised, to say the least. I immediately called Abbas to make my position clear lest he assume that I upstaged him. He told me that, when Fatemi was speaking to me, he was sitting in his office and that he was fully in the loop. As it turned out subsequently, he was offered London instead. My wife still often blames me for accepting New Delhi in haste. Had we waited in Berlin for a few more months, we could have gone to London. And I always disagree. Who knows what was awaiting us in London. For me the priority then was to leave Berlin though we loved the city and enjoyed our stay every bit. Germans are a great people. Their resilience and professionalism as a nation are second to none.

I had never imagined that I would be given the distinct honor of representing Pakistan in New Delhi. Honestly, I could not have asked for more. I was very excited. Though I had never served anywhere in South Asia before, my stint as spokesperson for over three years had given me a fair idea of our antagonistic relations with India and the regional dynamics. I was aware of the complexities involved and the centrality of India in our diplomacy. Undeniably, there were no shortcuts to changing the bilateral paradigm of mutual hostility. However, I had a few ideas to put the bilateral relations on a predictable trajectory. As it turned out, things were far more complex to trump even seemingly workable ideas.

I was told by the ministry and our high commission in New Delhi that it would take around four to six weeks to receive India's formal consent to my appointment. I, therefore, should finalize my travel plans accordingly.

Before leaving Berlin, I had left a small brief for my successor, Ambassador Syed Hasan Javed, on the state of our relations with Germany and the initiatives I had taken during the last two years and how they should be pursued. I was particularly keen on Chancellor Merkel's visit to Pakistan and the long overdue establishment of a bilateral chamber of commerce without which, as the German system worked, augmenting bilateral economic and commercial relations to their potential would remain a dream. Also, I particularly underlined the importance of working very closely with the Pakistani community as some individuals were well entrenched in the German system and could be of immense help in meeting our politico-economic objectives vis-à-vis Germany and the European Union.

I had thought to first go to Islamabad, get briefings on bilateral relations, pay courtesy calls on the leadership and from there travel to New Delhi. However, the ministry did not acquiesce. They asked me to reach New Delhi from Berlin and, after I had presented my Letter of Credence, I would be called to Islamabad for consultations and calls on the president and the prime minister. Accordingly, I left for New Delhi on 2 March arriving there the same day.

2

2014

"If you don't stand for something, you will fall for anything."

Gordon A. Edie

Onboard the flight to New Delhi, I couldn't help thinking about how one felt helpless in front of one's destiny. We human beings can claim many things bordering on hubris and narcissism but the fact of the matter is that we can only make plans and strive. The Almighty is omnipotent and ubiquitous. He knows what is good and bad for us while we are generally impatient and often get antsy when we find our aspirations and goals unrealizable. People who resign to His will remain content and focused and ultimately successful in many different ways.

On arrival in New Delhi, my wife and I were given a very warm welcome by the high commission officials and their spouses. I had visited New Delhi only once before as part of the Pakistan delegation led by Salman Bashir in February 2010.

In fact, I had to request him to include me in the delegation and he did agree, although with some reluctance. No wonder, when he visited New Delhi again, he kept me out but this time I would not go and request him for the same. As foreign office spokesperson, I was a familiar face in India and often upbraided for my strong statements, especially on Kashmir.

When Bashir was visiting New Delhi the second time, the Indian officials and media were totally focused on the Mumbai attack of 26 November 2008 as if that was the root cause of all the bilateral problems. In order to put things in perspective, the day our delegation left for New Delhi, I, with the foreign minister's approval, issued a press release underlining that terrorism was also Pakistan's major concern, adding that India was showing no seriousness of purpose to bringing the culprits of the Samjhauta Express blast (18 February 2007), in which 42 Pakistani nationals were killed, to justice. That was in my view necessary to push forward our narrative conveying to India that Islamabad was not approaching the New Delhi talks from a position of weakness. Indeed, the two sides must discuss Mumbai if India so desired but Samjhauta could not be put on the back burner either.

My press release created a huge storm in New Delhi. Some commentators suggested that the statement was issued to sabotage the talks as there was no comparison between the two situations. I had already calculated how the Indians would bristle and blame Pakistan for avoiding Mumbai. However, my statement went down extremely well with the people of Pakistan. It also, in a way, strengthened the hands of our delegation in New Delhi by telling our Indian interlocutors how much public pressure there was on the government on Samjhauta. As Pakistan was fully cooperating on Mumbai, India must also meet its obligations regarding terrorism.

Our diplomacy lacked coherence and the requisite aggression vis-à-vis India. Resultantly, our narrative was not gaining much traction at the global level. Frankly, I didn't find much appetite within our own system to do things differently and meaningfully.

It saddens me to see we haven't changed much even after the lapse of over a decade. We go on doing the same things again and again and expect different, better results. The world is changing very fast. We need new thinking and creative ways for our diplomacy. There is no denying that challenges abound and thus there is all the more reason for us to be innovative. More about this will be covered in the last chapter.

Some of the healthy traditions in our foreign office have either disappeared or are fast dissipating. For instance, ambassadors, when they take over their assignment abroad, should, as a matter of good practice, write down their mission statement and share it with Islamabad. It serves two purposes. Firstly, this brings clarity to what he or she would like to achieve during the limited tenure of usually three years. Secondly, the headquarters would not only be able to evaluate the ambassador's performance against his/her own mission statement but could also write back to the ambassador to rejig his/her priorities in tune with the systemic and sub-systemic foreign policy objectives. While some of our ambassadors may still be writing their mission statements and sharing them with Islamabad, the practice has, by and large, become a thing of yesteryears.

As I did in Berlin, my first communication from New Delhi to Islamabad was to convey my mission statement. I met all my officers on 3 March. The idea was to know about their respective areas of duty; where did the state of bilateral relations stand; and what were the realistic prospects. The detailed discussion helped me prepare my mission statement which I sent to MoFA on 4 March.

It goes without saying that all ambassadors are supposed to use their tenure to expand their country's clout in their respective host countries by enhancing relations in all possible areas. And then the nature and contents of relations vary. For instance, mission statements for China, US and India cannot be the same. Our bilateral relations with each country are underpinned by a myriad of dependent and independent variables including also their respective political systems. There is no-one-size-fits-all formula, though diplomacy in its essence, does conduct itself in familiar ways.

Diplomacy is one of the oldest professions in the world. There are several diplomatic practices that remain relevant and useful to this day, far-reaching and mind-boggling technological developments notwithstanding.

My mission statement in New Delhi was easy and difficult at the same time. When the bilateral relationship is riven by disputes and conflicts; mutual trust is at the lowest; and the public opinion on both sides is etched in almost intractable hostility, there is thus not much that can be done. Calcified and skewed narratives cannot be remolded easily especially when heavy historical baggage is also involved. However, I was not to keep low and just manage the status quo. From my own personal perspective, this was the only opportunity for me where I could make a positive difference in Pakistan-India relations. I was immensely excited and looking forward to making contributions towards opening spaces for the two countries to make significant and irreversible progress.

I was fully cognizant of the enormity of the task given the entrenched positions and rigid views on both sides. The two countries had tried many approaches but every time they ended up back to square one. Most bilateral energies are then spent in either preventing stalemates or breaking gridlocks. This is, however, not to say there have been no meaningful developments but they have been in fits and starts and unsustainable. There was a need to put this unquestionably difficult inter-state relationship on a predictable trajectory by gradually moving from conflict management to conflict resolution.

In essence, my mission statement had four interlocking parts. First, to persuade India that Kashmir was the core issue and, sans its fair resolution, there was, as far as I could see, no way that the two hostile nations could ever develop a trust and broad-based relationship. Second, to convince the Kashmiri resistance leadership how their bridgeable differences were diluting their legitimate struggle and how unity amongst them was the sine qua non for building pressure on New Delhi to consider exploring a tenable solution to the long-standing dispute. Third, to preserve and consolidate the existing confidence-building measures (CBMs) and fourth, to put in place a bilateral dialogue process that was reasonably balanced and tenable and had the potential to yield concrete results even if marginal in the beginning. We could not wait indefinitely for a deus ex machina to fix our bilateral relations overnight. It had to be an incremental and sustainable process that would need ample patience and more importantly intrepid leadership on both sides of the border.

******

The structured Composite Dialogue with eight segments that started in 2004 had suddenly come to a halt following the Mumbai terror attacks on 26 November 2008. The attack killed 166 people including four Americans. India was quick to blame

Pakistan and then it became a good talking point for India not only to keep hammering Pakistan on terrorism but also to avoid constructive talks on Kashmir.

The first opportunity that came to break the impasse after the Mumbai attacks was in July 2009 when the prime ministers of the two countries, Syed Yousuf Raza Gilani and Dr Manmohan Singh, met at Sharm el Sheikh, Egypt, on 16 July 2009 on the sidelines of the 16th Non-Aligned Movement (NAM) summit. A joint statement (Annex II) was issued that, inter alia, talked about terrorism including the Mumbai attacks but there was no reference to the Samjhauta Express blasts. The two leaders also "recognized that dialogue is the only way forward. Action on terrorism should not be linked to the Composite Dialogue and these should not be bracketed."

Significantly, Prime Minister Gilani also raised the issue of India's interference in Balochistan and this was also reflected in the joint statement in the following anodyne words: "Prime Minister Gilani mentioned that Pakistan has some information on threats in Balochistan and other areas." While in India, Prime Minister Singh was lashed out for the inclusion of this reference in the joint statement, people in Pakistan were gratuitously exhilarated about Balochistan without realizing that the joint statement did not contain any reference to Jammu & Kashmir. It only mentioned: "Prime Minister Singh said that India was ready to discuss all issues with Pakistan, including all outstanding issues."

This, in my opinion, was a huge blow but Salman Bashir was of the view that "all outstanding issues" also covered Kashmir and that our success was the inclusion of Balochistan. I was surprised at this line of argument. The Indian prime minister never acknowledged that his country was interfering in Balochistan. The joint statement contained what Prime

Minister Gilani had said about Balochistan. In my view, the statement was heavily in favor of India but, since Prime Minister Singh was drawing unending flak from the Indian opposition, nobody in Pakistan had really reflected as to what we had lost. I was the foreign office spokesperson then and was equally responsible for building misplaced excitement.

The two sides had then agreed to have bilateral talks under the "resumed dialogue" process. India was not willing to use the term Composite Dialogue as that would, as per their contention, give the impression that the situation was back to as it was prior to the Mumbai attacks. In fact, during this period, much was accomplished. Most importantly, the two countries were able to agree on relaxing the bilateral visa regime and Pakistan had agreed to extend the Most Favored Nation status to India under the name of Non-Discriminatory Market Access (NDMA) by 2012-13 as the two were gradually moving towards trimming the negative list of tariff lines meaning that now fewer and fewer goods were left outside the bilateral trade.

As for the back-channel diplomacy, expectations on both sides remained unfulfilled. While Pakistan had arrested the seven accused in the Mumbai attacks, India had been prevaricating on Kashmir.

As claimed by Pakistan's former foreign minister Khurshid Mahmud Kasuri, in his voluminous book, *Neither a Hawk Nor a Dove,* that the two countries were very close to reaching a modus vivendi on Kashmir, I had always had my serious apprehensions. After having lived in India and talking to insiders including the Indian interlocutor on the back channel, Ambassador S.K. Lambah (had my first one-on-one lunch with him on 13 May 2014), I could not convince myself that India was genuinely willing to change the status quo in Kashmir.

India was playing deftly. It could show to the world that, despite Mumbai, it was still talking to Pakistan behind-the scenes and that it was Pakistan that was culpable of procrastination. Ambassador Shahryar Khan, who was the last interlocutor from our side after Tariq Aziz and Ambassador Riaz M. Khan, had shared with me the details of his meetings with Ambassador Lambah. I could gather that the discussion on the back channel had turned into a dialogue on terrorism and Mumbai. It was regrettable that, even on the back channel, we could not negotiate anything worthwhile and conclusive on Kashmir and, at the end, got inveigled into making unilateral, unworkable commitments. Even President Musharraf's four-point formula that envisaged a solution without changing borders and making the LoC irrelevant had become unpalatable. India was not interested in seeking compromises but led Pakistan up the garden path. Musharraf was no doubt serious in finding a mutually acceptable solution to Kashmir but he floundered about in diplomacy.

I was scheduled to present my Letter of Credence to President Pranab Mukherjee (he passed away on 21 August 2020) on 2 April. As per the tradition, I was asked by my hosts to not engage in any media activity till then. Meanwhile I, in consultation with my team at the high commission, postponed the official reception of the Pakistan Day on 23 March. It was decided to host the reception on the evening of 2 April, that is, the day I would officially present my credentials. However, we did have a simple flag hoisting ceremony at the high commission in the morning that was attended only by our own officials, some Pakistani students at the SAARC University and a few Kashmiris.

******

Hoisting the green and white Pakistan flag in India is an experience a Pakistani diplomat can never forget. I was feeling like walking on the moon. We cannot pay enough tribute to our founding fathers led by Quaid-e-Azam Mohammad Ali Jinnah for creating a separate homeland for the Indian Muslims. Pakistan's story is remarkable. We literally started from scratch and despite humongous internal and external challenges, have still been able to come a long way. We are a relatively young nation of only 74 years old but we take great pride in being the custodians of the world's two oldest civilizations, namely, Indus Valley and Gandhara.

In India, unlike Pakistan and so many other countries, the ceremony of presenting credentials is rather vapid, lacking the traditional ostentation. A group of usually six high commissioners/ambassadors arrive at Rashtrapati Bhavan (official residence of India's President) in their own respective cars along with their spouses and maximum four officials. They present their credentials one-by-one followed by separate meetings not lasting more than ten minutes.

I was dressed in a black shirwani and wearing the Jinnah cap. I thanked President Mukherjee for accepting my credentials and conveyed felicitations from our president and prime minister. I also assured him that it would remain my endeavor to better the bilateral relationship underlining how important his support and guidance would be on this. While the president assured me of his full support, he also mentioned the importance of extirpating the menace of terrorism that, in his view, was gnawing at the prospects of creating a propitious bilateral environment. Fully agreeing with him, I then also stressed on the need of resolving all the bilateral issues including the Jammu & Kashmir dispute.

Since it was my first call on the president and that too in the context of presenting my Letter of Credence, I did not intend to raise any specific controversial issue. But when the president, who had also been the external affairs and finance minister at different times, had himself raised specific issues, I then had to politely respond. My call on the president thus went over and above the allotted time.

A pleasant surprise for me at the presidency was to see Ms Gaitri Issar Kumar serving as Joint/Additional Secretary at the presidency. We were together in Geneva dealing with arms control and disarmament matters from 2001–2003. I must hasten to add that she was one of the most delightful and courteous diplomats I had come across in my diplomatic career. We had enjoyed many parties at each other's homes in Geneva.

******

Earlier on 16 March, I quietly went to see an indefatigable Kashmiri leader, Syed Ali Shah Geelani, at his modest Delhi flat. He was unwell. I also thought to personally invite him to the Pakistan Day reception to be held on 2 April. Needless to say, I was overwhelmed. Here was a man who was totally committed to Pakistan and the cause of Kashmir. This was my first meeting with him as High Commissioner. I had met him once earlier at the high commission when he came to see Foreign Secretary Salman Bashir in February 2010.

Though there was nothing new about our meetings with the Kashmiri leaders, there is always some hoopla around them in India. As was the practice, I invited all of them to our Pakistan Day reception and they all came, including Syed Geelani, Mirwaiz Umar Farooq and Yasin Malik. I also had detailed meetings with them at the high commission. They were divided in their views about Modi's Kashmir policy should the Bharatiya Janata Party (BJP) win the upcoming Lok Sabha elections. Some opined the BJP would be better than Congress and that one could expect Modi to be another Atal Bihari Vajpayee who might revive his three-pronged policy of humanity (Insaniyat), democracy (Jamhooriyat) and Kashmiriness (Kashmiriyat) in settling the Kashmir dispute.

Syed Geelani, however, strongly differed. He was also shirty with President Pervez Musharraf for he thought he went out of his way to pander to India. He termed his four-point formula a huge setback causing immeasurable damage to the Kashmir struggle. Similarly, he would contend that the 6 January 2004 India-Pakistan Joint Statement (Annexure III) issued in Islamabad was an unpardonable faux pas that did nothing but only blighted the freedom movement as "cross-border terrorism". He had no doubt that the ultimate objective of New Delhi was to convert Jammu & Kashmir also into a Hindu-majority state and, in view of Pakistan's own political and economic mess, India would literally have a walkover. Syed Geelani would always insist that Pakistan was far more important than Kashmir. The latter would be able to free itself from Indian shackles only if Pakistan was stable and strong.

However, Mirwaiz and Professor Abdul Ghani Bhat would view the situation differently. They thought the BJP, since it was a Hindu nationalist party, was better positioned to resolve the Kashmir dispute. They, however, recognized that, for such parties, moving away from their ideological moorings was never an easy proposition. Nevertheless, if Modi was handled cogently and his pathological hubris was somehow managed gently, there could be some movement forward. I could see that, as in the case of Syed Geelani, they, too, were worried that the BJP under Modi, who was definitely not a Vajpayee and far more into pursuing the RSS agenda, could become a huge problem not only for the Kashmiris but also Indian Muslims.

As for Musharraf, they would give him the benefit of the doubt. In their opinion, Musharraf's four-point formula should have been taken as the starting point for negotiations and not the end game. However, the Congress party and the Indian government under Prime Minister Manmohan Singh were not the right interlocutors for resolving such a complex and religiously divisive issue. But then who knew in 2004 that the BJP under Modi would ever be able to win so convincingly in the May 2014 general elections.

The BJP election manifesto was clear on Kashmir which talked about revoking Article 370 of the Indian constitution and stripping the state of its special status that was granted to it by the so-called instrument of accession signed by Maharajah Hari Singh. Like Syed Geelani and other Kashmiri leaders, I couldn't help but worry about the BJP's future plans under Modi. But Islamabad seemed to be in total denial and mostly insouciant. Unfortunately, I ended up fighting on many fronts.

******

One other important issue that occupied me during my initial days in New Delhi was the grant of NDMA to India. Our Commerce Minister, Khurram Dastagir Khan, had visited New Delhi in January and it was decided that Pakistan would extend the NDMA (read as MFN status) to India soon. For this purpose, his Indian counterpart, Anand Sharma, was very keen to visit Pakistan at the earliest, that is, prior to general elections that were being held in several phases in April/May 2014.

While the dates for his visit to Pakistan were being worked out, I was approached by a person (Non-Resident Indian living in the US, I cannot disclose his name in deference to his desire) who claimed to be a close friend of both Mohan Bhagwat, Chief of RSS, and the BJP's prime ministerial candidate Narendra Modi. He was visiting Pakistan (as recommended by our Ambassador in Washington DC) on 3-6 April. He was in New Delhi and wanted to see me before leaving for Pakistan.

I invited him for lunch on 1 April. He conveyed a goodwill

message from the BJP leadership and thought he could play a positive role in bringing the two countries together. Coming to the main point, he contended that granting NDMA to the outgoing Congress government would be wasteful. Islamabad should defer the matter. Since the BJP would most likely form the next government, it would make eminent sense to oblige the incoming set-up. This would help make a good beginning. He said he knew Modi very well. Once he was convinced that Prime Minister Nawaz Sharif meant well, Modi would go out of his way to reciprocate and reach out to Pakistan. "Modi never forgets a favour," he claimed.

Without committing anything, I proposed that we meet again after he had returned from Pakistan. He was very happy with his discussions in Islamabad, especially in the MoFA where he was received by Fatemi. However, he wasn't sure if we were willing to acquiesce to his proposal of deferring the NDMA. I told him that the NDMA was not a very big deal. Should the BJP win, there would be many other opportunities to work together for peace and development in South Asia as envisioned by Prime Minister Nawaz Sharif. As for the NDMA, I also kept the door ajar as I was inclined to his viewpoint. However, I wanted to be absolutely sure that BJP's victory was a foregone conclusion. After much homework, I finally wrote to Islamabad that postponing the NDMA would be wise as the Congress party was in deep water and in no position to win for a third consecutive time.

Islamabad agreed with my recommendation. However, Commerce Minister Sharma was unhappy. At a social event in New Delhi, he conveyed his disappointment to me at Pakistan's kind of backing off from its commitment and being driven by Indian domestic politics. He found it strange that Pakistan had totally forgotten what happened to Babri Mosque in 1992 and how thousands of Muslims were massacred in Gujarat in 2002 under Modi's watch. He was of the clear view that Pakistan's approach was short-sighted and would likely boomerang.

Sharma did make the right noises in private. But the fact of the matter was that, in Pakistan, too, there were strong lobbies averse to the idea of NDMA. I myself was apprehensive. Despite the fact that India had granted us the MFN status back in 1996, the balance of trade continued to be growing in favor of India. Our exports to India went through discriminatory non-tariff barriers including stringent visa procedures for Pakistani businessmen and unduly long sanitary and phytosanitary tests leaving our exporters with endless agonies and, in the end, making our exports non-competitive.

In my subsequent recommendations to Islamabad, I would support extending the NDMA to India but with the caveat that Pakistan should also apply all those non-tariff barriers on Indian imports that India unilaterally invoked in our case. My argument was that we must take a leaf out of the Indian playbook rather than cribbing about non-tariff barriers. Diplomacy is not about only adopting and articulating hard positions when it comes to an adversary but also playing hardball and return in kind. Later developments, however, overshadowed the initial bonhomie that was generated by Prime Minister Nawaz Sharif's two-day visit to New Delhi (26-27 May) to attend Modi's inauguration.

******

Narendra Damodardas Modi emerged from the May 2014 Lok Sabha elections as an indisputable leader. BJP's election slogan "Sab Ke Saath Sab Ka Viqas" (development for all) paid off. The BJP won 282 seats whereas it needed 272 seats to form the next government. The Congress party could bag only 44 seats, its worst ever electoral performance.

In the run-up to the elections, I had kept a very busy schedule of meetings and media interactions. I called on Foreign Secretary Sujatha Singh (7 April), who I had known from before as we were both in Berlin more or less during the same period of time. From Berlin she returned to New Delhi to take over as foreign secretary in August 2013. She had invited me to her farewell reception. When I congratulated her on her elevation, she tersely said: "I am hearing that you, too, are being made foreign secretary." I was sort of caught unawares as I had no clue whatsoever by then. But still I facetiously responded that my intelligence sources were not as efficient as hers and, for a change, I would wish her intelligence people to be on the mark.

Sujatha was a pleasant person and easy to talk to. I felt quite bad for her when she was unceremoniously removed by Prime Minister Modi as he wanted to accommodate Dr Subrahmanyam Jaishankar who was to retire from the service on 31 January 2015. As per the Indian system, a foreign secretary is appointed for a minimum of two years. However, the appointment should be notified and effected before the officer reaches his/her superannuation. Jaishankar took over as Foreign Secretary on 29 January 2015, just two days before his retirement.

On the same day (7 April), I also called on National Security Advisor Shiv Shankar Menon, who had also served in Islamabad as high commissioner and then as foreign secretary. An illustrious and suave diplomat, our meeting was more about taking stock of the bilateral relations as he was to step down with the change of government in New Delhi. His message was clear: India and Pakistan had to find sustainable ways and means to build tension-free, if not friendly, bilateral relations. In response to my question as to why the back-channel diplomacy on Kashmir did not yield the desired results, he thought it was not easy for India to ignore terror issues. He also opined that by 2007, President Musharraf had become too enervated politically to take such a major decision on Kashmir. Overall, he was of the view that the good opportunity had been lost, and now it would be for the new government in New Delhi to carry forward the work so far done, or do things differently. He gave me the impression that neither Congress nor the BJP would be able to win enough seats; he was seeing a hung parliament that he reckoned would hold no promise for India-Pakistan relations.

Some opinion polls were, however, predicting a clear victory for the BJP. I thought to meet Subramanian Swamy, India's well-known political figure who joined the BJP in 2013. He is also known for his extremely anti-Pakistan views and openly talks about splitting Pakistan into four pieces. In a recent TV interview, referring to Muslims, he shamelessly asserted that that all human beings are not equal and thus Indian Muslims should not expect equal rights. Interestingly, his daughter Suhasini Haidar, one of India's prominent journalists, is married to a Muslim, Nadeem Haidar, son of Salman Haidar, India's former foreign secretary. I had met Suhasini and Salman many times during my stay in New Delhi but never got a chance to meet Nadeem Haidar.

We met over lunch on 14 April. Swamy was confident that the BJP would trounce the Congress in the upcoming elections. When I asked him did he see any role for himself in the new government under Modi, he was seeing himself as either the next finance or external affairs minister. He was also very critical of Arun Jaitley. In the final event, it was the latter who became India's next finance minister. Swamy did not get any portfolio in the Modi dispensation. Jaitley died in August 2019.

I also met Ram Jethmalani (originally from Sindh), one of India's top lawyers at his residence on 22 April. Also member of the Rajya Sabha, he assured me of contributing positively towards normalizing Pakistan-India relations. He was not a great fan of Modi but expected him to consult him on important issues. I would meet him off and on, and found him to be getting gradually disappointed with Modi for his sectarian and divisive policies. I had enjoyed many lavish parties at Jethmalani's beautiful residence, which would be attended by movers and shakers in New Delhi. He passed away on 8 September 2019, aged 95.

As suggested by my Press Counsellor, Manzoor Ali Memon, who was very effective and by now had made excellent ingress into the Indian media, I started my media interaction with the Indian Women Press Corps at the high commission on 23 April. I spoke extensively on bilateral relations including Jammu & Kashmir followed by a question-answer session, all on the record. The next day, the Indian press was full of positive stories with banner headlines in almost all national and regional newspapers.

I found *Mail Today's* headline: "Modi finds new supporter in Pak High Commissioner", most interesting. As opinion polls were now clearly suggesting that the BJP would win the forthcoming election, I was inundated with questions on Modi, especially how Pakistan would deal with him given his well-known views which were not very encouraging. In my response I would emphasize that it was for the Indian people and not for Pakistan to decide who should form the next government. As for Mr Modi, "I welcome his comments that he would pursue the policies followed by former BJP premier Atal Bihari Vajpayee."

I also underlined that Islamabad was committed to change the bilateral narrative of conflict into one by cooperation and mutual trust, adding "it takes two to tango".

While my team and I in New Delhi were extremely happy with the most positive coverage we got, Islamabad never ceased to surprise me. To my utter shock, I would receive a call from Aizaz in the morning of 24 April. He would tell me that I "scale down" my media engagement and that I should stop reminding the ministry again and again of an inter-ministerial meeting on India.

I could have argued with him but avoided it. It was no secret that all our telephones were tapped. Indians were listening to our conversation. It would hardly behoove a foreign secretary to call a high commissioner in New Delhi and issue him instructions. Aizaz had just done that. I was flabbergasted, to put it mildly. If he was concerned and had felt so strongly about my media interaction, he could have conveyed to me in writing. I don't doubt his intentions but calling me like this and admonishing me on the landline was hardly professional. It must have been a good day for the Indian intelligence officials. However, I was not to be deterred. I knew what I was doing. A Pakistan high commissioner could not just sit behind his desk and write long-winded communications. I was neither shy nor lacked the confidence for engaging in public diplomacy. On the contrary, I felt the need for more of it in India.

Now, more to my amusement, Aizaz would call me again on 23 May. He told me that he was sitting in Fatemi's office and he wanted to convey that "the highest authorities are upset with my active media engagement." I found that absolutely bizarre. Why on earth would the prime minister feel offended at his high commissioner's constructive activities? As on the previous occasion, I remained quiet as arguing with him on the telephone would have made no sense.

On 29 April, I paid my first visit to Mumbai where, besides media interactions, I also had speaking engagements at the Gateway House and the Asia Society. The event at the latter in a jam-packed room was moderated by Shekhar Gupta, then editor-in-chief of *The Indian Express*. I could see how positively the audience was reacting to my candid remarks. Such constructive interactions in Mumbai for a Pakistan high commissioner against the backdrop of 26/11 was a rarity. I was thankful to the people of Mumbai for their warm welcome and affectionate hospitality though there were scores of people who gathered outside the Mumbai Press Club to protest against my visit.

The only thing that saddened me during my visit to Mumbai was the Jinnah House on Mount Pleasant Road, Malabar Hill, that was lying deserted and in a dilapidated state. The board hanging at the gate of the house read: "Proposed site of SOUTH ASIA CENTRE FOR ART AND CULTURE". The gate was locked. I asked my security officials if I could go inside the house given the emotional attachment of Pakistanis to this place. They consulted the guards but to no avail. We were told that the house was not open for visitors and that written permission from the Indian Ministry of External Affairs (MEA) was a must.

The house on Malabar Hill, one of the most premium neighborhoods in Mumbai, was built by our founding father in 1936. He lived there for about ten years and had retained it even after he had moved to Karachi in August 1947. India did not agree to hand over this property to Pakistan for the residence of Pakistan Consul General. Pakistan closed down its consulate in 1994. Some efforts were made in 2006 to reopen the consulate but Pakistan could not find a suitable place as most landlords were reluctant to rent out their property to Pakistan. After the Mumbai attacks, whatever little possibility for reopening the consulate existed had also disappeared. I did raise this issue with National Security Advisor Ajit Doval in one of my meetings with him but found him disinterested. In strict reciprocity, the Indian consulate general in Karachi was also closed down in 1994.

******

After winning the election so convincingly, Modi soon gave us another surprise, this time on the diplomatic front, throwing up a quandary of sorts. He wanted his inauguration to be ostentatious in political terms and remembered for its contextual significance. He was to take oath along with his cabinet on 26 May. He floated the idea of inviting all the SAARC leaders to attend his inauguration ceremony. Invitation letters were sent to the SAARC leaders on his behalf by Foreign Secretary Sujatha Singh on 21 May. Prime Minister Sharif called Prime Minister-elect Modi on 17 May to greet him on the unprecedented victory of the BJP. He also expressed the hope that they would be able to work together towards promoting peace and prosperity in the region.

The next day (18 May) I was invited for a lunch by Mr Sajjan Jindal of JSW Group of Companies. I didn't then know that he was a close friend of Prime Minister Nawaz Sharif. Jindal, India's steel tycoon, comes across as an affable person. His eyes speak of his dynamism. We were able to establish a good personal equation instantly and I was looking forward to keeping him engaged as I was now aware of his free access to Modi.

During the conversation, he told me that he had spoken both to Modi and Sharif and that it was he who had facilitated the telephone call between the two leaders the day before. Among other things, he also floated the idea with me of releasing some Indian fishermen being held in Pakistan as a goodwill gesture to the Indian prime minister-elect. Though he didn't share it with me, I was sure that he must have already discussed this with our prime minister, too, and convinced him to extend the goodwill gesture and oblige Modi at the very outset.

On 25 May, Pakistan unilaterally announced the release of 150 Indian fishermen although after meeting Jindal, I had proposed to Islamabad that we could discuss this with the Indian side to make it a reciprocal step that could be announced after the two leaders had met in New Delhi. Even the year earlier, Pakistan had released over 300 Indian fishermen unilaterally but to no positive effect or response from India.

Modi, because of the horrific Gujarat episode of 2002, was a reprehensible and despicable figure for Pakistanis in general. In Pakistan he was called the "butcher of Gujarat".

Most commentators in Pakistan, as well as opposition politicians, reacting largely emotionally, argued against Prime Minister Sharif accepting Modi's invitation to attend his inauguration. They contended that Modi was behaving like an arrogant imperial leader who had summoned India's smaller SAARC neighbors to his darbar. Pakistan was not just any neighbor to be bullied or denigrated by India. There was tremendous pressure on Nawaz Sharif to turn down the invitation. I was thinking differently and, perhaps, rationally if I may say so myself.

As I had arrived in New Delhi only recently, I was looking for ways and means to break the ice and let the bilateral matters move forward. Perhaps this was a godsend to test Modi's intentions especially in the context of Kashmir. Would he be willing to work with Pakistan to make a new beginning or would he turn out to be like his immediate predecessor, Manmohan Singh. The latter did not visit Pakistan during his ten years as prime minister. He was even reluctant to visit Pakistan as a private person. Prime Minister Nawaz Sharif had sent him an invitation in 2014 to visit Pakistan, including his birth place Gah at Chakwal, at his own convenience as a state guest. I reminded him at least twice but he would avoid talking about it.

I was of the view that Pakistan would not lose anything by attending the inauguration. We would rather convey to the international community our good intentions and willingness to work for regional economic cooperation and connectivity within the SAARC framework. And then should the prime minister agree, we could prepare a decent visit program focusing also on public diplomacy. So, in short, I was strongly in favor of the visit as building a personal rapport between the two leaders would also help diplomacy at the working level and push the difficult relationship forward no matter how grudgingly in the beginning. The important thing was to bring the two leaders together, let them discuss issues informally and, if possible, agree on how to move forward even by taking small steps. Nevertheless, I had no doubt in my mind that Modi was a difficult character committed to the RSS and its extremist agenda and, in all likelihood, would prove to be a hard nut to crack. But, as Pakistan high commissioner, I was still looking for reasonable opportunities without compromising on principles. Accordingly, in a message to Islamabad, I strongly recommended that Nawaz Sharif accept the invitation.

It had almost become a cliffhanger whether or not Prime Minister Sharif would attend Modi's swearing-in. Other SAARC leaders had already confirmed. On 22 May, our foreign office spokesperson, in her weekly press briefing responding to a question, said: "A decision will be taken sometime today." There was, however, no announcement that day or the next. The Indian media was quick to speculate. Some news reports even falsely claimed that the Pakistan establishment was not convinced of the merit of the visit. Therefore, Sharif was highly unlikely to come to New Delhi. Thus, Pakistan would be the only SAARC country that would be conspicuous by its absence.

Lo and behold, I would receive an SMS from Jindal, who was in Tanzania, informing me that Mian Sahab had decided to attend Modi's inauguration and that he would also visit Jindal's residence in New Delhi on 26 May at 4.30 pm before leaving for the oath-taking ceremony at Rashtrapati Bhavan. Feeling embarrassed, I pretended that I was already in the know. Finally, before informing the high commission, MoFA made an announcement on 24 May at around noon that the prime minister would attend Modi's inauguration. I was upbeat. The prime minister was coming and, in my view, that was the right decision.

No sooner had the news of Prime Minister Sharif become public than the high commission was literally inundated with requests for meetings and interviews. Most interesting, however, was a request for an urgent meeting with me by a former R&AW Chief A. S. Dulat. He made the request through our Minister (political) Rahim Hayat Qureshi with whom he had been meeting socially. Both had developed a good personal relationship; it was good to know that my officers had been moving around and reaching out to the relevant people. I would always tell my officers that, when abroad, they were in the field. Thus, they should be spending more of their time in meeting and cultivating people from all walks of life rather than remaining in their offices writing long-winded reports as we do at headquarters in Islamabad. Field-work requirements are different from what we do at the secretariat.

I met Dulat the same day (24 May) at 4 pm at Taj Mahal Hotel over a cup of coffee. We later became good friends and would often meet to discuss topical issues, especially Kashmir. Not surprisingly, he would always vouch for a solution along the lines of President Musharraf's four-point formula. He once told me that he had met almost all the well-known Kashmiri leaders but Geelani Sahab. The latter had never obliged him. I would appreciate Dulat for his respect for the Hurriyat leader as he would always address him as Geelani Sahab.

Dulat quickly came to the point. He recommended that, since Prime Minister Sharif had shown magnanimity and that his goodwill gesture could go a long way in improving bilateral relations, it would be helpful if the Kashmir issue was kept aside to make a positive beginning. He added that meeting the Hurriyat leaders at the inauguration would be an unnecessary distraction which would kill the very purpose of the visit. He said that if Pakistan obliged and the two leaders were able to develop a personal equation and felt comfortable with each other, Modi, given his personality, could be expected to go the extra mile even on Kashmir. Dulat was of the strong view that it was necessary that the two leaders met in an environment free from stress and strain; a meeting with the Hurriyat leaders would spoil everything.

Agreeing with him that both sides should be keeping the atmospherics congenial, I asked Dulat if that was his personal view or he was conveying an official message unofficially. As expected, he parried the question saying it didn't matter. It was vital to make a good beginning and he would strongly pitch for that. He also left me with the impression that, perhaps, the message had already been conveyed informally to Prime Minister Sharif and that he was inclined to the suggestion.

As I myself wasn't sure what the thinking in Islamabad was, I remained non-committal. Moreover, I still did not know whether the prime minister was coming for a day trip or would also stay overnight. I nevertheless told Dulat that the prime minister would be under tremendous domestic pressure to meet the Hurriyat leaders as not meeting them would be unprecedented and, since Indians were the hosts, we expected them to be more accommodative. I also stressed that keeping a good atmosphere largely depended on India as our prime minister, by agreeing to attend the inauguration, had already demonstrated Pakistan's sincerity and readiness to work with India's new leadership. I also hoped India would not make any public statement to embarrass Pakistan because such a statement would not go unanswered. I also mentioned that one way was to go for a joint statement to which Dulat replied that he would let me know if there were any takers of the suggestion in MEA.

Later I learnt that Jindal did convey a message to the prime minister and Indian High Commissioner Dr T.C. Raghavan also had a meeting with Fatemi and Aizaz together in the foreign office and made the same request. The subsequent events did corroborate that Nawaz Sharif's approach was different. He had genuinely believed that he could do business with Modi as he was able to with Atal Bihari Vajpayee. No wonder, when he visited New Delhi, he made a point to visit the ailing former Prime Minister Vajpayee with whom he had also shared his birthday, that is, 25 December. Vajpayee died in August 2018.

Interestingly, several Kashmiri leaders (I am deliberately not mentioning their names) also enquired whether the prime minister would be meeting the Hurriyat leaders. Some suggested he should; others thought that, since he would be here for a very brief visit and it was not bilateral either, they would understand if he could not meet them. There was also a view that Modi should be tested. We should not give him any pretext to blame Pakistan for vitiating the atmosphere and undermining the first meeting between the two leaders.

By now I could calculate that there was no appetite in Islamabad for a meeting with the Hurriyat leadership. Nor was there any time left to make arrangements for a meeting as almost all the Hurriyat leaders would have to come from Kashmir. The foreign office had also by now conveyed to me who the prime minster would be meeting or would like to meet during his two-day sojourn. The high commission made the program accordingly.

On arrival in New Delhi on 26 May, we warmly welcomed the prime minister and his entourage including Sartaj Aziz, Fatemi, Political Secretary Asif Kirmani, Principal Secretary Javed Aslam, Aizaz and the prime minister's son Hussain Nawaz. The Indian high commissioner in Islamabad and Jindal were also present to welcome the prime minister. On the way to the hotel, I gave the prime minister my take on Modi and what we should expect during his premiership. In particular, I underlined that his ideological moorings did not inspire much hope. He was a staunch RSS man and strongly committed to its socio-political agenda. It was therefore imperative from our perspective that our every step vis-à-vis India must be well calibrated stressing that there was no room for unilateralism.

As per the program, the prime minister visited Jindal's residence. I was asked to stay back and come there with Sartaj Aziz, leaving together for Rashtrapati Bhavan for the oath-taking ceremony. The ceremony, held in the sprawling open area of the presidency, was quite long as, following the prime minister-elect, all the cabinet ministers also took oath individually. All the SAARC leaders then went on to the stage one-by-one to greet President Mukherjee and Prime Minister Modi and then had a group photograph. It was also a hot and humid day. The SAARC leaders sitting in the front row were visibly feeling uncomfortable.

The two prime ministers were to meet at the Hyderabad House the next day in the afternoon at around 12:45 pm. After visiting the Delhi Jama Masjid and Red Fort in the morning of 27 May, we got together at the prime minister's suite to finalize the talking points for the meeting.

Earlier, I had expressed my apprehensions to Fatemi that we could not trust the Indians. It was likely that they would immediately go public after the meeting and put forth their narrative on issues like terrorism and Mumbai. To preempt any such move by India, it would be better if a terse joint statement could be issued. (Daulat did not revert to me on the suggestion I had made to him.) I also gave him a draft statement which I had thought could be sent to the Indian side for their consideration. They might jettison the idea in which case we should be prepared to respond to their possible shenanigans about the meeting. I was emphatic that we must not let India steal a march on us.

Fatemi appeared to be in agreement and started tweaking the draft in consultation with the foreign secretary. He told me he would himself speak to the prime minister, show him the draft and seek his concurrence to send it across. I reminded him a couple of times but he would simply ignore it. I would not know whether he ever spoke to the prime minister on the subject and, if so, what was the latter's response.

As for the talking points, there were divergent views especially on Kashmir and terrorism. The prime minister kept listening and then instructed me to quickly write a few talking points on note cards which he returned to me after the meeting. I am retaining those cards as a memento from the former prime minister.

The meeting between the two prime ministers was suffused with incredible amiability. Our prime minister underscored the importance of not squandering this historic opportunity of building peace between the two countries. To address mutual concerns conclusively, he proposed a mechanism of regular consultations headed by the national security advisors. This mechanism could also include heads of security and intelligence agencies. The prime minister also talked about enhancing bilateral trade and people-to-people contact and moving from confrontation to cooperation. He, however, did not raise the issue of Kashmir and restricted himself to proposing that the foreign secretaries should meet as early as possible to work out modalities for resuming the bilateral dialogue process.

Surprisingly, he also referred to the Charter of Democracy and his political struggle which I thought was out of place especially in a meeting with the Indian prime minister who had blighted credentials and was well-known for his anti-Muslim outlook. Sharif was insistent that this was a historic opportunity for the two countries and must not be squandered.

Modi, on his part, thanked the prime minister for accepting the invitation and welcomed his desire for promoting bilateral peace. However, he was quick to mention that it was difficult to continue meaningful talks in an environment of terrorism. He also underlined the importance of concluding the Mumbai attack trial at the earliest. He agreed with our prime minister that the two foreign secretaries should meet and prepare a future bilateral agenda implying that the Composite Dialogue process, as far as India was concerned, had outlived its utility.

Now that Modi had raised the issue of violence and held Pakistan responsible for the conflictual relationship, I was expecting the prime minister to respond adequately and, at the minimum, mention that the root cause of all the bilateral problems was the long-standing Jammu & Kashmir dispute. But, to my utmost dismay, he did not do that. Nor did he raise the Samjhauta Express terror blasts. We did not know if the trial of the accused was making any progress. He appeared too soft and unnecessarily accommodative and, as he told Modi, he genuinely wanted to pick up the threads of the Lahore Declaration from where it had to be left off in October 1999.

The two prime ministers also had a 20-minute long one-on-one meeting. What the two leaders discussed was never shared, at least with me.

From the Hyderabad House, we went straight to Rashtrapati Bhavan for a call on President Mukherjee. As we came out of the meeting, we learnt that Indian Foreign Secretary Singh had already held a press conference and briefed the media about the meeting between the two prime ministers and the points Modi raised about Mumbai and terrorism. My apprehensions as I mentioned to Fatemi had thus come to be true.

At Taj Mahal Hotel, where the prime minister was staying, the media had already gathered in the lobby to get our version of the bilateral meeting between the two leaders.

I was of the view that it would be most appropriate if our foreign secretary engaged with the media rather than the prime minister himself. I even offered myself to be in the line of fire. However, others thought that the prime minister could read out a brief written statement himself and, without taking any questions, leave from there for the Palam Air Force Base for his departure. Though the prime minister appeared to be disinclined, he finally agreed when pushed very hard, especially by Fatemi and Aizaz. Accordingly, we informed the media that the prime minister would come down at around 3 pm and address them. The prime minister then directed Fatemi and Aizaz to prepare draft press remarks.

Earlier in a brief discussion on what should be included in the press statement, I opposed the idea of referring to the Mumbai attack trial as it would not go down well with the people of Pakistan especially when there would be no reference to Kashmir. I also insisted that, though Kashmir was not raised by us, we could still mention it in the prime minister's statement for it had been our consistent position that Kashmir was the root cause of instability in the region.

Interestingly, the statement in its final shape was neither shared with Sartaj Aziz nor with me. As it turned out, the statement was factually correct and retained the spirit of friendliness the prime minister had desired. He was somehow convinced that he could do business with Modi and was looking forward to his next meeting with him on the margins of the United Nations General Assembly session in New York in September.

On the way to the Palam Air Force Base, I informed the prime minister that I would be in Islamabad the following day for a week for some private chores. He asked me to see him to discuss in detail his talks with Modi and how to take the matters forward. Since there was an Indian protocol officer sitting in the front seat of the car, that was not the occasion to engage in substantive discussion. Referring to his tete-a-tete meeting, the prime minister did, however, laconically say that he found Modi quite forthcoming and that he liked his business-like approach. I listened to him but avoided engaging in any substantive discussion. I thought my call on him in

Islamabad would be the right time to share my thoughts with him after listening to what he had discussed with Modi in the one-to-one session.

I called on the prime minister on 2 June. His Principal Secretary, Javed Aslam, was also present but we also had some one-on-one moments. I gave my candid assessment about his visit to New Delhi underlining the importance of moving strategically as the resumption of talks, though important, would not be enough in themselves to build mutual trust. I also cautioned him about Modi and advised him to proceed with utmost circumspection lest the engagement process become one-sided. I told him that Kashmiris were looking up to him; we must not err to relegate the Kashmir issue in any manner.

In response to his question, I advised against resuming the back-channel diplomacy prematurely. I made a few recommendations to him on Kashmir and some other important matters. He listened attentively and appeared to have agreed with my views. He was, however, tight-lipped about his private conversation with Modi. When I asked him about the gist of their discussion, he only said that there was nothing substantive and they mostly discussed their personal political struggles, adding that Modi had assured him that he would find him a trustworthy interlocutor and partner in peace. As I was leaving his office, the prime minister directed me to see the ISI chief before I returned to New Delhi.

In an inter-agency meeting in the foreign office, which was chaired by Sartaj Aziz and attended by Fatemi, Aizaz, Additional Foreign Secretary for Asia-Pacific Mohsin Razi and two ISI and MO officers, I presented my take in detail on Pakistan-India relations following the Sharif-Modi talks. I also briefed them about my call on the prime minister. My principal argument was that we must now wait and see and not show undue keenness or make unilateral moves to appear as if we were begging for bilateral talks. I also underlined that diplomacy, particularly when it came to India, needed enormous patience. Avoiding haste and sticking to our principled positions, especially in the obtaining circumstances, were the prerequisites.

Besides, we must always remember that Modi was not Vajpayee. We must play the art of diplomacy intelligently and convey very clearly to Indians our red lines before they drew theirs. Modi should understand that, by resuming talks, he was not doing any favor to Pakistan. Peace was in our mutual interest and it could not be achieved unilaterally. I also strongly opposed back-channel diplomacy prior to the resumption of structured dialogue at the foreign-secretary level.

Alas, I was talking to the people with the apologetic mindset as substantiated beyond any doubt by the later developments. There was a clear division of views. Sartaj Aziz, Fatemi and Aizaz were on one side and the rest on the other. In my separate meetings, too, with the three I ingeminated my points with more emphasis. They all seemed excited. One thing that particularly struck me was their accepting Modi's contentions readily and working quickly to assuage his concerns. I was uncomfortable since I did not see my own foreign office concerned about Kashmir. Nor were they willing to listen to the need to have a plan of action. In varying degrees, they all thought the ball was in Pakistan's court which, in my view, was simply specious. They were all experienced people with more insights than I could ever claim. But I was convinced that we must first probe Modi; proceed gradually and avoid giving any unilateral commitment on any issue outside the structured dialogue process. Every step must be weighed rationally; there was no room to get carried away by the maiden friendly meeting between the two prime ministers.

As directed by the prime minister, I met ISI chief Lt Gen Zaheerul Islam and also called on Chief of Army Staff (COAS) General Raheel Sharif. I briefed them about the state of play and what I expected in the months ahead. They both agreed that while Pakistan should be doing whatever was possible to meet India's concerns, New Delhi should not expect improvement in relations sans progress on Kashmir. They also asked me whether there was any specific reason why the prime minister did not mention Kashmir in his statement to the Indian media. I sort of parried the question by saying that perhaps the prime minister had thought of not spoiling the atmospherics since he had gone to New Delhi primarily for Modi's inauguration and not a bilateral meeting.

I knew General Sharif from London where he, then as Brigadier, was doing a course at the prestigious Royal College of Defense Studies. We had a long chat not only on Pakistan-India relations but also Afghanistan, US and disarmament issues. I shared with him my ideas and, on some points, we did differ but I thought that was a healthy sign. I always found General Sharif easy to talk to. He would always listen patiently, ask questions and then share his views. That was our last meeting. He is now heading the Riyadh-based Islamic Military Counterterrorism Coalition founded in December 2015.

******

After considerable behind-the-scene diplomacy, it was decided that the two foreign secretaries would meet in Islamabad on 25 August. As per practice, I was asked to be in Islamabad two/three days before the meeting for consultations. I was preparing accordingly.

I was deeply concerned about Kashmir and had, on many occasions, conveyed to Islamabad that the BJP Government under Modi would be doing things differently in Jammu & Kashmir. They were openly talking about revoking Article 370 which was also contained in the party's election manifesto and trifurcating the state. I was getting vibes that the first step might be to separate Ladakh from the state and make it a Union Territory. However, the BJP government would wait till after elections in Kashmir which were scheduled to be held later in the year.

Kashmiris were also ambivalent over the exclusion of Kashmir in the Sharif-Modi meeting in New Delhi. Therefore, it was necessary to allay their concerns and reassure them that there was no change in Pakistan's policy. Any suggestion that Prime Minister Sharif was willing to put the issue on the back burner had no basis. Pakistan remained convinced that resolving the Kashmir dispute in line with the political aspirations of Kashmiris was fundamental to achieving peace in the region.

Moreover, the Indian suggestion, however informal, that Prime Minister Sharif should not be meeting the Hurriyat leadership during his visit to New Delhi was also at the back of my mind. And as the practice had been, the upcoming meeting of the foreign secretaries was a good opportunity to brief the Hurriyat leadership and take them into confidence. I also wanted to convey to the Indian side that, though our Prime Minister did not raise the issue of Kashmir with Modi out of courtesy, he remained committed to the Kashmir cause. The Indians must not be given any reason to misinterpret our goodwill as our weakness or that Pakistan could ever consider ditching the Kashmiris.

Keeping all this in view, I decided to invite the Hurriyat leadership to the high commission for meetings on 18-19 August, that is, before my departure for Islamabad. I also sent a pithy communication to Islamabad about my decision to meet the Hurriyat leaders before traveling to Pakistan.

The Indian media had literally gone bonkers. Led by Arnab Goswami, they were all out blazing their guns at me asserting that, while India was exhibiting immense goodwill by sending its foreign secretary to Pakistan, the Pakistan high commissioner at the behest of his real "masters", that is, the Pakistan establishment, was bent on scuttling the dialogue process before it could even begin. Most of them were shouting at the top of their lungs putting pressure on New Delhi to call off Sujatha Singh's visit to Pakistan should the high commissioner go ahead and host the Hurriyat leaders.

It was 18 August, and I was having lunch with A.S. Dulat at Oberoi Hotel. My personal assistant called me to say that the Indian foreign secretary wanted to speak to me urgently. I returned to the high commission at around 2:15 pm and called back Sujatha Singh at around 2:30 pm. Shabir Ahmad Shah, a Hurriyat leader, was already waiting for me at the high commission for our meeting at 3 pm.

When I mentioned to Dulat that the Indian foreign secretary wanted to speak to me urgently and most probably about my meeting with the Hurriyat leaders in view of the uproar created by the Indian media, he did not appear to be concerned. He was of the view that she would make a standard mild protest for domestic consumption and the matter would end there. Since he had been dealing with these issues himself as Prime Minister Vajpayee's focal point on Kashmir, as well as the R&AW chief, I expressed the hope that he was right though I had a feeling that this time it might be different from the past.

Sujatha Singh, in quite a harsh tone, quickly came to the point. She said: "I have been instructed by the highest authorities that if you go ahead with your meetings with the Hurriyat leaders, I will be constrained to call off my visit to Islamabad. We cannot accept Pakistan's interference in India's internal affairs. Pakistan has to decide whether it wants to engage with the Indian government or the Kashmiri separatists." In my terse response I told her that it was not the first time we were meeting the Hurriyat leadership and the fact of the matter was that, in the past, the Indian governments had even facilitated these meetings. I, therefore, thought India was overreacting and that cancelling the visit would be a mutual loss but it was for India to make the final call. I stressed there was no change in Pakistan's Kashmir policy.

As we were having this telephone conversation, the Indian media had started running the breaking news that the Indian foreign secretary had called the Pakistan high commissioner and conveyed to him the message in most clear terms. The media was also praising Modi for finally putting an end to the "anti-national practice" going on for years.

I immediately convened a meeting of senior officials of the high commission to discuss the matter. We all agreed there was no turning back. If we had submitted to the Indian demand, which had already been made public by them, we would only reinforce the impression that Prime Minister Sharif's Kashmir policy was indeed undergoing some undesirable modulation. India's ill-intentions were now manifest. Perhaps they had already wanted to wriggle out of the Islamabad meeting.

By appearing tough on the Hurriyat and Pakistan, the BJP was hoping to win, for the first time, a good number of seats in the forthcoming Jammu & Kashmir elections. They called it "Mission 44". There were a total of 87 seats. The BJP had never won a single seat in any previous state elections in Jammu &

Kashmir. Their strategy paid off. The BJP was able to win 25 seats in the Hindu-majority Jammu region and became part of the coalition government with the People's Democratic Party (PDP) which won 28 seats with Mufti Mohammad Sayeed of the PDP as chief minister. After his death in January 2016, his daughter Mehbooba Mufti took over in April 2016. The PDP-BJP coalition government, however, collapsed in June 2018, followed by a long governor/presidential rule as had happened many times in the past.

As I went ahead and met the Hurriyat leaders, the Indian government issued a statement that said: "The invitation to so-called leaders of the Hurriyat by Pakistan High Commissioner does indeed raise questions about Pakistan's sincerity, and shows that its negative approaches and attempts to interfere in India's internal affairs continue unabated, under the present circumstances, it is felt that no useful purpose will be served by the Indian Foreign Secretary going to Islamabad next week."

In response, our foreign office called India's move to cancel talks a "setback to the efforts to promote good-neighborly relations with India", and said the meeting with Kashmiri leaders was a "long-standing practice" prior to the Pakistan-India talks.

To go ahead and meet the Kashmiri leaders was not an easy decision for me especially when I knew how our own leadership was lukewarm on Kashmir. I was also aware of the fact of how my detractors in the foreign office would exploit the situation to my disadvantage. But I was determined to not let the Kashmiris and their leaders down. Though the Indian media and commentators by and large held me responsible for scuttling the prospects of bilateral dialogue, I was absolutely content and happy that I did not waffle. Kashmiris were also upbeat and felt reassured.

All the Hurriyat leaders whom I met on 18 and 19 August appreciated my decision. They also asked me to convey their gratitude to Prime Minister Sharif for making a clear choice in favor of the Kashmiris. Syed Geelani was particularly appreciative. He was extremely apprehensive of the BJP agenda vis-à-vis Kashmir and was of the view that Modi was using the bogey of dialogue only to bide time. Pakistan should be wary of what Modi was up to.

There were some sane Indian voices who disagreed with the Indian official viewpoint and termed India's reaction as out of proportion. For example, a well-known and respected Indian journalist, Vinod Sharma, writing in *Hindustan Times* on 20 August commented: "Making the envoy's invite to the Hurriyat as the prime reason for discarding talks seemed a trifle churlish. Grudgingly though, such meetings were allowed in the past including the 1998–2004 Vajpayee period."

Another well-respected journalist, Prem Shankar Jha, wrote an article under the title, "An Inept Pakistan Policy". carried by *The Times of India* on 21 August. He wrote: "Monday's action may make BJP look tough but it has severely hurt India's long-term interests. It has revoked the commitment previous governments, including Vajpayee's, made to keep the Kashmiris within the decision-making process. And it has sealed the doom of Hurriyat and all "separatists" who had tacitly accepted the Manmohan-Musharraf formula for peace."

A veteran Indian diplomat, Ambassador K.C. Singh, in an article in *The Asian Age* of 20 August stated: "Hurriyat leaders have been meeting the Pakistan envoy or visiting Pakistani political leaders periodically. High Commissioner Abdul Basit met them on 2 April 2014 on the eve of Indian elections. It hardly raised a storm. When PM Nawaz Sharif came for Mr

Modi's swearing-in ceremony on May 26-27, 2014, he skipped meeting them, perhaps to avoid a controversy in view of the context. The two PMs exuded bonhomie and announced that the foreign secretaries would follow up on their useful talks. It was assumed that all pre-conditions had been thrashed out."

Ambassador Singh had raised the pertinent issue but at least I was not aware if any understanding had been reached between Pakistan and India on not meeting the Hurriyat leaders. The problem from my perspective then was that Prime Minister Sharif's one-time concession of not meeting the Hurriyat was being misconstrued by India that Pakistan had agreed to keep the Kashmiris at bay in order to keep the bilateral environment positive and constructive.

The Hindu in its editorial of 20 August had also upbraided New Delhi for cancelling the talks: "..... the proper course would have been to express displeasure at the Pakistan High Commissioner's invitation to the Hurriyat for consultations before the talks between the Foreign Secretaries. But to have cancelled the talks shows a shockingly inadequate grasp of history, and is short-sighted."

Quoting unknown official sources, some Indian newspapers wrote that, "In fact, mindful of India's sensitivities, Pakistan Prime Minister Nawaz Sharif did not meet the Hurriyat leaders when he visited India to attend Modi's swearing-in ceremony on May 26. When Sharif did not meet the Hurriyat leaders, what was the need for the Pakistan High Commissioner to meet them?"

Most commentators in Pakistan were also critical of the Indian decision. The government was being commended for standing its ground on Kashmir. Many thought that the mistake of not raising Kashmir at the New Delhi meeting had been rectified. India should not be under any illusion that the bilateral relationship could move towards normalization without tangible progress on finding a just solution to the Kashmir dispute. My meeting with the Hurriyat leaders had clearly conveyed to the newly-elected Indian government that Kashmir was central and that there could be no compromise on our principled position.

******

I was already scheduled to have an interaction at New Delhi's Foreign Correspondents Club as arranged by Press Counsellor Manzoor Memon on 20 August. After the cancellation of the foreign secretaries meeting, some of my colleagues in the high commission advised that it would be desirable to cancel the event as it could lead to engendering more controversies. However, agreeing with my other colleagues, I decided that cancelling the event was not a good option. This was an opportunity for us to explain and put things in their right perspective. The foreign secretaries' meeting was cancelled by India by using a lame pretext and not Pakistan. We must not be seen as being apologetic. This was indeed the right time for more public diplomacy rather than hiding behind the big walls of the high commission.

I asked Minister (Political) Rahim Hayat Qureshi and Manzoor Memon to accompany me. The place was jam-packed and the event, Memon told me, would go live and would also be seen in Pakistan. As a diplomat, I was trained to handle pressures. However, I must admit I was feeling drained because I was not only facing Indians but also wasn't sure what Prime Minister Sharif was thinking. There was no room for a lapsus linguae. At the end, I thought I had managed the event reasonably well. I kept my cool and composure and, after my initial remarks, responded to all and mostly provocative questions with diplomatic unflappability.

I was particularly flattered by an article by Nayanima Basu in the daily *Business Standard* of 22 August under the heading, "His cool-headedness serves him well". She wrote: "Audacity, or as some would call it, chutzpah, is a facet of diplomacy. Abdul Basit practices it well. He may be a diplomat by profession, but the art of saying the right thing at the right time is almost inborn in Basit.

"Basit obviously has many qualities as the practitioner of the art of finesse. Therefore, it is doubly interesting to see how he makes both ends meet when the going has just got that much tougher for the neighboring countries."

My message at the Foreign Correspondents Club was loud and clear: The Hurriyat leaders were the legitimate stakeholders in efforts to find a solution to the Kashmir dispute; Pakistan would, therefore, continue talking to Kashmiri leaders; the sudden change in India's position was neither comprehensible nor helpful. I added that, while the situation was complex, there was no need to be pessimistic about it. The setback should not discourage us from finding ways and means to take the process forward in line with our leadership's vision on both sides of the border.

There was also a question about Hafiz Muhammad Saeed, chief of Jama'at-ud-Da'wah (JuD), who is a household name in India about why he was roaming about freely in Pakistan despite his involvement in many terror actions. My response to the effect that Pakistan could not put its citizens behind bars just to please other countries became a media headline immediately. A judicial process could go nowhere without evidence and, in his case, there was not enough evidence to arrest and try him.

In response to my overall remarks at the Club, MEA spokesperson, Syed Akbaruddin, said that "only India and

Pakistan are stakeholders and this was a principle which is the bedrock of our bilateral relations and which was also reaffirmed in the 1999 Lahore Declaration."

This statement by the MEA spokesperson was a clear indication that the BJP government had made up its mind that more of the same would not work or would not be allowed to work. At one level I was satisfied that I was able to expose the BJP early in the game and that, if Prime Minister Sharif had any illusions or had committed anything to Modi about which I was not aware, this was the right time to dispense with the euphoric tendency that, if Pakistan had accommodated India on Hurriyat, Prime Minister Modi would go out of his way to favor Sharif and resume the bilateral dialogue on Kashmir.

I had always been of the view that we must disabuse India of the notion that Pakistan was begging for dialogue and that peace in the region was only in Pakistan's interest. Because of our own flawed narrative, India had been leveraging the process of bilateral engagement to build pressure on us, especially on Kashmir, and we had been unwittingly weakening our Kashmir policy. Thus, throughout my stay in India, I had always emphasized that talks were not a favor by one country to another; they should be held without preconditions and, as our friend, Mani Shankar Aiyar says, should be "uninterrupted and uninterruptible." Aiyar, diplomat-turned-politician, also served in Karachi as India's first consul general from 1978 to 1982. He resigned from the service in 1989 and joined the Congress party. Very impressive, Aiyar is a treasure of knowledge and clarity of vision. We share the same date of birth, 10 April. (Aries are generally nice people. I know many non-Aries readers would hardly agee.)

I would also argue that both the countries had invested heavily in cobbling together a myriad of CBMs. We must work together to build on them and move forward irreversibly rather than disrupting the dialogue every now and then, and raise questions about the CBMs. We must also not allow the bilateral dialogue to become hostage to terrorism as violent extremists on both sides of the border who had their own respective agendas would always look for ways to not let mutual hostility give way to mutual understanding and affinity.

However, whereas New Delhi was hubristic, Islamabad had the masochistic ability to be delusional. My own take when it came to India had always been that Pakistan must be patient and talk less but coherently. We had the tendency of making hoary and pleonastic statements and, since statements about India would usually grab headlines, our politicians, whether in government or opposition, would not miss an opportunity to be in the limelight by lashing out at India.

India also had its own issues. Whereas its tactics were aimed at avoiding meaningful talks on Kashmir and keeping Pakistan under pressure on terrorism, it could not avoid talking to Pakistan indefinitely. It was after all aspiring to be a regional and global power and, by cancelling the foreign secretary-level meeting on a flimsy ground, it was not helping its own systemic diplomatic objectives. I had no doubt whatsoever that India itself would find a way to reach out to Pakistan.

On 9 September, External Affairs Minister (EAM) Sushma Swaraj speaking about talks with Pakistan said: "There was no full stop in diplomacy". She also changed the Indian position slightly by saying that India was opposed to Pakistan meeting "Kashmiri separatists" before India-Pakistan talks conveying implicitly that India would not demur to post-talks meetings. I thought Pakistan was never so adamant about the sequence of meetings. If that was the Indian position, Foreign Secretary Singh could have been more diplomatic and nuanced rather than threatening me of the consequences if I had met the Hurriyat leaders.

On 11 September, I inaugurated the second edition of the lifestyle show "Aalishan Pakistan" jointly put together by the Trade Development Authority of Pakistan and the Federation of Indian Chambers of Commerce and Industry (FICCI). In my address and in response to questions, I made two basic points. Firstly, I could not agree more with Sushma Swaraj that we must keep the diplomatic door ajar if we were serious in pursuing peace. Secondly, "Sky is the limit if India and Pakistan got together." (*The Hindu*, 12 September 2014). My remarks were received positively across India. Nevertheless, I could see even then that the Hurriyat episode was not yet over and it would resurface at some point pushing the engagement process back into a cul-de-sac.

I was asked to come to Islamabad for consultations and, before leaving, I wanted to meet both the newly appointed National Security Advisor (NSA), Ajit Doval, and Foreign Secretary Singh.

My first meeting with NSA Doval took place on Saturday, 13 September. Doval had spent over 6 years in Pakistan under cover and knew Pakistan well but, inevitably, as a former intelligence officer, was trained to look at things mostly from an intelligence lens. I was also aware of his "defensive-offence strategy" vis-à-vis Pakistan which he had articulated in his lecture at Sastra University in Tamil Nadu in February 2014. In simple terms, his doctrine sought to weaken Pakistan from within through terrorism. He had also conveyed in that lecture that Pakistan should understand that, if there was another Mumbai, Pakistan would lose Balochistan.

It was our first meeting and it was important from my viewpoint to establish a good rapport with him since, as the grapevine had it, he would be driving India's Pakistan policy. He made the following interesting points:

1. Modi was sincere and genuinely wanted to reset relations with Pakistan.
2. Once a commitment was made, it should be delivered no matter what. But if there were problems, those should be discussed truthfully.
3. Modi would go all out for Pakistan if he was convinced of Pakistan's sincerity.
4. India-Pakistan destinies were interlinked. There was no option but to work together for peace.

In my response, I told him that, given his vast experience, he would agree that the distrust was mutual. And then there were some fundamental issues. The impression in Pakistan was that India was not sincere in resolving the Kashmir dispute. Even the back-channel diplomacy could not deliver. I also assured him that Prime Minister Nawaz Sharif, too, wanted to make a new beginning but the Hurriyat episode and the cancellation of the foreign secretary-level meeting by India unilaterally did not augur well. I expressed the hope that India would soon find a way out of the present stalemate.

Neither of us raised the possibility of a meeting between the two prime ministers in New York as the two leaders had agreed in their first meeting in New Delhi on 27 May.

Doval also gave me his private number to contact him directly whenever required. I thanked him for that saying that I looked forward to working with him closely in the interest of peace between our two countries and the prosperity of our region as a whole.

My meeting with Foreign Secretary Singh was on 15 September. I told her that I was going to Pakistan for consultations and was interested in knowing what her thoughts were on the present bilateral situation. While repeating India's position on our meetings with the Hurriyat, she mentioned that the Indian side was encouraged that Prime Minister Nawaz Sharif had accepted their request and did not meet the Hurriyat leadership during his stay in New Delhi. Therefore, my meetings with the Hurriyat leaders had come as a total surprise. Now she had surprised me since I was not informed about this by Islamabad but I had to feign knowledge about it.

I responded to her that we were shocked at the way New Delhi reacted to my meeting. If the prime minister did not meet the Hurriyat leadership because of the special occasion and the limited time at his disposal, how could India deduce that the Pakistan position vis-à-vis the Hurriyat had changed?

Sujatha also asked me to remind Islamabad about the Mumbai attack trial and their request to keep their high commissioner in Islamabad au currant with the progress. I said we were fully cognizant of our obligations. However, she would appreciate that the trial could not be concluded without India's active and full cooperation. I also reminded her of the Samjhauta Express terror blasts trial hoping that India would also keep us posted as the trial, which seemed to be going nowhere, was of immense concern to Islamabad.

We both agreed to meet again after I had returned from Pakistan. There was no mention from either side about the upcoming UNGA session in New York. By now it was clear that the neither side would make the first move and suggest a meeting between the two prime ministers.

My meetings and discussions in Islamabad were quite useful. I argued that Modi would eventually agree to resuming talks provided we stood our ground firmly. Adding a note of caution, I said we must not expect this happening anytime soon. Modi would ratchet up the rhetoric and also tension along the Line of Control in the run-up to the state elections in Kashmir in November/December this year. The BJP was confident of performing well in Jammu though the Kashmir Valley was a different story.

I would also emphasize that the Indian narrative of Pakistan had not changed. It sought to portray Pakistan as a problem country which was stoking "terrorism" in Kashmir, using dilatory tactics on the Mumbai trial and that the Pakistan establishment was the biggest impediment in settling issues between the two countries. Even my meeting with the Hurriyat leaders was being projected as if I had received direct orders from Rawalpindi.

To my utter surprise, nobody in the foreign office was ready to give me a clear response to my question of whether we had given any word to New Delhi on our interaction with the Hurriyat. They would beat about the bush. It seemed that, even our in-charge additional secretary, Mohsin Razi, was not in the loop. He was a coursemate and friend and would keep the high commission posted wherever it was necessary. After his promotion in September, he was moved to head the Foreign Service Academy (FSA). Thereafter, the high commission was totally on its own. As I could easily assess, the ministry had clearly made up its mind that they would continue working through the Indian high commission in Islamabad and not me. In diplomacy, there could not be anything more Kafkaesque than this; a state undermining its own established channels of communication. It simply proved that the MoFA leadership was totally bankrupt professionally and I was considered to be an outsider.

During my consultations in Islamabad, I also advised that Pakistan should not request a meeting between the two prime ministers in New York. But if there was any suggestion from New Delhi or some mutual friends tried to arrange a meeting, Pakistan should be amenable though I did not realistically see that it was likely to happen. I also said that we should not seek a bilateral meeting on the margins of the SAARC Summit being held in Kathmandu, Nepal, in the last week of November. In my considered opinion, India was highly unlikely to have any meeting before elections in Jammu & Kashmir.

But there is no end to surprises in Pakistan. Sartaj Aziz was in New York along with the prime minister. Giving an interview to an Indian TV channel (NDTV) from there on 28 September, he threw a bombshell by saying that the "high commissioner's meeting with the Hurriyat leaders in New Delhi ahead of the foreign secretary-level talks in August was perhaps not totally right. If India had sent its request a little earlier, probably it could have been considered. The message came at a time when one Hurriyat leader was already in Pakistan's High Commission in New Delhi.' (*The Indian Express*, 29 September 2014). Just after a day he tried to rectify this by saying that his statement was twisted as there was no reason Pakistan should not be interacting with the Hurriyat leadership.

I had no clue as to what prompted Sartaj Aziz to make these gratuitous remarks especially when we had had in-depth discussions in Islamabad just 10 days ago. I felt very embarrassed indeed. Press Counsellor Manzoor Memon was also very upset as his Indian journalist friends had deluged him for the high commissioner's reaction. I decided to stay quiet for it would have ill-behooved me to contradict Sartaj Aziz. I left it to the foreign office to handle.

The most befitting rejoinder, however, came from one of my senior colleagues, Ambassador Asif Ezdi, who was now retired and would write off and on for *The News*. He was also one of my predecessors in Berlin. In his article published on 14 October, titled "Calculated escalation", he wrote: "What Sartaj said was not only unfair to the high commissioner, it was also very ill-advised, to put it mildly. And it would be nothing short of disastrous if the government were now to act upon the Indian suggestion to recall Basit from his post in Delhi, something that Nawaz is quite capable of doing. It would not only be unfair to him but, far worse, it would confirm the impression that his government lacks the spine and the nerve to stand up to Indian pressure and bluster."

Ambassador Ezdi also commented, "Of course, there was nothing wrong with the timing of the high commissioner's meeting." In conclusion, he said, "Modi will of course not change his policies towards Pakistan. He is the prime minister of India and will do what he thinks is in his country's interests as he sees them. Our problem is not Modi, but our own leaders who are too timid and too weak-kneed to stand up for Pakistan's interests in the face of external pressure. The people of Pakistan surely deserve better."

At her weekly press briefing on 2 October, the foreign ministry's spokesperson had a difficult job trying to defend Sartaj Aziz's indefensible comments and she did well to restate Pakistan's policy that "we will continue to meet Kashmiri leadership whenever we consider it necessary."

While there was no meeting between the two prime ministers in New York, eyes were now set on Kathmandu where the 18th SAARC summit was scheduled to be held on 26-27 November. Some well-placed sources in New Delhi had told me that Modi was ready to meet Sharif in New York had the latter agreed to not mentioning Kashmir in his UNGA session address. I was not aware of that but that was, in any case, a cockamamie idea. Sharif could not have taken the risk of igniting enormous domestic wrath by excluding Kashmir from a statement on the world's biggest multilateral stage.

But SAARC was different and was not the forum where country speeches would mention bilateral issues. I was still of the view that Pakistan must not seek a meeting and that was also our official position. However, I was keen to know what the Indians were thinking. I requested Dulat if he could enquire and let me know. He returned to me in the last week of October. His impression was that, while the Indian side was positive about a bilateral meeting, they were unsure of the outcome. I said a meeting could be taken as an icebreaker rather than thinking of outcomes at this stage.

Here I may mention my first and last meeting with Ram Madhav, General Secretary of the BJP and a former member of the National Executive Council of the RSS, on 24 October. Deputy High Commissioner Mansoor A. Khan accompanied me to the meeting. Madhav was the point man for Kashmir and he had subsequently negotiated with the PDP the "Agenda for Alliance" that helped form the PDP-BJP coalition government in Jammu & Kashmir in March 2015 under Mufti Mohammad Sayeed.

When I asked him about the BJP election manifesto, he claimed that the Modi government was committed to revoking Article 370 and that would happen sooner or later no matter what Pakistan said or did.

I realized immediately that Madhav was a difficult guy. I did, however, respond politely to all his self-serving and stereotypical arguments. In particular, I stressed that Kashmir was not about a territory but the people living there under interminable and abominable oppression. I made it absolutely clear to him that, whatever the BJP was planning, Kashmiris would never accept unilateral and illegal actions. Moreover, Pakistan-India relations would never move from confrontation to cooperation irreversibly without the resolution of the Jammu & Kashmir dispute. It was not a pleasant meeting but Madhav was an important person in the BJP dispensation with strong roots in the RSS.

I am sure I did not impress him either. Hence, my subsequent repeated requests for a meeting with him were never answered. We could always be forceful in making arguments but I had always believed in being courteous even in the most hostile of circumstances though there had been occasions in my career where I did seem to have lost my cool but that, too, I would do purposely; practising diplomacy needs patience and poise but tantrums, too, have a place in this delicate profession depending on the situation. I'll write more on this in a later chapter.

On 6 November, Ajit Doval called me to greet and also thank me for the gifts I had sent to him on Diwali. He also showed interest in seeing me to which I said, "I am at your disposal". However, he never called me back. I had thought that a meeting between us before the SAARC Summit would be useful in exploring if there was any possibility for a meeting between Sharif and Modi though I did not see India agreeing to a bilateral meeting at this critical point in time. Multi-phased elections in Jammu & Kashmir were to begin on 25 November. The late Arun Jaitley, who was then Finance Minister, made a public statement repeating the mantra of no talks in an environment of violence and that Pakistan had to either talk to New Delhi or "Kashmiri separatists".

However, a well-known Indian journalist, Barkha Dutt, claimed in her book, *This Unquiet Land* (pp 246–50) that the two prime ministers did meet in Kathmandu "in the privacy of Jindal's hotel room in Nepal where they are said to have spent an hour together. Elections in the sensitive state of Jammu & Kashmir were just a month away and Modi explained that, while he was keen to find ways to reopen some formal channels, circumstances did not permit him to do so immediately. Sharif, in turn, told him about the constrictions imposed on him by the security establishment in Pakistan — his negotiating power with the army had been gradually whittled away. Both agreed they needed some more time and greater political space to move forward publicly."

I still do not know whether what Barkha is claiming is correct. She also asked me post-Kathmandu summit but, since I was unaware myself, I couldn't confirm nor deny it. I did try to get to the bottom of her claim but failed. There was no one in Islamabad who would know or was willing to share information. However, all said and done, how was it possible for the two main SAARC leaders to be away for more than an hour and the meeting could still be kept under wraps and how could the hosts, who were responsible for the security of their guests, not come to know about it. In today's world, keeping confidentiality around such high-profile meetings is well-nigh impossible.

More than six years have elapsed since the Kathmandu summit. Sharif is no longer in power and we still do not know for sure if the two leaders had indeed met. I do not rule out the possibility that Indians might have used Barkha and planted the story to widen chasms between Prime Minister Sharif and General Raheel Sharif. However, I am not in a position to completely rubbish her story either. I did ask one of the Pakistan officials, who was part of the Pakistan delegation, about the claim Barkha had made. He told me that he, at least, had not come across any such information in Kathmandu. He, however, added it was possible that, during the retreat at the Delkhel resort, the two prime ministers were given some exclusive time by the other SAARC leaders to chat privately.

I did try to contact Jindal post-Kathmandu summit but apparently he was reluctant to see me as he knew I would ask him about the secret meeting in Kathmandu as was being claimed by Barkha. He must have thought it was better to avoid me for some time rather than to deny or confirm.

******

The 16 December terror attack on the Army Public School in Peshawar by the Tehrik-i-Taliban Pakistan (TTP) that killed 145 young students and staff, including the principal of the school, was a tragedy that had jolted not only Pakistan but also the entire world. In India, too, people were expressing their grief and visiting the high commission to sign the condolence book. In many cities, vigils were organized in memory of the victims. First Ajit Doval (17 December) and then Sujatha Singh (18 December) came to the high commission to record condolences on behalf of the government of India. I thanked them for personally visiting the high commission and signing the condolence book.

While that was not the occasion to indulge in political issues and discuss the state of bilateral relations, both agreed to have a cup of tea and the discussion of bilateral relations then became ineluctable. Sujatha thought the time was not still propitious for her visit to Pakistan, Doval thought differently. When I suggested to the latter to review the state of bilateral relations, he asked me to visit his office on 19 December for a detailed discussion. We met at 2:20 pm.

To my surprise, Doval asked me if Pakistan would be agreeable to receiving Sujatha on 22 December, that is, just in two days time. He added that he had not run the idea through the prime minister but he would do so if he received a positive response from Pakistan. He stressed that it was high time to break the ice and move forward. I welcomed the proposal adding that, since the notice was too short, we should keep the possibility open for a visit a week later as well. I undertook to get back to him at the earliest possible.

I immediately contacted Aizaz. I told him that we must get back to India with a concrete date if 22 December was not possible, suggesting that in any case, we should not be agreeing to the proposed date as Pakistan was still going through the pain of the APS tragedy. The proposed foreign secretary's visit so soon after 16 December was intriguing, to say the least.

Aizaz got back to me on 22 December and proposed 29 December for the proposed visit. I conveyed that to Doval instantly. He would run it now officially in the system. He also suggested somewhat out of the blue that the two sides should consider resuming the back channel to which I replied that we should first resume the formal diplomatic channel and then we could consider the back channel in due course. Interestingly, I never heard back either from him or the MEA though I did send him messages to respond to our proposed date either way. I also decided to not go into overdrive lest Doval misconstrue that Pakistan was desperate to have a foreign secretary level meeting or that we were at the receiving end.

******

I may conclude this chapter by mentioning two gentlemen with whom I interacted closely but they were opposite to each other. Let me first talk about Ved Pratap Vaidik, a journalist who claimed to be a friend of both Modi and Sharif. As soon as I arrived in New Delhi, he contacted me and then continued inviting me for informal chats. I found him to be a well-meaning person and thought he could act as a bridge between the two leaders. In June/July 2014, he visited Pakistan at the invitation of Prime Minister Sharif. He told me he was carrying a goodwill message from Modi. However, during the visit, he also met Hafiz Mohammad Saeed of JuD on 2 July and that created a huge controversy in India. Whereas Vaidik kept on explaining that he met Saeed as a journalist and interviewed him for his paper, there were few in India who would endorse his meeting the alleged mastermind of the Mumbai attacks.

In short, a person who intended to play a positive role and serve as a bridge between the two leaders ended up becoming irrelevant. However, I did maintain contact with him as I always appreciated his courage to speak up his mind and his genuine desire to seeing Pakistan-India relations improve to their mutual benefit.

The other person is a well-known historian and constitutional expert, A.G. Noorani, whom we all know for his courage in writing what he strongly believes in. His extensive books on Kashmir and Babri Mosque and many other highly valuable works are a treasure trove for those who are interested in Pakistan-India relations and India's political and constitutional issues. Whenever he visited New Delhi, we would invariably meet over lunch and discuss Kashmir and Pakistan-India relations. He would always surprise me with his memory and command over details. Born in 1930, he still writes passionately about issues without losing his objectivity as a constitutional expert and historian. I always cherished our long discussions and the ideas he shared with me on how to push Pakistan-India relations forward. One thing he would perennially grouse about was that Pakistan had such a strong case on Kashmir but the country had, by and large, failed to do much about it. He would also sometimes be critical of the founding father of Pakistan but do it obliquely in deference to my sensitivities.

Noorani is unapologetically anti-Modi and BJP/RSS and expresses his views openly and with remarkable intrepidity. Once he saw me having lunch with Pratap Vaidik. As a friend, he thought that it would tarnish my image as there was no point in entertaining such people. I would listen to him respectfully but not necessarily agree with him. I wish him a very long life and hope he continues writing and sharing his thoughts and wisdom on topical issues not only for our benefit but also posterity.

3

2015

"Diplomacy is the art of accepting the feasible in order to advance the desirable."

President Kwame Nkrumah

My meetings and discussions in Islamabad were quite useful. I also called on the prime minister on 28 January 2015. He seemed a little perturbed about my decision to meet the Hurriyat leadership but, when I explained the rationale of my decision to meet them, he appeared to be in agreement. However, he still thought that a way should be found to break the impasse. I respectfully submitted to him that the key was to remain steadfast and not show impatience. I had no doubt that Modi would eventually agree to talks, provided we firmly stood our ground.

Modi was a maverick politician and mavericks were attention seekers. He would reach out to Pakistan also to show the world that he was a man of peace but he would do that somewhat differently and dramatically. He was a man of theatrics; we would be well-served to wait and see.

Briefing him further, I said the Indian narrative of Pakistan had not changed. It continued to portray Pakistan as a problem country which was stoking "terrorism" in Kashmir using dilatory tactics on the Mumbai trial and that the Pakistan establishment was the biggest barrier in settling issues between the two countries. Even my interaction with the Hurriyat leaders was being projected in the context of civil-military relations in Pakistan. I underlined the importance of consistency and coherence in our India and Kashmir policy. There was no room to waver. I assured the prime minister that India could not stay disengaged for too long. I requested him to have faith in my assessment.

Since the prime minister himself had thus far not volunteered the information about his much talked-about meeting with Modi in Kathmandu, I was double-minded whether to ask him. During the course of our conversation he kept on referring to his meeting with Modi in New Delhi and not even once mentioned Kathmandu. I then let it go in the hope that I would be able to get the factual position from someone in the foreign office.

However, taking advantage of the meeting, I did submit to him that keeping the Pakistan high commissioner in the loop was essential for effective diplomacy. I would be grateful if the foreign office was directed to keep me posted on everything related to India and Kashmir to which he said, "I will ask Fatemi."

Towards the end of the meeting, the prime minister asked me to send him a very brief but comprehensive paper on Pakistan-India relations covering the key issues and how to manage them which I did on my return to New Delhi. As directed by him, the paper was only for the eyes of the prime minister.

While I was in Pakistan, Dr S. Jaishankar took over as foreign secretary on 29 January. On return to New Delhi, the first thing I did was to place a request for a courtesy call on him. We met on 13 February. I briefed him about the gist of my discussion with Prime Minister Sharif and how serious he was to move on with India and settle all the bilateral issues including Jammu & Kashmir. I underscored that no one had a magic wand to change things overnight. Prime Minister Sharif fully understood the complexities on both sides but he was willing to make a new beginning and reshape the bilateral relationship through incremental steps.

Jaishankar couldn't resist mentioning that the Pakistan side had miscalculated in the context of my meeting with the Hurriyat leadership last year but hastened to add that Prime Minister Modi, too, wanted to develop normal relations with Pakistan. However, Islamabad had to make some adjustments in its approach vis-à-vis the Hurriyat so that bilateral matters could be pushed forward without interruptions.

I told him that we were open to ideas but expecting Pakistan to change its Kashmir policy was a non-starter. It was India which had overreacted as most Indian commentators had also argued. At the end, we both agreed that it was important that both sides should avoid embarrassing each other publicly.

Interestingly, Jaishankar did not give me even the slightest of hints that Modi would be making a phone call to Sharif tomorrow. Modi used the pretext of the ongoing cricket championship in Australia and New Zealand to call his counterparts in Pakistan, Afghanistan, Sri Lanka and Bangladesh and wish their respective teams well in the tournament. Modi also conveyed to Sharif that he wanted to send his new foreign secretary to SAARC countries, including

Pakistan, in the near future. Jaishankar embarked on his so-called "SAARC Yatra" on 1 March with Bhutan and then visited Bangladesh followed by Pakistan and Afghanistan.

It was clear that India was using the SAARC cover to reach out to Pakistan and cleverly taking the opportunity of bilateral talks away from us so we could not insist on meeting the Hurriyat leadership. At the same time, the SAARC cover would also help Modi respond to the opposition's criticism that he did not have a Pakistan policy and that he was capitulating to Pakistan while getting nothing in return.

While I could appreciate the Indian move, I was sure it could not be sustained and the visit might eventually turn out to be an exercise in candy floss diplomacy. We might not meet the Hurriyat leaders this time but every bilateral visit in either direction could not always have the SAARC cover. As a diplomat, I was all for exploring newer possibilities and understood the importance of small and incremental steps in a hostile relationship but I was also aware of the hazards associated with slap-dash approaches. I was more interested in an uninterrupted and constructive dialogue process.

It was Modi who was trying to dictate new rules for bilateral engagement. They overreacted last year. The ball was in their court. Pakistan could accommodate them in different ways but they were mistaken if they had expected us to give up our interaction with the Hurriyat in the face of New Delhi's minatory statements and imprudent steps.

Islamabad was excited about Jaishankar's visit and, in my view, the excitement was misplaced. Beneath their excitement lurked some fear that Basit might again decide to meet the Hurriyat leaders and the process of engagement would yet again come to a halt before it could even begin. Although I had already conveyed to Islamabad that, since the visit was taking place in the context of SAARC, and that no significant development had taken place since August last year, I could see the Kashmiri leaders after the visit, that is, when they came to attend the Pakistan Day reception next month. I could even meet them before the reception if the situation so warranted.

Moreover, I genuinely thought that Islamabad was being carried away by Jaishankar's upcoming visit but there was no harm in letting them have a reality check. In any case, Islamabad was wrong to blame itself or its high commissioner, even by implication, for the August setback. It was the Indian side which had trampled upon all the diplomatic norms and practices and tried to bully us publicly. Kashmir was no ordinary issue. Both sides had well-established positions. I was even ready to resign but was not willing to pander to Modi at the cost of Kashmir.

Be that as it may, the political leadership in Islamabad was not ready to take any chances. Fatemi asked me to report to Islamabad immediately and I was in the beautiful capital a week before Jaishankar was to come. I met Fatemi, Sartaj Aziz and Aizaz. I soon came to know that the Indian high commissioner had met Fatemi and requested that no meeting should be held with the Hurriyat whereas some in the government were still of the strong view that I should return immediately to New Delhi, meet at least Syed Geelani and the Mirwaiz, who were already in the capital, and return for Jaishankar's visit.

I had to argue against this. My point was that we were not living in an isolated world. The international community, including our strategic partner, China, was watching the developments very closely and desired us to resume bilateral engagement. We must avoid taking any diplomatic step that could not be explained rationally and convincingly. We should play the game deftly and not only emotionally. By meeting the

Hurriyat leaders in August last year despite India's handling of the issue in a wayward and churlish manner, we were able to convey to Modi that Kashmir was too important to be handled casually. It was, however, important for us to be consistent and forceful. Conveying contradictory signals to New Delhi would damage the Kashmir cause irretrievably. All of us must be on one page and conduct our relations with India cohesively.

Jaishankar was given a very warm welcome. Besides talks with the foreign secretary, he called on Fatemi, Sartaj Aziz and the prime minister. Talks were mostly on bilateral issues and the prime minister in particular was concerned about frequent exchanges of firing on the LoC which he thought must come to an end to enable the two countries to work together in a relatively peaceful environment. Both sides reiterated their respective positions on almost all the issues ranging from Kashmir to Mumbai. The prime minister ended his conversation by asking Jaishankar to tell Prime Minister Modi: "If we can do anything, let us know and I am saying this with sincerity."

Jaishankar also delivered a letter from Modi to Sharif. The letter, inter alia, asked our prime minister to suggest a way forward. Our reply was, to put it mildly, a futile exercise in humdrum. It ignored almost all my suggestions. So much so that the ministry denied me an opportunity to call on Modi and deliver the letter to him personally. This was in spite of my making the request to deliver the letter. Instead, the letter was handed over by Aizaz to the Indian high commissioner in Islamabad on 31 March. This was bizarre and simply non-professional, to say the least. I was deliberately being undermined by my own colleagues back home and fighting on the two fronts was never easy.

I thought Jaishankar's visit had gone well in general but I was still not sure if this artificial congeniality could be sustained in the face of harsh ground realities. I was back in New Delhi and had already decided to see Syed Geelani at his Malviya Nagar flat on 9 March. I briefed him on Jaishankar's visit and invited him to the Pakistan Day reception. While the Indian government did not react, the media, as expected, went berserk taking pot shots at me for yet again vitiating the atmosphere and derailing the engagement process resumed with the so-called "SAARC Yatra".

I also met all the Hurriyat leaders on the occasion of the Pakistan Day reception. The Chief Guest from the Indian side was General V.K. Singh, a former Indian army chief and now Minister of State (MoS) for foreign affairs. One could see he was feeling very uncomfortable and was in a hurry to leave. He hardly stayed with us for 15 minutes. I invited him on to the stage. In my brief address, I thanked him for gracing the occasion expressing the hope that our two countries would continue working for peace and development not only in our mutual interest but also in the interest of the region at large. I had earlier asked him if he would be willing to speak but he regretted saying that he had to leave early as he had some other engagement.

As his host, I looked after him well and extended all the required courtesies but he didn't eat or drink anything. The most interesting part was that he came to our reception wearing white clothes with a green waistcoat, the colors of the Pakistan flag. That was obviously inadvertent but some Indian journalists did not spare him even for that in their write-ups the next day.

As soon he left the Pakistan high commission, V.K. Singh tweeted: "#DUTY A task or action that a person is bound to perform for moral or legal reasons". This was followed by two more tweets on similar lines: "#DUTY The force that binds one morally or legally to one's obligations", and "#DUTY A job or service allocated". (*The Indian Express*, New Delhi, 24 March 2015.)

These tweets were indeed in bad taste. Now that he had attended the reception, he could have stayed quiet. However, soon he kind of retracted his tweets. An hour later (around 11 pm), reportedly under pressure from the Prime Minister's Office, he tweeted: "Disgusted to see how certain sections of the media are twisting the issue". Earlier, when asked about his presence at the event, Singh told reporters: "The Government of India has to send an MoS. They sent me and I went there and came back." (*The Indian Express*, New Delhi, 24 March 2015.)

******

I visited Kolkata on 17-19 March and had a wonderful meeting with the charismatic chief minister, Mamata Banerjee. I was accompanied by my wife, Trade Minister Irfan Tarar, Political Counsellor Ubaid-ur-Rehman Nizamani and Press Counsellor Memon. I briefed her in detail about the issues that continued to bedevil the bilateral relationship expressing the hope that, given her strong political credentials, she would take more interest in this relationship and guide us on ways and means to avoid logjams and move forward uninterruptedly. I also invited her to visit Pakistan.

She did not speak a single word against Prime Minister Modi or the BJP government and, to my admiration, while hoping that the two countries would be able to settle the bilateral issues through dialogue, mostly talked about West Bengal and what important initiatives she had taken to improve the lot of her people. She also asked if we had tried the best mutton biryani in Kolkata. When I said not yet, she asked her staff to send it to our hotel for dinner. Indeed, the biryani was delicious.

I had a very busy schedule in Kolkata that included talks at local think tanks, media interactions, and meetings with business chambers. I also visited the central mosque as well as St. Xavier's College and addressed over 400 students. The visit could not have been better arranged. I returned to New Delhi fully impressed by chief minister Banerjee and wished that we had political leaders like her in Pakistan. She was literally the people's person. No wonder the BJP had not been able to dislodge her Trinamool Congress Party despite vicious campaigns against her. I also wrote her a thank-you letter for her warm hospitality with a copy endorsed to the Indian foreign office.

We returned to New Delhi on 19 March, and the next day we learnt that India had denied visa to a Pakistani couple who had lost their five children in the Samjhauta blasts and were buried at Panipat. The couple wanted to visit the graves of their children. The high commission did take up the matter with the MEA repeatedly, but they would refuse to oblige giving no reasonable explanation. Perhaps, the government did not want the Samjhauta terror attack to get any attention, especially now that there was the government in place that was trying to get acquittal for the four accused including RSS pracharak Swami Aseemanand.

On 8 April, I received at the Delhi airport 11 Indians who had been evacuated from Yemen and brought home in a special Pakistani plane. This humanitarian gesture was duly acknowledged and appreciated in India. Modi tweeted: "Thank you PM Nawaz Sharif for your humanitarian gesture". (*The Indian Express*, New Delhi, 9 April 2015.) My presence at the airport to personally welcome the evacuees was also widely reported and commended in the Indian media. I was wondering how long this favorable coverage would last. There must be some controversy brewing and I wasn't wrong.

Indian MoS for Home Affairs, Haribhai Parathibhai Chaudhary, while replying to a question in Lok Sabah on 5 May said, "The subject [Dawood] has not been located so far. His extradition process would be initiated once he is located." (*Mail Today*, New Delhi, 7 May 2015.) I was already scheduled to have an interview with Karan Thapar which was aired on 6 May. When he asked me about the whereabouts of Dawood Ibrahim, I referred him to the statement made in the Indian parliament on the previous day. I underscored that India had been accusing Pakistan for years without any concrete evidence and that it was good to see New Delhi finally acknowledging the reality that nobody knew about his whereabouts. (Dawood Ibrahim, originally from Mumbai, known to be a gangster, is currently on the run and on the most wanted list of Interpol. He is widely believed to have masterminded the March 1993 bombings in Mumbai in which 257 people died and more than 700 were wounded. In 2003, the Indian and US governments declared him a global terrorist. India has also put a reward of $25 million on his head.)

The Dawood issue would chase me also during my visit to Lucknow on 10-12 May. The media there continued asking me about him. A day earlier, Home Affairs Minister, Rajnath Singh, once again asserted that Dawood Ibrahim was in Pakistan. He told the Lok Sabha that "India had credible information of Dawood's presence in Pakistan. We will do whatever it takes to get him. Pakistan failed to take any action against Dawood or track him down". (*The Times of India*, Lucknow, 12 May 2015). I kept repeating my line of argument.

I called on Uttar Pradesh (UP) Chief Minister Akhilesh Yadav on 11 May. I briefed him on the state of Pakistan-India relations hoping that the trajectory set by the two sides would be pursued steadily. I also invited him to visit Pakistan as with

UP, India's biggest sate, there were numerous possibilities for cooperation. From Agra to Lucknow, these places were very close to the hearts of Pakistanis. When I told the chief minister that my father had studied at Darul Uloom Nadwatal Ulama (Nadwa College) and I would be visiting the place after our meeting, he instructed his staff that special arrangements be made for the high commissioner's visit. Mrs Dimple Yadav also appeared briefly and exchanged pleasantries with us.

I wished Yadav many more political successes in his career. He appeared confident that, despite intra-Samajwadi Party frictions, the party was well placed to win the next state elections on the basis of his unprecedented development work. However, in the elections held in 2017, the BJP had literally trounced the Samajwadi Party, and Yogi Adityanath, became UP's next chief minister.

My visit to the Nadwa College was simply remarkable and an unforgettable experience. On learning that the Pakistan high commissioner was visiting the college, the students came out of their classes in hundreds to greet me, shake hands and take selfies. My colleagues and I were overwhelmed.

In Lucknow, wherever I went and spoke, my message was terse and clear. "We cannot live in the past. We have to be forward-looking and bring in young people to move ahead uninterruptedly. Counsellors Memon and Farrukh Habib and Second Secretary Muhammad Adeel Pervaiz agreed with me that the Lucknow visit had gone extremely well. Despite the Dawood issue, we were able to keep our focus on the positives by reaching out to all important institutions in UP's beautiful capital which had so far managed to retain its legendry *Lucknow tehzeeb*. How could we, therefore, not have *tundey ke kebab?*

The local media was ubiquitous and followed our every step of the visit. Whenever my colleagues and I meet, even after my retirement, we still relish the warm hospitality the people of Lucknow extended to us. Politics apart, when human beings reach out to each other, they generally do create an immutable bond. I can only say, thank you Lucknow!

******

I visited Pakistan from 29 May to 14 June primarily for a restricted SAARC-ECO envoys' conference on 9-11 June. In our system, envoys' conferences appear to have lost their utility. Many good and practical recommendations are discussed and formulated but barely implemented. This is the irony of our system. Our institutions have, over the years, lost the capacity to sustain initiatives and processes to their successful end. I have witnessed and participated in many such conferences which have, for all practical purposes, become an exercise in futility. The prime minister will inaugurate, share his/her vision and then return to hear the recommendations at the concluding session, appreciate the work done, and wait for another envoys' conference a couple of years down the road. Nobody bothers to see what has been implemented and where there are gaps and to hold the weak links accountable.

It is not just about the foreign office. In fact, achieving foreign policy objectives is the work of the government as a whole. MoFA, unfortunately, more often than not, find other institutions and departments least cooperative. From trade to foreign investment and culture to promoting helpful narratives, the foreign office is inevitably dependent on others. Our diplomacy will continue to be performing less than its inherent potential if everything is left to the foreign office. We need tenable inter-ministerial mechanisms to ensure that government decisions involving more than one organization are executed in all their aspects.

Also, a reorganization of the foreign office is long overdue. The world is changing incredibly fast. Without massive structural and organizational changes, the foreign office would never be able to keep pace with the rest of the world and step up to the massive and multiple challenges the country is facing in many spheres. Frankly speaking, the foreign office has long not seen the leadership it has justly deserved.

During my spokesperson years from 2009–12 with a short interruption as I discussed earlier, and as additional foreign secretary, I had realized that our ministry must focus more on economic and public diplomacy. There was also no well-knit plan with regards to overseas Pakistanis; how to mobilize them and channel their activities towards promoting Pakistan's interests in a systematic manner. However, the foreign office and our diplomatic and consular missions abroad never walked the talk to deliver.

When I was posted to Germany as Ambassador, I made sure to bring the Pakistani community together despite their divisions along political lines. I would often tell them, "Abroad we should not be doing the politics of Pakistan but for Pakistan." I also made sure they had easy access to me and I am glad they always responded to my calls, whether on Kashmir or any other national issue.

I had also established an economic advisory council consisting of German-Pakistanis to seek their guidance on a regular basis since my main agenda in Berlin was to augment trade and economic relations. It was a pity that no one had earlier thought of establishing a bilateral chamber of commerce which was one of the prerequisites in the German system as chambers worked as official guarantors to private investments abroad. With the advisory council, we had immediately started working on the proposal. My early transfer from Berlin, however, did not allow me to see the proposal materialized.

At the envoys' conference, I made a presentation on the subject that was assigned to me which was followed by an animated discussion. Most people in the foreign office still thought that I would most likely replace Aizaz later this year or early next year. However, I was not living in a cloud-cuckoo land. I was aware of the vicious campaign against me and how the deeply-entrenched mafia in the foreign office was trying to promote their own candidate for the post. I would quietly watch, praying to Allah that whatever finally happened should be good for all of us. Sometimes you wish for something but you don't know how it turns out to be for you. I have always believed in hard work but the Almighty knows best what is good or bad for us. We must always submit to His will and be content with His countless blessings and pray for His forgiveness.

My call on the prime minister had already taken place on 3 June. Fatemi was also asked by the prime minister to join the meeting along with his Principal Secretary Javed Aslam. I briefed the prime minister on the state of bilateral relations underlining that our "patient diplomacy", as proposed by me, was working. Although Prime Minister Modi was being criticized by the opposition for his "flip-flop" on Pakistan, he, nonetheless, understood that he could not bully Pakistan and had to be accommodative. We also discussed many other issues and the prime minister more or less agreed with me. He had thought that it was important to have the engagement process in place and the sooner the better and especially the NSA-level mechanism that he had proposed to Modi in New Delhi.

In particular, I updated him on my focused endeavors to bring the Hurriyat factions together. It was being done in a subtle way as there were grievances on all sides though all of them did agree that the Hurriyat needed to work in unison. I told the prime minister that Syed Geelani, Mirwaiz Farooq and Yasin Malik had addressed a joint rally in Badgam on 20 April after offering condolences to the bereaved family of Suhail Ahmad Sofi. The Hurriyat leaders had shared the stage after almost seven years. This in its own right was a good development and boded well for the future of the Kashmir struggle. Subsequently on 11 July, the Hurriyat leaders were also together at an Iftar party hosted by Syed Geelani; our collective efforts were gradually yielding good results.

On a different note, when I told the prime minster that I would be visiting Mumbai later that month, he asked me to also meet his favorite legendary actor in Bollywood, Dilip Kumar, and convey to him personally his best wishes and present a bouquet of flowers to him on his behalf. I did that when I visited Mr Kumar at his residence on 19 June where Summiya and I, our daughter Umamah, and Second Secretary Muhammad Adeel Pervaiz were warmly welcomed by his wife, Saira Bano. When Dilip Kumar (Yusuf Khan and originally from Peshawar) came to know that I, too, was from Peshawar, he immediately started speaking in the local language called Hindko. Instead of 30 minutes, we stayed there for almost two hours as Dilip Kumar, despite being sick and frail, would not let us leave. Saira Bano later told me that he was incredibly thrilled with our visit. She asked me to visit again but, unfortunately, I didn't get an opportunity to do so.

While in Mumbai, we also went to see another Bollywood legend, Amitabh Bachchan. I was aware of his mostly negative views about Pakistan but that never discouraged me to reach out to such people. In fact, we needed more interaction with them to remove misgivings and persuade them to chip in as, being stars, their words counted. I must confess here that the way we were welcomed by the Bachchan family had far exceeded our expectations. Both senior and junior (Abhishek) Bachchans were at the gate to receive us and we stayed with them for over an hour. Mrs Aishwarya Bachchan, daughter-in-law of Amitabh and a Bollywood star in her own right, herself served us tea impeccably. We were deeply impressed by their warm hospitality.

Besides many other points, we discussed possible collaboration between the film and television industries of the two countries. Amitabh was very positive. When I mentioned several anti-Pakistan Indian movies, he said Bollywood was not working in a vacuum though he himself would prefer to keep art insulated from politics adding, in a lighter vain, how that was possible when he could not ensure the same in his own house. His wife Jaya, another great Bollywood actor, was now a politician and member of Rajya Sabha, upper house of the Indian parliament. To my invitation for him to visit Pakistan as he had a huge following there, he said, "let us wait for the right time." We also exchanged gifts and left their place with memories which I still cherish. Artistes on both sides of the border do have an important role to play in bettering bilateral atmospherics but it is easier said than done when it comes to Pakistan and India as their deeply-entrenched mutual hostilities do not allow enough space to take initiatives and sustain them smoothly.

I apologize for this slight but important distraction from Islamabad to Mumbai. Let us get back to Islamabad where I had come to attend the envoys' conference.

I had also called on National Assembly Speaker Sardar Ayaz Sadiq, Defense Minister Khawaja Asif Ali and Interior Minister Chaudhry Nisar Ali Khan. While my meeting with the defense minister was a slight disappointment as he paid scant attention to what I discussed with him regarding Siachen and Sir Creek, I found the interior minister focused and interested in issues. From Kashmir to Mumbai, I briefed him on all the important matters. I was glad that not only was he listening but also giving his views and advice candidly. I had then made a point to call on him without fail whenever I visited Pakistan from New Delhi. I tried to keep him in the loop as, being interior minister, his role in Pakistan-India relations could not be underestimated.

I also had a meeting with the chairman of the Kashmir parliamentary committee, Maulana Fazlur Rahman, at his residence in the Ministers Enclave. I had met him twice earlier when I was posted to London as deputy high commissioner and always enjoyed our conversations. Though the Maulana was a clever politician, somehow his performance vis-à-vis Kashmir had not been up to the mark. When politics is overplayed on national causes and people are placed in critical positions with no conviction, then the results are bound to be either unattainable or minimal at best.

******

Back in New Delhi, I convened our weekly officers' meeting on 16 June. I briefed my team about the sense I had brought back from Islamabad, underlining that the prime minister was keen to move ahead and that I would seek an early meeting with Jaishankar to discuss if a meeting between the two leaders could be worked out at Ufa, Russia where they would be attending a Shanghai Cooperation Organization (SCO) summit meeting.

Before my meeting with Jaishankar, Modi had already called Sharif on 16 June to felicitate him on the beginning of the holy month of Ramadan but, more importantly, to implicitly convey to him that he was ready to meet him at Ufa to which Sharif responded positively. Meanwhile, I had invited guests, including the Hurriyat leadership, for an Iftar dinner on 4 July which I had to cancel on 26 June in view of over 800 deaths in Karachi alone due to a heat wave. By 2 July, the death toll in the province of Sindh had crossed 1,400 people. Many Indian journalists, when they came to know about the telephonic conversation between the two prime ministers much later, interpreted my decision of cancelling the Iftar dinner in the context of the Sharif-Modi meeting in Ufa. They did not know that even the Pakistan high commissioner was not aware that the two leaders would be meeting in Ufa when I had cancelled the Iftar dinner. Ordinarily, I should have been asked by the ministry to be in Ufa for this important meeting but here I was not even being kept informed about important things like a telephone conversation between the two prime ministers let alone being asked to attend a meeting between the two leaders.

I met Jaishankar on 22 June accompanied by Deputy High Commissioner Mansoor Khan. During the discussion, I said that, though I did not have any instructions from Islamabad to discuss this with him, I was personally of the view that a meeting between the two leaders could help break the ice after a long hiatus of more than a year. Overall, Jaishankar was positive. After saying that releasing one of the seven accused in the 2008 Mumbai attack, Zaki ur Rehman Lakhvi (on 10 April, glad the Indian media didn't link his release to my birthday) on bail was a setback, he made the following points:

1. Bilateral problems could not be settled quickly and easily.
2. Two countries needed to look constantly at possibilities and focus on what was achievable.

3. Whenever a dialogue began, PM Modi wanted to move forward in a mutually comfortable manner and pace.

I responded to him adequately. As for the release of Lakhvi on bail, I underlined that it was part of the judicial process and had to be handled legally. I also briefed him about the recently held envoys' conference in Islamabad and Prime Minister Sharif's keen interest in settling all the issues with India and also removing impediments to regional connectivity and economic cooperation. As we were coming out of the South Block, I asked Mansoor to check with Islamabad whether there was any progress on the Ufa front as we still did not know that the two prime ministers had spoken to each other a week ago.

As always, I reported the account of my meeting with Jaishankar to Islamabad, recommending that any proposal for a meeting in Ufa if made by the Indian high commissioner in Islamabad should be considered favorably. However, MoFA, as on earlier occasions, kept me in the dark. I learnt through a senior colleague in the ministry that the Indian high commissioner had a meeting in the foreign office on 3 July and had proposed a meeting at Ufa either on 9 or 10 July.

I came to know about this on 6 July. I immediately sent a message to Aizaz to which he pithily responded "work in progress". He never replied to my message asking him to confirm if my Indian counterpart had a meeting with him or Fatemi last week. Nor did the ministry's South Asia Division bother to keep their high commission informed of the developments taking place at their end. Like all other Pakistanis and Indians, we had also learnt through the media that the two prime ministers would be meeting in Ufa on 10 July.

This was a clear indication that Islamabad would not ask me to come to Ufa for the meeting. I also showed no interest nor did I propose to the ministry that I should be attending this important meeting knowing that they would either not respond at all or say no.

Be that as it may, I did send a communication to Islamabad with suggested talking points for the prime minister. However, 10 July, contrary to the general expectations, turned out to be a bad day from Pakistan's perspective. By and large, Pakistanis were outraged at the way the meeting was conducted as well as at its unsettling outcome.

First, our foreign office apparently could not anticipate and left the protocol details unattended. In a big hall, our prime minister was forced to take a long walk up to Modi which was unacceptable in the context of Pakistan-India relations. We, as Pakistanis, felt very insulted. Modi kept standing at his place and waited for Sharif to come to him. Those long-walk visuals were played again and again by both the Pakistani and Indian TV channels obviously for different reasons. I sincerely hope such protocol details would not be given short shrift by our foreign office in future.

The outcome document of the meeting, negotiated by the two foreign secretaries, was also a setback from our standpoint. A joint statement issued by the two countries (Annexure III) did not explicitly mention Kashmir as was the case in the Sharm el Sheikh joint statement of 16 July 2009. That was the failure of the then Foreign Secretary Salman Bashir and Ufa reflected how Aizaz could not rise to the challenge to protect Pakistan's core interest in the joint statement. Even at the most difficult of times for Pakistan, for instance, after the 1971 war, our delegation had managed to include Kashmir in the Simla Agreement of 2 July 1972.

The second paragraph of the Ufa joint statement read: "They agreed that India and Pakistan have a collective responsibility to ensure peace and promote development. To do so, they prepared to discuss all outstanding issues." Jaishankar must have quoted the Sharm el Sheikh precedent to outsmart Aizaz. However, precedents are not sacrosanct. We all knew what India under Modi was up to in Kashmir. Therefore, he should have fought tooth and nail to have Kashmir included in the joint statement. And if the Indians were not willing to accommodate this, we should have told them loud and clear that Pakistan was not that keen to have a joint statement. Frankly, I do not know if Jaishankar even mentioned the Sharm el Sheikh joint statement in support of his arguments against including Kashmir. And if he did not, the Ufa joint statement was all the more disappointing and deplorable from our standpoint.

Our senior colleague, Ambassador Ashraf Jahangir Qazi, in an article in the daily *Dawn*, titled "The Ufa goof-up" (14 July 2015), wrote, "Has Ufa helped? As a starting point towards resumed dialogue, possibly. But the joint statement was an unnecessary disaster. It was the first prime minister-level joint statement in which Kashmir was not specifically mentioned. Kashmir was specifically mentioned in the Simla Agreement of 1972, the joint statement in New York in 1998, the Lahore Declaration of 1999, the draft Agra declaration of 2001, and the joint statement in Islamabad in 2004. Not this time."

He further wrote, "Terrorism in the India-Pakistan context is largely Kashmir related. Accordingly, mentioning one without the other is unhelpful even though terrorism is a concern of both countries. Nuances matter in diplomacy."

Ambassador Qazi was spot on but, as was obvious, he did not remember the Sharm el Sheikh joint statement which also did not mention Kashmir explicitly.

On terrorism, too, the joint statement was one-sided as if it was only India's concern. While talking about the Mumbai case trial specifically, it conveniently ignored the Samjhauta Express terror attack in India (18 February 2007) in which 42 Pakistan nationals were killed. Moreover, the two sides also agreed to a "meeting in New Delhi between the two NSAs to discuss all issues connected to terrorism." Another big mistake was to commit ourselves to providing to the Indian side voice samples of Lakhvi without perhaps knowing the background of the case and how India had been using delaying tactics to keep Pakistan under pressure. Undoubtedly, the Ufa joint statement was a huge setback for Pakistan.

As Pakistan high commissioner, no matter how incensed I was at the joint statement, I had to defend it publicly. I was interviewed by several Indian English and Hindi TV channels and newspapers on the Ufa meeting and the joint statement by explaining that "all outstanding issues" did cover Kashmir and that no one in the subcontinent could ever imagine that the two countries could make irreversible progress on other issues unless Kashmir was settled.

However, in my communications to Pakistan, I did politely convey the problems in the joint statement urging Islamabad that we should dispense with our delusional unilateral approach in the hope that Modi was some sort of a saint who would reciprocate and accommodate our concerns once he was fully convinced of our good intentions and that the establishment was also on board the process. We had also, it seemed, agreed to ditch the composite dialogue framework as I had feared all along.

The painstaking work of our seniors, especially Foreign Secretary Shamshad Ahmad Khan, was being consigned to the dustbin of history without being clear as to what the end game was. As I had witnessed in New Delhi, none of the prime minister's foreign policy advisors had the gall to say things which they knew the prime minister would not like to hear.

******

On 12 July, I attended an Iftar party hosted by New Delhi's chief minister, Arvind Kejriwal, where Vice President Hamid Ansari was also present. When I arrived at the venue, the Indian media immediately spotted me and literally converged on me to take me to task so they could make their headlines. As expected, most of them were interested in knowing when Pakistan would share the voice samples of Lakhvi and whether there was any change in Pakistan's Kashmir policy.

I would not run away. As a diplomat, I have learnt that if you avoid the media especially these days when everything is telecast live, you lose half of your narrative to begin with. Modern media is no doubt a tricky game with up and down sides. They will usually pick up one thing, mostly out of context and report it and then, no matter what you do, you are doomed to live with that. But I always tried to give them my punch lines; sometimes I succeeded and sometimes failed but I always engaged the media and that is mostly helpful depending not only on the substance of one's talk but also on one's demeanor. The key is never to get provoked and lose composure.

In Pakistan, the government had come under extreme political pressure from the opposition and was at its wit's end to justify that the phrase "all outstanding issues" did cover Kashmir. Technically, the government was right but failed to realize that their negotiating team had brought the Kashmir dispute down to any other bilateral issue. That was unpardonable but our systems had become so ineffective and inefficient that, instead of holding people accountable for their failures and incompetence, we reward them for their obsequiousness. But, to be fair, and, as mentioned earlier, this was not unprecedented.

Under unending domestic pressure, the foreign office principals went all-out in the media to explain and justify the joint statement. I could only sympathize with them as they had no solid arguments to make a convincing case. 10 July 2015 would be remembered as one of the days in Pakistan-India relations when our diplomatic skills were unarguably at their lowest as we failed both on Kashmir and terrorism.

Interestingly and, as far as I know, nobody talked about the Sharm el Sheikh statement in the government's defense which people in Pakistan believed was our success as it had mentioned Balochistan—naivety manifests itself in many ways but, when it is at the national level, then it should be a matter of great concern. I accept I was equally responsible at least in knowingly propagating the false narrative and misleading our own people as the foreign office spokesperson during that period.

A communication by our Ambassador in Moscow, who attended the Ufa meeting, which I received after a week or so, had given good details of the meeting. In fact, Sharif did mention Kashmir in the meeting along with Siachen and Sir Creek but did not do so as forcefully as Modi was on Mumbai. The two leaders agreed as under:

1. A meeting in New Delhi between the two NASs to discuss all issues connected to terrorism.
2. Early meeting of DG BSF and DG Pak Rangers, followed by a meeting of Directors General Military Operations. (Sharif suggested inclusion of Foreign Office representatives in these meetings.)

3. Release of fishermen and boats.
4. Measures to facilitate religious tourism.
5. Discuss ways and means to expedite the Mumbai trial, including additional information like providing voice samples.
6. Resumption of back-channel diplomacy.
7. Meeting of the two commerce ministers to discuss ways and means to enhance trade, including NDMA to each other's markets.

Except the last two points, the rest were all mentioned in the joint statement.

Despite the regrettable diplomatic setback at Ufa, we were all now looking forward to implementing the joint statement but divergent interpretations were inevitable. And the way the statement had become controversial instantly, no sane person with some knowledge of Pakistan-India relations would dare wager on its success.

The first casualty of Ufa was my Eid Milan party on 21 July that was boycotted by Syed Geelani, Yasin Malik and Asiya Andrabi. Kashmiris were understandably upset as to why Pakistan should sign a joint statement with India sans Kashmir. Their anger was justified. Mirwaiz Farooq, however, did come and we had a detailed discussion on Ufa and Kashmir. I assured him that Pakistan was fully behind the people of Kashmir and the Ufa statement must be seen in its proper context. Without settling the Kashmir dispute, there was simply no possibility of peace between the two countries. I added that Pakistan's tactical flexibility should not be misconstrued as if Pakistan had given up its strategic objectives. I also reminded him of the Sharm el Sheikh joint statement.

******

On 15 July, NSA Ajit Doval called me to convey that Pakistan was engaged in heavy firing on the LoC which should be stopped immediately. He added that, as agreed in Ufa, the Indian side was showing restraint and, if the firing from the Pakistan side continued, India would have no option but to retaliate; the situation could escalate and only Pakistan would be responsible for that. I listened to him with patience and, without entering into any argument, asked him to let me check with Islamabad and I would get back to him, hopefully, before the end of the day.

I immediately called Aizaz and informed him of Doval's angry call and a veiled threat. I asked him to let me know of the actual situation so that I could respond to him cogently. I did not hear back from him that day. The next day, Jaishankar also called me to reiterate what Doval had told me the day before. I again called Aizaz to know what was actually happening. Meanwhile, I also asked our Defense Advisor to check with Rawalpindi and see if we could get some response that could be conveyed to our hosts. The same day, that is, 16 July, Aizaz conveyed to me that he had just summoned the Indian high commissioner and lodged a protest against the unprovoked ceasefire violations by India which had killed three people on our side. We also claimed to have shot down an Indian drone on the Pakistan side of the LoC which India, as expected, denied.

I did call Doval back and convey to him what I was told. The general impression being created through the Indian media was that, since the Pakistan establishment was upset with the Ufa joint statement, it was now stymying the peace process by escalating tensions on the LoC.

Surprisingly, I wasn't summoned by Jaishankar to the South Block to lodge a formal protest on the LoC firing. There was also a "terrorist attack" in Gurdaspur, Punjab, on 27 July in which, according to the Indian official position, all the 4 to 5 terrorists, who allegedly entered either from Kashmir or Pakistan, were killed. The media had gone out all guns blazing at Pakistan and termed it yet another conspiracy by the Pakistan establishment to sabotage the upcoming NSAs meeting.

This resulted in the cancellation of my scheduled visit to Chandigarh, the joint capital of the states of Punjab and Haryana, as the chief ministers of both the states regretted their inability to see me. I also subsequently cancelled my visit to Kerala as my meeting with the chief minister could not be confirmed.

Moreover, the Indian side also refused to give permission to my officers who would usually travel with me outside New Delhi. That was clearly being done to convey India's displeasure both over the LoC firing and the Gurdaspur incident but there was no desire to take matters to the level where the so-called "Ufa spirit" could be decimated.

While all this was happening, Sharif sent a gift of mangoes to Modi and I would also receive an Eid hamper from Ajit Doval. We also met at an Eid Milan party hosted by Jamiat-i-Ulama-e-Hind on 23 July. I was also invited by Jaishankar to his Eid party for the Muslim high commissioners/ambassadors on 25 July where EAM, Sushma Swaraj, was also present. I was given an opportunity to sit next to her. I quickly went through the bilateral agenda including the upcoming meeting of NSAs, a possible meeting between the two prime ministers in New York, and then her own visit to attend the Heart of Asia Conference on Afghanistan (HoA) in Islamabad in December. In a lighter mood, she said, "High Commissioner, I hope the roadmap you are giving can be pursued but you know we can never be predictable on Pakistan-India relations." Agreeing with her, I said it would be very disappointing if the two sides could not sustain the positive momentum, adding that we also counted on her leadership."

It was there that Jaishankar told me that they had directed their high commissioner to propose 23-24 August to our side for the NSA-level meeting in New Delhi. I thanked him for the information. He also thought it would be helpful if meetings between DG Rangers/BSF and Military Operations could be held before the NSAs meeting.

From the party, I decided to go the high commission and send a message to Islamabad. And the next day I would receive a terse message from Aizaz that the Indian high commissioner had already conveyed that to us. This time I was neither shocked nor surprised because it was quite clear by now, as I was also told by an officer in the foreign office, that the foreign secretary had instructed them not to send any communication to the high commission without his prior permission. But I was clear in my mind that, so long as I was in New Delhi, I would continue pursuing my mandate actively no matter how much Aizaz tried to undermine me.

******

There is many a slip between the cup and the lip. Since the NSA-level meeting was being held within the framework of the Ufa joint statement, I was not very confident of its success or the sustainability of the entire process itself. Accordingly, I made four specific suggestions to Islamabad. First, our delegation must come fully prepared to respond to India's terror allegations including on Mumbai, and also bring along a comprehensive dossier on India's terror involvement in Pakistan.

Two, we must not agree to a second NSA-level meeting unless India had agreed to resuming a comprehensive dialogue process. Three, our delegation should include the foreign secretary and we should also suggest a separate meeting between the two foreign secretaries. This was important as the dates suggested by India was a clever move to avoid a meeting between Sartaj Aziz and Sushma Swaraj as the latter was to be leaving for Egypt on 23 August. The Modi government looked determined not to broaden the discussion beyond terrorism. And last but not least, Sartaj Aziz should meet the Hurriyat leadership.

The fact that we had played our hand so badly in Ufa, it was imperative to prevent another setback. The Indian strategy was to keep the focus on terrorism and discuss Kashmir also in that context. Interestingly, on 5 August, India claimed to have arrested another Pakistani, Mohammad Naved, in Udhampur who, they claimed, was a Lashkar-e-Taiba (LeT) operative. In our measured response, we put the onus on India to prove what they were claiming both on Gurdaspur and Udhampur. By levelling such baseless accusations, India was not helping the cause of peace and unnecessarily vitiating the bilateral environment just before the upcoming meeting.

I am still baffled as to why Sartaj Aziz would call in the Indian high commissioner (14 August) and convey to him himself that India's proposed dates for the NSA-level meeting were acceptable to us. Instead, according to the desirable diplomatic practice, our ministry should have asked its high commission in New Delhi to convey the message to the Indian side. But that was too much to expect from the ministry. When the house is divided and headed by people who nurture grudges and do things beyond their bailiwicks, such weird things become normal and there is little realization of their long-term negative effects for the institution as a whole. For MoFA, the Pakistan high commission in New Delhi did not exist.

As the situation on the LoC was still bad, I was summoned

to the South Block on Sunday 16 August by the acting foreign secretary as Jaishankar was on a visit abroad. As Counsellor Nizamani and I stepped out of the South Block, we were surprised to see a huge presence of the Indian media there. They started pummeling me with questions about what the Indian secretary said to me. I was double-minded whether to engage with the media at that point when the NSAs were to meet in ten days. I then decided to go ahead and use that opportunity to put forth our narrative and change the media headlines overshadowing the Indian demarche.

In my brief interaction, I told the media that it was not for me to tell them what the Indian secretary had told me. Nonetheless, I could tell them that I informed the secretary that India had violated the November 2003 ceasefire understanding 70 times in the past two months and that an effective mechanism was required to determine who was responsible for unprovoked firing. As my interaction with the media was being telecast live, my remarks immediately became headlines with the crowding out effect for the Indian protest. The next day, almost all the mainstream Indian newspapers carried headlines covering what I said rather than the Indian protest. Thereafter, and till my departure from New Delhi, I was summoned to the South Block several times but never again did I see the media waiting for me outside.

In diplomacy, as I see it, there is always some space in a given situation to use it to your advantage. Diplomacy cannot be a profession for people suffering from trepidation.

Meanwhile, the Indian media also started speculating whether the Pakistan high commissioner would invite the Kashmiri leaders for a meeting with Sartaj Aziz during his two-day stay in New Delhi. I kept the media guessing as I was still waiting for instructions from Islamabad to go ahead or otherwise. On 19 August, we made phone calls to the Hurriyat leadership and invited them to attend a reception I would be hosting for Sartaj Aziz on 23 August, the same day the two NSAs were scheduled to meet. This was obviously done after I had received clearance from Islamabad. My timely communication to Islamabad had perhaps left no option for them to say no to a meeting with the Hurriyat leadership.

We had changed the format slightly without losing the spirit of our interaction with the Hurriyat leadership. It was decided that, after the reception, the Hurriyat leaders would stay back and meet the advisor. While inviting the Hurriyat leaders immediately became a controversy, the other moot point had arisen that India would talk only on terrorism and not Kashmir. They also refused to have a separate meeting between the two foreign secretaries to work out modalities for all-encompassing bilateral talks. The two sides were yet again finding themselves in a gridlock.

The Indian side, adopting a more aggressive posturing this time, also decided to not allow the Kashmiri leaders to meet Sartaj Aziz. They were either not allowed to leave Kashmir or detained on arrival at the Delhi airport. (Source: https://www.thehindu.com/news/national/countdown-to-nda-talks-in-flipflop-hurriyat-leaders-held-let-off/article7562395.ece) The situation was thus boiling to the point where it was looking increasingly difficult to hold a constructive meeting but neither side was willing to take the blame for cancelling the visit.

On the other hand, the Indian foreign office was showing reluctance in meeting the high commission officials to finalize the logistics of the visit. The first request was made by us on 15 August, i.e., the day after we had confirmed the proposed dates for the visit. Despite our repeated reminders, we could get a meeting at the MEA only on 21 August. That was indeed a pro forma move. By then they must have already decided to set preconditions for the visit and make them public.

At a press conference on 22 August, Sushma Swaraj, adopting quite an aggressive tone, said that Sartaj was welcome to New Delhi but India would discuss only terrorism and that he should also not meet the Hurriyat leadership. This was the end of the cliffhanger. Sartaj Aziz, in a response presser in Islamabad, announced that, in view of India's inflexibility on the agenda of the talks and setting pre-conditions for the visit, it would serve no useful purpose for him to visit New Delhi. This was quite a setback but I was still convinced that "patient diplomacy" was the name of the game. We must not compromise on principles and, in any case, the Ufa joint statement was not a balanced document and needed to be replaced with something fair and realistic. In hostility there is barely any space for unilateral flexibility. But Prime Minister Sharif and his advisors in Islamabad were thinking differently.

After the cancellation of the visit, I gave many interviews to the Indian print and electronic media, explaining our rationale for calling-off the visit. I underlined particularly that we had never insisted that the two NSAs should discuss Kashmir. As provided for in the Ufa statement, it was only appropriate that, while the two NSAs were discussing terrorism, the visit was also a good opportunity for the two foreign secretaries to talk about future talks. Secondly, how was it possible for Pakistan to accept the Indian contention that Kashmiris were not the stakeholders in the Kashmir dispute? I still hoped that diplomacy would be able to find a way out as there was no alternative to talks if we were to promote peace between the two countries.

In spite of the setback, the two sides went ahead with a meeting between the Directors General of India's Border Security Force (BSF) and Pakistan Rangers in New Delhi on

9-12 September. The meeting was seen by many in the Indian media as an indication of a thaw and, perhaps, a prelude to a possible meeting between the two prime ministers in New York. But that was not to happen. Modi left New York after attending the Sustainable Development Summit. India's statement at the UNGA session was made by Sushma Swaraj.

In his address at the UNGA session on 30 September, Prime Minister Sharif once again tried to reach out to India by making the following four specific proposals.

The two countries:

1. formalize and respect the 2003 understanding for a complete ceasefire on the Line of Control;
2. reaffirm that they will not resort to the use or threat of use of force under any circumstances;
3. take steps to demilitarize Kashmir; and
4. agree to an unconditional mutual withdrawal from the Siachen Glacier.

In her address on 1 October, Sushma Swaraj, responding to Prime Minister Sharif, said: "We do not need four points, we need just one — give up terrorism and let us sit down and talk. She also referred to the 2008 Mumbai terror attacks alleging that nothing was being done to bring the perpetrators to justice.

On the other hand, Sartaj Aziz, giving an interview to CNN-IBN on 4 October, divulged that some messages were exchanged between Pakistan and India to have a meeting of NSAs in New York but Pakistan did not agree as it also wanted a meeting between the two foreign ministers to which India was not willing.

Yet again the high commission was not being kept in the loop. I wrote to Aizaz to share details. As usual there was no response. Earlier on 3 October, I had recommended to Islamabad that Sartaj Aziz might invite Sushma Swaraj to visit

Pakistan to discuss Prime Minister Sharif's four-point peace proposal. It was a foregone conclusion that India would not agree but there was no harm in testing waters and showing to the world that Pakistan made the proposal in New York with full sincerity of purpose. We would lose nothing if India had chosen not to respond or even if they responded negatively. In diplomacy one cannot give up pushing the envelope even in a stalemate. Islamabad never responded.

******

Pakistan's former foreign minister, Khurshid Mahmud Kasuri, was in New Delhi for the launch of his book *Neither a Hawk Nor a Dove* on 7 October. I was also invited to speak on the occasion along with former Indian Prime Minister Manmohan Singh, BJP patriarch L.K. Advani and former chief minister of Kashmir, Farooq Abdullah. In my brief remarks, I expressed the hope that India would respond positively to Prime Minster Sharif's proposals. I also emphasized that setting preconditions for talks would never work. It was important for the two countries to engage comprehensively and resolve all the bilateral issues while preserving and consolidating the existing confidence-building measures.

Kasuri spoke more about how close the two countries were to striking a deal on Kashmir through the back channel but the political circumstances in both the countries did not allow that to happen. He thought that, whenever the two sides had agreed to resolve the Kashmir dispute, it would be more or less along the lines of President Musharraf's four-point formula which was:

1. Border to remain as it is (on maps) and people on either side of the LoC to be allowed to move freely.
2. Self-governance or autonomous status (not independence) to Jammu & Kashmir

along with Pakistan-administered Kashmir for internal management in all areas like trade, tourism, waters, etc., to maximize socio-economic development of the region through cooperation.

3. Withdrawal of troops from the region in a phased manner.
4. A joint mechanism to supervise the implementation of such a road-map, comprising Indian, Pakistani and Kashmiri representatives.

We will perhaps never be able to answer the question whether the Congress party-led coalition government under Prime Minister Manmohan Singh was genuinely negotiating on Kashmir or biding time to weaken the freedom movement both politically and militarily. Whatever the case, there is no doubt that President Musharraf, by making his proposed plan public, had greatly damaged Pakistan's principled stand on the dispute. Even if a state is ready for a compromise, that is done through sub rosa diplomacy rather than discussing it in the open and depriving yourself of the room for plausible deniability.

However, it is also a fact that most Hurriyat leaders, including Mirwaiz Umar Farooq, had implicitly or explicitly supported the Musharraf formula. The lone voice of dissension was of Syed Geelani who never budged from the right to self-determination. Even for talks with New Delhi, he laid down five conditions, to wit:

1. India should openly acknowledge that there existed the Jammu & Kashmir dispute;
2. withdrawal of Indian forces from Jammu & Kashmir;

3. revocation of the draconian laws (such as Armed Forces Special Powers Act {AFSPA}, Public Safety Act and Disturbed Areas Act);
4. release of all Kashmiri political prisoners; and
5. tripartite talks between Pakistan, India and the Hurriyat.

While the book launch ceremony in New Delhi went smoothly, the one scheduled in Mumbai on 12 October was not an easy affair. Hindu extremists belonging to Shiv Sena succeeded in smearing black paint on Sudheendra Kulkarni for hosting Kasuri. When push came to shove, Kulkarni, former BJP leader and the chairperson of the Observer Research Foundation (ORF), an international policy think tank, exhibited great courage and refused to buckle under pressure. He managed to reach the venue and attended the event with the blackened face. The state BJP government also came into action and ensured the event did not face any further incident.

As I know him, Kulkarni is a genuine person keen on realizing peace between the two counties. I subsequently invited him to the high commission to give a talk on Pakistan-India relations as part of the High Commission Lecture Series on 27 November. It was a treat to listen to him. I continue to admire him for his clarity of vision, courage and wholehearted commitment to building bridges between the two arch-enemies.

But Shiv Sena members did succeed in blocking a meeting between the chairpersons of the Pakistan Cricket Board (PCB) and the Board of Control for Cricket in India (BCCI) on 19 October by storming the BCCI office in Mumbai. The PCB chairman, Ambassador Shahryar Khan, who was invited by his Indian counterpart, Shashank Manohar, for talks in order to resolve the issues apropos the bilateral cricket series as per the MoU signed between the two countries in 2014, returned to Pakistan without a meeting or even a telephone conversation with his Indian counterpart. There was quite an uproar in Pakistan on the humiliating treatment meted out to Ambassador Khan.

Insofar as cricket is concerned, if India remains adamant about not playing with Pakistan, it is not because of Shiv Sena. It is part of the BJP government's Pakistan policy to keep the latter under pressure on Kashmir and other issues. It is as simple as that.

Here it may be congruent to mention that I ran into Farooq Abdullah many a time during my stint in New Delhi. I would always exchange pleasantries but never engaged with him in any substantive discussion on Kashmir. On one occasion he briefly remarked that "Mr High Commissioner I know you do not like to meet us; and I fully understand your position." I only smiled and avoided to give him any response.

I may also mention here that Farooq Abdullah and my father-in-law Dr Abdul Haseeb had worked together at the Black Gate Hospital, Great Yarmouth, England, in the 1960s. When my wife reminded him of those days in England, Farooq Abdullah did recall, especially the delicious food cooked by my mother-in-law. They would often visit each other as they used to live in the same premises.

******

The Heart of Asia (HoA) conference was scheduled to be held in Islamabad on 9-10 December. The question was whether India would attend and, if so, at what level. Islamabad was keen to have a successful conference which meant that all member countries attended at the foreign-minister level. In case of India, the conference was also an opportunity to resume the bilateral dialogue should India decide to send Sushma Swaraj to the conference.

As for India, my assessment was that, since the conference was on Afghanistan, it would be difficult for India to stay away from the conclave or attend at a lower level as that might not go down well with the Kabul government. Moreover, India had always considered itself an important stakeholder in the landlocked Afghanistan. And if that could also help resume talks between Pakistan and India, the latter should be willing to consider the possibility provided there was a new framework more or less along the lines of the Ufa Joint Statement. So, attending the conference made perfect sense from India's standpoint. However, India was not ready to commit itself too early in the game. It wanted to first ensure that Pakistan, despite the cancellation of the NSA-level meeting in August, was still willing to play ball.

I sought a meeting with Ajit Doval and he immediately agreed to see me. We met in his office on Saturday, 7 November and the meeting lasted for about two hours. We reviewed and discussed the state of bilateral relations, including his Defensive-Offence Doctrine, and agreed that the two neighbors could not live in a state of perpetual stalemate. I encouraged him to respond positively to a bilateral cricket series in UAE next month as well as to Pakistan's invitation to Sushma Swaraj to attend the Afghanistan conference in Islamabad. He didn't commit on either but did undertake to mull over our discussion and help create a congenial bilateral atmosphere.

We also discussed Kashmir in detail. He was of the view, like Ram Madhav, that the Hurriyat had almost lost its relevance. India understood Pakistan's compulsions perfectly. However, Islamabad had to revisit its Kashmir policy and denude it of violence. India's Kashmir policy was now rooted in its parliamentary resolution of 22 February 1994 and no party in India could ever deviate from that. It was for Pakistan to rethink and encourage Kashmiris under its influence to come to terms, accept the Indian constitution and move on. He concluded by saying that Prime Minister Modi was doubtless very much interested in achieving peace with Pakistan but there was no room for making unconstitutional compromises. He hastened to add that Modi also realized that good and normal relations with Pakistan were essential for India's own growth and development. Therefore, he had been consistently trying to reach out to Pakistan but Islamabad had always misinterpreted his intentions.

I reiterated our well-known position, mentioning that as he had lived in Pakistan for several years, he would understand how strong the public opinion in Pakistan was on Kashmir. No government in Islamabad could ever take the risk of making unnatural and unconstitutional compromises. I reminded him of Article 257 in the Pakistan constitution that committed Pakistan to seek the will of the people of Jammu & Kashmir on what kind of relations they would like to have with Pakistan even after a decision was taken by them in favor of Pakistan in a United Nations-supervised plebiscite. I also told him that, if India had thought to weaken Pakistan through Afghanistan as per his own doctrine, this policy could not deliver on Kashmir. It was necessary for India to improve the human rights situation in Kashmir and engage with Pakistan to find a workable solution. I emphasized that a solution that did not respect the political aspirations of Kashmiris was bound to collapse under its own weight.

When I asked him about his views on the four-point formula and whether back-channel diplomacy was a better option, he paused for a moment and then said: "I would go by your advice on the back-channel". As for the four-point formula, he was almost dismissive as, according to him, it was impractical given the fast-changing realities on the ground. He was confident that the resistance movement was losing ground from under its feet; Kashmiris were exhausted and weary of the long conflict and wanted to live in peace.

Agreeing with him that Kashmiris had long been suffering and wanted an end to the extended conflict, I told him that this, however, must not be interpreted as if they were willing to give up their legitimate struggle. I underlined that India must not misread Kashmiris and avoid arriving at erroneous conclusions. The fact was that Kashmiris had made massive sacrifices, every household had suffered in one way or another and it looked almost impossible for India to win their trust. I added that, for India to realize its great potential in the region and beyond, resolving Kashmir was essential. I ended by saying that I wished this could happen sooner rather than later and that the two prime ministers could be standing together and sharing the Nobel Peace Prize.

He smiled at the last thought but then asked whether the Pakistan establishment was ready for a compromise and reminded me of the Kargil episode. In reply I said this was another misplaced view in India. I assured him that the military establishment was as keen on attaining bilateral peace as one could be. These misgivings could be removed gradually as the two sides engaged in a focused dialogue to make tangible progress. I added that it was, after all, General Musharraf who had put himself in a difficult situation by trying to find an out-of-the-box solution. It was also General Musharraf who had signed the 6 January 2004 statement with Prime Minister Vajpayee.

I also reminded him that it was the Indian establishment that had obstructed the almost finalized agreement on Siachen between Benazir Bhutto and Rajiv Gandhi in 1989.

I told him that, from my own experience, I could tell him that Pakistanis across the board desired peace with India but were not sure about India. New Delhi was still setting preconditions for talks and the plight of Kashmiris was continually going from bad to worse. I stressed that we must help our respective leaders to leave an eternally peaceful legacy in South Asia. I hoped that, with the visit of Sushma Swaraj to Pakistan in December, a good, solid beginning could be made.

Later, on 19 November, at a dinner hosted by Jaishankar at his residence, I had a brief conversation with Sushma Swaraj. When I asked her whether we should make arrangements to welcome her in Islamabad, she responded by saying, "let us wait and see". I could gather from our conversation that she would most probably attend the conference and the Indian side was also comfortable now to engage with Pakistan bilaterally.

By then I did not have any information relating to Sajjan Jindal's efforts towards facilitating an informal conversation between the two prime ministers on the margins of the upcoming climate summit in Paris nor did I know that India had proposed a meeting between the two NSAs at a neutral place so that the sticking point of meeting the Hurriyat leaders could be kept aside. I came to know about the two events just a day before each meeting took place in Paris on 30 November and Bangkok on 6 December, not from Islamabad but through my well-placed sources in New Delhi.

When I asked Aizaz on 4 December as to why I was not informed of the Bangkok meeting, he was kind of shocked as to how I came to know about it. When he could not come up with anything convincing, he, at the end, said it was the prime minister himself who wanted to keep the meeting confidential. When I asked even from the high commissioner he responded in the affirmative. I did tell him even then that it beggared belief that the prime minister would ask MoFA to keep his high commissioner out of this. I also sent a message to one of the aides of the prime minister and he assured me there was no such thing.

In any case, Islamabad never shared with its high commissioner as to how these meetings were arranged or what was discussed in them. Frankly, by now, I had become some what used to this grotesque practice. But, as a professional, I was finding it difficult to digest. It was not about Abdul Basit, but about conducting our India and Kashmir policy effectively. That only reflected professional and intellectual bankruptcy on the part of the foreign office. It was simply incomprehensible that they could even think that by keeping their own high commissioner out of the loop in most matters related to India happening at their end, they could achieve their objectives vis-à-vis India. Perhaps, they needed a refresher course at the Foreign Service Academy.

What I leant subsequently was that the two to three minutes' conversation between the two prime ministers in Paris was mostly one-sided. Modi spoke and Sharif listened. It was there that Modi proposed a meeting between the two NSAs in Bangkok. Prime Minister Sharif did not say yes then and there but thought it was a good idea. The only thing Pakistan wanted was to include the two foreign secretaries in the meeting as well so that some discussion could also take place about talks. India readily agreed to the proposition. In Paris, Modi also assured Sharif that, once the Bangkok meeting had taken place, and hopefully successfully, he would send Sushma Swaraj to

Islamabad for further bilateral discussion on the sidelines of the Heart of Asia Conference. Accordingly, Sushma Swaraj's visit to Pakistan was formally announced by India just a day after the Bangkok meeting had concluded. The ice was thus broken.

At the Bangkok meeting, the NSAs and foreign secretaries had also exchanged WhatsApp numbers with a view to staying in touch and bypassing the diplomatic missions. After Bangkok, as per my information, they had met twice, once in Bangkok and the second time in Moscow. This was in effect the resumed back-channel diplomacy. Now we were looking forward to Swaraj's visit. To my pleasant surprise, my ministry agreed to my suggestion that I should be present in Islamabad for a bilateral meeting.

******

Swaraj's call on Prime Minister Sharif on 9 December at around 4.30 pm was brimmed with mutual affection. Swaraj was full of praise for the prime minister, saying that Prime Minister Modi had told her after the two prime ministers' meeting in New Delhi that Nawaz Sharif was a sincere person who spoke from his heart. When the discussion turned to Mumbai, the prime minister said Pakistan wanted to conclude the trial but needed solid evidence. To that Jaishankar said he would consult with his NSA. Sharif also added that a joint statement to be issued after the bilateral talks should not become hostage to trivial language issues as people in both the countries wanted peace and prosperity. Swaraj insisted it would help their side if Kashmir was not referred to, specifically in the statement as mentioning of "comprehensive bilateral dialogue" should suffice to satisfy the people of Pakistan.

As we were leaving the prime minister's office, the prime minister directed Aizaz that we could be flexible on including

Mumbai in the statement if India had agreed to the resumption of a comprehensive dialogue. From there, we came to the foreign office for bilateral talks headed by Sartaj Aziz from our side. It was a marathon session starting at 5:45 pm and concluding at around 8 pm.

Par for the course, the draft proposed by India was clearly one-sided. Aizaz and Jaishankar were leading their respective sides while Sartaj and Sushma continued with their informal conversation in a separate room. I told Aizaz that the Indian draft had specific problems from our viewpoint. Firstly, the word "bilateral" before "dialogue" would be used by India as if Pakistan had committed to give up its insistence on talking to the Hurriyat and would talk only to New Delhi. It would also be interpreted as recommitment on the part of Pakistan to not raise the Kashmir dispute internationally as per India's interpretation of the 1972 Simla Agreement.

Secondly, the Indian formulation almost exonerated India of any responsibility putting the entire burden on Pakistan to conclude the Mumbai trial. The prime minister, while talking to Swaraj, had clearly stated that, though Pakistan wanted to conclude the trial expeditiously, it was waiting for solid evidence from India. In other words, the Mumbai trial could not be concluded without India's meaningful cooperation.

Thirdly, the bilateral dialogue should not be linked to progress on the Mumbai trial. It should be a standalone paragraph. I thought the word "accordingly" in the third paragraph of the joint statement was problematic.

Fourthly, the way Jammu & Kashmir had been mentioned in the Indian draft had brought the dispute to the level of other peripheral issues like people-to-people exchanges and religious tourism. I thought we could have borrowed the agreed formulation from the 1999 Lahore Declaration but the Indian negotiators proved too skillful for the visibly flexible and accommodative Pakistan side.

I was glad that Aizaz, at least ostensibly, did see merit in all the points that I had made. We put forth our views and suggestions but the Indians had already and rightly calculated how desperate Pakistan was to have the dialogue process back on track as was also mentioned by the prime minister that "the joint statement should not be made hostage to trivial language issues". But these were not trivial issues. When we failed to agree on the draft, we came back to the room where Sartaj and Sushma were sitting. They were informed of the sticking points.

I could not help but say explicitly what I felt about the draft, almost saying that it would be better not to have a joint statement if the Indian side remained inflexible. I kept telling both Sartaj and Aizaz, almost whispering in their ears, that, if the Indian side continued to be unreasonable, then it was better to not have a statement. This was, however, too much for our side as they wanted to deliver no matter what because the prime minister had told Aizaz that Pakistan should have no problem including Mumbai if India had agreed to a bilateral dialogue. But the prime minister, I am sure, did not mean to have a joint statement at any cost. Of course, our three principals (Sartaj, Fatemi and Aizaz) knew better than me what the prime minister actually meant.

As I was quite insistent on changing the proposed formulations, Swaraj, looking somewhat irritated, remarked that the high commissioner was a very tough negotiator and would not listen. Let me here confess, and somewhat with a heavy heart, that our side failed to protect Pakistan's principled positions and, like the Ufa Joint Statement, our side was yet again inveigled into diluting our national positions on Kashmir and Mumbai. At the end, India got what it had wanted and got it rather easily. It would be unfair to blame Aizaz alone. Sartaj appeared to be too weak, and Fatemi, though he was not in the meeting, was shown the final draft version by Aizaz to which he gave his consent. This was what Aizaz told Sartaj when he returned to the meeting room.

The way we handled the Indian draft in my view reflected very poorly on our working culture. In retrospect, I regret having requested the ministry to come to Islamabad for the bilateral meeting. Our side had already made up its mind to go the extra mile and accommodate India. The Indian side must have also realized that, at the end, nobody listened to me and I was overruled on almost everything. The Islamabad Joint Statement (Annexure III) was not what I thought we could agree on. Retrospectively, I tried to find some solace in the fact that I was not asked to attend the bilateral meeting in Ufa.

It is often said, and I think rightly so, that diplomacy cannot be conducted without showing flexibility and making compromises. But this, if we call it a general principle, cannot be applied to all situations. Many variables drive diplomatic decisions. And, in any negotiations, much also hinges on the opposite side. If the latter is not ready to budge an inch and expects the other side to be unilaterally flexible, how can one expect balanced and mutually palatable outcomes? Understandably, diplomacy is also about using pressure tactics on the weaker side to extract concessions. Whether it was Sharam el Sheikh, Ufa or Islamabad, Pakistan clearly went out of its way to accommodate India. Whereas Pakistan talks excessively about the necessity of talks, India has refined its position that, even talking to Pakistan, is a big concession to Pakistan.

On 14 December, Swaraj made statements in both Houses of Parliament on her recent visit to Pakistan. She said: "Her meetings with Sharif and Sartaj Aziz were held in the backdrop of the constructive talks between the NSAs in Bangkok on December 6. Both sides condemned terrorism and resolved to cooperate to eliminate this menace. There we dwelt on the need for Pakistan to expedite the Mumbai terror attacks trial. The Indian side was assured of the steps being taken to expedite its early conclusion." (*The Times of India*, New Delhi, 15 December 2015)

The same day, I met Hurriyat leaders Syed Geelani and Mirwaiz Umar Farooq separately to brief them about the recent bilateral exchanges. India didn't react to my meeting despite the usual din in the Indian media on such occasions. An Indian journalist later told me that, in an off-the-record-meeting with the Indian media on 21 December, Swaraj told them that India-Pakistan talks would take place irrespective of Pakistan's engagement with "the Kashmiri separatists". This was a positive development. Our perseverance had at last made India realize that this was an issue on which Pakistan would never compromise. Yes, we could accommodate them by meeting them in Bangkok but could not give up the right to meet Kashmiris who were the principal stakeholders in the dispute.

If this was true, then my apprehensions as I expressed on the word "bilateral" in the Islamabad Joint Statement were perhaps somewhat inflated. Perhaps, India was insistent on the word in the context of the Simla agreement, and not Hurriyat. But the way India had cancelled the two important meetings on the ground of our interaction with the Hurriyat, I was right to be forceful in my interpretation. In any case, I was not privy to all that was being discussed between the two sides in Islamabad. Still, I considered as my professional and national duty to express my concerns freely and honestly. I was not in a position to dictate to the foreign office to act upon my advice.

******

I was on leave in Pakistan when Prime Minister Modi made a surprise stopover in Lahore on 25 December on his way to New Delhi from Kabul to attend Prime Minister Nawaz Sharif's granddaughter's wedding ceremony. This was definitely the handiwork of Jindal who also attended along with many other personal guests of Prime Minister Sharif from India. I was in my hometown Peshawar when I was informed by my Press Counsellor, Manzoor Memon, in the morning that Modi would come to Lahore and spend a few hours with Sharif. I am not privy to what was discussed though the ministry knew that I was in Pakistan and, if they had wanted, they could have asked me to come and be part of the meeting like the Indian high commissioner was asked to be present in Lahore.

Be that as it may, according to the media in both countries, there was no discussion on substantive bilateral matters. Both leaders were satisfied with the 9 December Joint Statement and resolved to move forward. Aizaz told the media that both leaders agreed that Jaishankar would travel to Islamabad to carry forward the dialogue process. (*The Times of India*, New Delhi, 26 December 2015.)

Earlier, that is, on 19 December, Aizaz had informed me that Jaishankar wanted to visit Islamabad and that Aizaz had suggested to him the timeframe of 12-15 January 2016. He was likely to visit Islamabad on 15 January but that day was never to come.

The year 2015 concluded on positive notes boding well for future bilateral engagement. However, the Pathankot crisis at the very beginning of the next year brought us back to square one. Again, we got busy consuming our energies in containing another crisis and breaking another logjam.

4

2016

"Take time for all things: great haste makes great waste."

Benjamin Franklin

On 2 January an Indian Air Force base in Pathankot, Punjab, was attacked reportedly by a group of six militants. They were all killed in a counter-operation that lasted almost three days and also claimed the lives of ten Indian security personnel but caused no major damages to aircraft or other assets at the base.

Not unexpectedly, the Indian media immediately started accusing Pakistan for the attack. It was claimed that militants had crossed over from Pakistan and that the attack was planned and perpetrated by Jaish-e-Mohammad (JeM) headed by Maulana Masood Azhar. Azhar was one of the three men who were released by India in exchange for 150 Indians who were onboard the Indian Airlines flight IC-814 that was hijacked to Kandahar, Afghanistan in 1999. The JeM was proscribed by Pakistan back in 2002. While India was holding the JeM responsible for the attack, it was the Kashmiri United Jihad Council that claimed to have carried out the attack.

The NSAs of the two countries immediately got in touch with each other lest the crisis spiral out of control. They spoke to each other several times. According to some media reports, Ajit Doval also shared with his Pakistan counterpart Lt Gen. Nasser Janjua (retd.) some intercepts and leads which they asserted led to JeM.

Meanwhile, Prime Minister Sharif, who was travelling to Sri Lanka on an official visit, called his Indian counterpart from Colombo on 5 January. A press release issued in Colombo, inter alia, stated:

> The Prime Minister appreciated the maturity shown by the Indian government in its statements issued after the unfortunate incident took place. His government was working on the leads and information provided by the Indian government. The Pakistan government would investigate this matter. Prime Minister Nawaz Sharif pointed out to the Indian Prime Minister that whenever a serious effort for bringing peace between the two countries was underway, terrorism tried to derail the process. Both the Prime Ministers agreed that a cordial and cooperative relationship between the two countries would be the most appropriate response to the nefarious designs of the terrorists.

New Delhi also issued a press release the same day which stated:

> Prime Minister Narendra Modi received a call this afternoon from Prime Minister Muhammad Nawaz Sharif regarding the terrorist attack on the Pathankot airbase. Prime Minister Modi strongly emphasized the

> need for Pakistan to take firm and immediate action against the organizations and individuals responsible for and linked to the Pathankot terrorist attack. Specific and actionable information in this regard has been provided to Pakistan. Prime Minister Nawaz Sharif assured Prime Minister Modi that his government would take prompt and decisive action against the terrorists.

On the basis of the initial information provided by India, we immediately put Maulana Azhar under protective custody. We also offered to send a Special Investigation Team (SIT) to Pathankot and New Delhi to take the matter forward. This was done, however, without invoking the Joint Anti-Terrorism Mechanism (JATM) that was established in 2006 but left to atrophy after a few initial meetings at the additional-secretary level.

Meanwhile, our side was keen that a meeting between the foreign secretaries scheduled in Islamabad for 15 January should not be postponed or cancelled as that would amount to playing into the hands of those who did not want the two countries to sit across the table. Whereas India was circumspect in its official statements, the Indian media continued regurgitating the hackneyed narrative that it was the Pakistan deep state which was behind the attack as Prime Minister Sharif was moving too fast without thinking through. In any case, it was announced by India on 14 January that the "talks have been deferred to near future with mutual consent." (*The Indian Express*, New Delhi, 15 January 2015.)

"Asked why have the talks been rescheduled if India was welcoming the Pakistani action against JeM, Vikas Swarup (MEA spokesperson) said the foreign secretaries felt that more time was required before they meet "away from the shadow" of the investigations into the Pathankot terror strike." (*The Indian Express*, New Delhi, 15 January 2015.)

Meanwhile, I cautioned Islamabad that we must be careful as deferring the talks by mutual consent and the narrative that the two foreign secretaries were in touch with each other to finalize new dates for a meeting in Islamabad may eventually turn out to be counterproductive. In my view, it would be better if, after some time, we formally propose a new date for the Indian foreign secretary's visit and let India say no or yes. In short, we should not ourselves be linking the visit to progress on Pathankot. Nor should we share the responsibility if India kept on delaying the talks for no valid reason.

Secondly, our SIT should not visit India with a limited mandate both in terms of visiting the Pathankot airbase and meeting and cross-examining the most relevant people. Our side should be fully satisfied with its mutually agreed mandate before leaving for India. Otherwise, the team would visit but return with an inconclusive work and the entire exercise, instead of being helpful, would become controversial and a liability for Pakistan.

In the first week of February, I also recommended to Islamabad not to file an FIR (First Information Report) in Pakistan in haste. I argued that, if our SIT was visiting at the end of March, an FIR could be filed thereafter. However, I never received any response nor was I asked to come to Islamabad for consultations.

Nevertheless, Islamabad decided to go ahead and, as far as I could see, without thinking through its implications, filed an FIR at Gujranwala on 19 February. The Indian media regarded this as a step in the right direction but regretted that the FIR didn't name JeM or Maulana Azhar. As I looked at it, by filing the FIR, Pakistan had implicitly and prematurely accepted the culpability of JeM in the attack.

On 13 March, India formally asked us to accept the mortal remains of four of the six terrorists killed (the bodies of the remaining two as per Indian officials were completely burned) in the Pathankot counter-operation. We responded to the Indian side that their suggestion was unacceptable as there was no evidence that the terrorists were Pakistan nationals. India subsequently buried them locally.

At the end of March, our SIT visited Pathankot airbase as well as New Delhi for almost a week and all the team members had unanimously expressed their reservations to me about the team's Terms of Reference. Their access to the airbase was extremely limited and they were not even allowed to meet, let alone to cross-examine, the main characters in the entire Pathankot episode including a senior Punjab Police officer and Superintendent of Police, Salwinder Singh, who had claimed that he was kidnapped by the terrorists and that his official car was used by the terrorists to access the Pathankot airbase.

Salwinder Singh, his friend and cook, who were travelling with him, had made so many loose statements full of discrepancies that our SIT could not have reached any plausible conclusion without meeting the three of them. Still, the Indian side denied those meetings. In February 2019, Salwinder Singh was sentenced to 10-year imprisonment for rape and bribery. Interestingly, he was booked for these crimes in August 2016, i.e., seven months after the Pathankot attack.

I learnt afterwards to my dismay that the Indian high commissioner in Islamabad had a meeting in our foreign office where he was given to understand that Pakistan would allow a reciprocal visit by a team of India's National Investigation Agency (NIA). This commitment, even if it was verbal, was not only absolutely uncalled for but also too vacuous to digest and was akin to jumping the gun. It was simply baffling as to how a country could commit to such absurdities. Even though, for a moment, we accepted the Indian allegation of JeM's involvement and the need for them to cross-examine the JeM chief and other accused, we should have waited for the outcome of the SIT findings now that we had, though again unnecessarily, agreed to its visit to India. It seemed we were willingly being entrapped by India and there was no one in Islamabad who could restrain the growing solipsistic foreign office.

I was invited by the Foreign Correspondents Club of South Asia in New Delhi on 7 April. Pakistan had announced on 25 March that it had captured an Indian naval officer, Commander Kulbhushan Jadhav, in Balochistan on 3 March and he was being tried in a military court. There at the club, in response to questions by journalists on bilateral talks and the NIA team's visit to Pakistan, I said that, as far the bilateral talks were concerned, though the two foreign secretaries were in touch with each other, there were no dates yet. I said talks appeared to have been suspended adding that Pakistan was keen to have a meeting of the foreign secretaries as soon as possible. On the latter question, I said that, in such matters, my personal view was that, more than reciprocity, the two countries needed to retain the spirit of cooperation in order to establish undeniable facts.

These remarks had stirred a hornet's nest. I was castigated by the Indian media for being undiplomatic and some even commented that I was an ISI agent. The question of reciprocity was still a riddle for me and how come a journalist would ask a question about it. Since I was not aware of any such commitment by Islamabad, I could not respond better than the way I did. As for the question itself, that was planted by the MEA beyond a shadow of doubt, especially when the issue was not even being discussed in the public sphere.

I could find only one sane voice and that was of India's former high commissioner to Pakistan, Satyabrata Pal, who, in response to a question by a correspondent of *The Hindu*, said: "Basit stated the factual position which is that there are no talks at the moment. There should not be a big controversy as he has pointed out the reality of the moment." (*The Hindu*, 9 April 2016.)

Ambassador Pal had always impressed me with his impeccable, polite manners and remarkable intellectual sophistication. He was one of India's finest diplomats who had the unmatched ability of saying the harshest of things mellifluously. I would envy him for both his perspicacity and unflappability. We first met in London in 2004 where both of us were serving as deputy high commissioners. From London, he went to South Africa as high commissioner in 2005. He passed away on 24 September 2019. It genuinely saddened me when I read about his demise.

The next day (8 April) I would receive an unexpected letter from the foreign office in Islamabad reprimanding me for my remarks which, according to them, had caused considerable confusion on the two issues and that, in future, I should seek prior clearance from MoFA before making policy statements. The letter, signed by a junior officer, was very insulting, to say the least.

In my response addressed to the foreign secretary on 13 April, I took strong exception to the letter telling him how systematically I was being kept out of the loop and the ministry's preference to deal with India through the Indian high commissioner in Islamabad rather than using the office of their high commission in New Delhi was most unfair. I also asked the ministry to let me know if I had said anything that was at variance with the national interests of Pakistan. It was for the ministry to reflect on how it was conducting the matters with India rather than sending a gratuitous and insulting letter to me. While I never heard back from him on this subject, the ministry was still sticking to its illogical and ill-served position.

On 14 April, in a statement, our spokesperson, instead of explaining the rationale of my remarks, parroted the same trite line that the two foreign secretaries were in touch with each other to finalize the modalities of talks. I again sent a communication to Islamabad the same day to the effect that we should not let India hide under the veneer of diplomatic niceties. Pakistan should clearly say that it was waiting for India to suggest dates for a meeting rather than allowing them to keep linking talks to progress on Pathankot.

However, on 18 April, in his interview with *CNN-18 News*, Sartaj Aziz said that the bilateral talks were suspended though not canceled. But he stopped short of saying that it was India which was not suggesting new dates. He also, and this was something mind-boggling for me, left the door ajar for a reciprocal visit to Pakistan by a team of NIA. The visit could never materialize. Yes, diplomacy is the art of the possible but not about turning deceptive illusions into realities.

The Indian government acted smartly by letting the Pakistan SIT visit India with Terms of Reference of no consequence, and thus took the moral high ground. For us it was not an easy decision. By allowing the NIA team to visit Pakistan, we would have implicitly conceded that our team's visit to India was productive and, secondly, what would the Indian team have done in Pakistan except seeking interviews with the chief of the proscribed JeM and some of its operatives. How could Pakistan let these people to be cross-examined by Indian officials who never allowed our team to even meet the relevant people? From the very beginning, we got our foot caught in the Indian trap. The most damaging was to move an FIR in Pakistan without calculating its possible repercussions.

One must read Elias Davidsson's *The Betrayal of India-Revisiting the 26/11 Evidence* which raises most pertinent questions about the Mumbai attacks and effectively punctures the Indian claim about Pakistan's connivance.

In a first public reaction to the Pathankot attack, the PIA office in one of New Delhi's posh areas was vandalized by a group of Hindu extremists reportedly belonging to the Hindu Mahasabha and Vishva Hindu Parishad. As the news was reported in the Indian TV channels, it was also picked up by the Pakistani media and some of the Pakistani channels started contacting the high commission spokesperson, Manzoor Memon. I authorized him to speak to them but asked him to focus only on what measures the high commission had taken including the demarche we had made with the MEA, asking them to beef up security of the premises and take action against the miscreants.

No sooner had Memon spoken to the first Pakistani TV channel than we received a message from one of the top aides of Prime Minister Sharif that no statement should be made against the Indian government on the PIA issue. The message was uncalled for. Memon never took potshots at the government. His interaction with the Pakistani media was to apprise the people of Pakistan of what actually happened and that the PIA staff were safe. When Memon stopped entertaining Pakistani TV channels' requests, I received calls from several journalists from Pakistan enquiring whether the Prime Minister's Office had given any instructions to the high commission to not speak against the Indian government on the PIA office issue. Two of them also tweeted that the Prime Minister had instructed the high commissioner to direct his spokesperson not to talk to the Pakistani media. I vehemently denied this saying that the foreign office in Islamabad had already issued a press release on the subject so why would the prime minister issue such instructions to me? In any case, after the issuance of the press release, there was nothing for the high commission to add.

The Indian government was also not extending the visas of PIA officials in New Delhi and Mumbai despite our repeated requests. Their visas expired in early January and they and their family members were literally stuck in India. Not only this, their phones were disconnected and an official, whose son was seriously ill in Pakistan, could not visit him until his visa was extended.

There was also another matter on which I was quite baffled to have received a telephone call from our Prime Minister's Office. That was about the issuance of a visa to a Bollywood actor Anupam Kher. He was invited along with 17 other Indian nationals to attend the Karachi Literature Festival on 5-7 February. The organizers of the festival had already sent us the list as per our procedural requirement. We started receiving visa applications forms along with their passports separately from the invited guests. Anupam Kher never sent his documents but went public with a tweet that Pakistan's Ministry of Interior had refused to issue a No Objection Certificate (NOC) in his case and therefore he would not be able to attend the festival in Karachi.

His tweet was quite a surprise. I tweeted back saying:

"Sorry Sir I don't know who told you about this so-called NOC; we are still to receive your visa application and passport." I also spoke to him on the telephone but by then it was clear to me that he was playing politics.

I explained to our Prime Minister's Office that I had already spoken to him and that he was using the issue as a political stunt but they insisted that the prime minister still wanted me to talk to him again and issue him a visa. As instructed, I called Anupam Kher again. He thanked me for the call but said that he had taken up other assignments on the scheduled dates. He posted another tweet reporting our telephone conversation and thanking me for the call. The matter ended there.

Then came the T20 World Cup. Pakistan rightly refused to play its first match with India at Dharamshala, capital of Himachal Pradesh, on 19 March. A local ex-servicemen organization had threatened not to allow the match as that would hurt the feelings of soldiers and martyrs from the state. The chief minister of the Congress party-led government there had also publicly regretted that he could not give security guarantees for the Pakistan team and that the venue be shifted from Dharamshala. We wanted explicit assurances from the Indian side for the safety and security of our team.

A two-member team from Pakistan which visited Dharamshala on 7-8 March to assess the overall security risk to our team, had also recommended against playing at Dharamsala. I had requested a meeting with Home Affairs Minister, Rajnath Singh, to discuss the issue with him and also to be assured of the security of the team for their entire stay in India for the tournament. I was keeping our Interior Minister, Chaudhry Nisar Ali Khan, who had told me that he would go by my final advice, informed.

This was important because the Pakistan Cricket Board was somewhat restless and wanted the team to leave for India as per the schedule.

India then decided to shift the Pakistan-India match to Kolkata on 9 March, and the chief minister of Bengal, Mamata Banerjee, in a letter to ICC and BCCI had guaranteed foolproof security cover to all the teams, including Pakistan. But we would still not commit our participation unless we had blanket security assurances from the Indian side for all the venues where the Pakistan team might play depending on its program.

The same day, I was offered to meet the home affairs secretary, Rajiv Mehrishi, instead of the home affairs minister of which I readily agreed. All hinged on that meeting. People in both Pakistan and India were impatiently waiting to know whether or not Pakistan would play in the world cup.

I thanked the secretary for the meeting and said that Islamabad was waiting for my recommendation and I hoped that our meeting would conclude on a positive note enabling me to advise my authorities favorably. The secretary responded by saying that security was a state subject as well as the responsibility of the Union Government to pitch in where needed. I reminded him that Pakistan was a peculiar case and, in view of the threats being received, we would not be able to permit our team to play in India without security assurances from the Union Government. To this the secretary responded that he fully understood our concerns and he could assure me that he would personally supervise and coordinate security arrangements for the Pakistan team including for a match in Mohali, which was in the Union Territory.

I then asked the secretary whether the Indian side would issue any statement on our meeting. He said they would not but that he might talk to the media if there was any such request and would brief them along the lines of our discussion. Our interior minister was waiting for my go-ahead. I immediately called him to convey the good news. The PCB Chairman, Najam Sethi, was with the minister. After my call, the latter addressed the Pakistani media saying that High Commissioner Abdul Basit had met the Indian authorities and the Pakistan team would participate in the tournament.

The MEA immediately issued a press release on my meeting with the home secretary which attempted to suggest that there were no security assurances specific to the Pakistan team. Interestingly, when I came out of the meeting, the Indian media was there. I told them that I would send my recommendation to my interior minister and that it would be his call. When pressed by the media as to what would be my recommendation, I said tersely that my meeting with the home secretary was positive.

I asked my deputy high commissioner, Nizamani, to send a brief informal message to the MEA spokesperson, Gopal Baglay, who had recently returned from Pakistan after serving there as India's deputy high commissioner that the issuance of a press release by the MEA was in bad taste and contrary to the mutual understanding of the two interlocutors. According to my recollection, he never responded to the message.

I went to Kolkata for the match between India and Pakistan on 19 March which the Indian team won rather easily. Imran Khan, Chairman of the Pakistan Tehreek-e-Insaf (PTI), was also there along with a senior Pakistani politician, Sheikh Rashid Ahmad. I went to their cabin to greet them and asked them if they needed any facilitation.

On the downside, the Indian government denied permission to five officials of the high commission, out of the list of ten, including our Defense Attaché, to go to Kolkata for the match. But that was something usual and, by now, we had become used to it and would keep Islamabad informed with the view to observing strict reciprocity.

Similarly, during my entire stay in New Delhi, I was never given an opportunity to call on the external affairs minister and the prime minister despite our repeated requests. Accordingly, I continued recommending to Islamabad to ensure reciprocity in this matter as well. However, Islamabad would never listen. For instance, when High Commissioner Sharat Sabharwal was leaving Pakistan in July 2013, he was received by all including our Prime Minister-elect Mian Nawaz Sharif in Lahore as well as President Asif Ali Zardari. When the new high commissioner Gautam Bambawale took over in early 2016 he was also received by Prime Minister Sharif. Prime Minister-elect Imran Khan received High Commissioner Ajay Bisaria.

In my considered view, it was the foreign office that was responsible for this anomalous situation but, with weak people at the helm, expecting them to suggest anything perceived to be contrary to the inclination of the prime minister was asking for too much. An organization led by successive weaklings starts losing its credibility and, in turn, its relevance. This is what is happening to MoFA for years and it hurts all those who care about this once great institution.

Here I may mention, for the sake of record, that I invited Jaishankar many times to have lunch or dinner at the Pakistan House but he never obliged me. It was good to receive a message from Aizaz about whether he should accept an invitation from my Indian counterpart in Islamabad and, when I told him how Jaishankar had regretted my invitation every time I extended it, Aizaz also declined. As far as I know, Aizaz never obliged the Indian high commissioner for as long as he remained the foreign secretary.

Let me here once again stress that, as a diplomat, I fully understood the importance of flexibility in diplomacy. However, in a hostile inter-state relationship, diplomacy has to be conducted with utmost circumspection lest the other side misconstrue. I am of the firm view that, when it comes to India, unilateral gestures and going into overdrive at times actually made India more stubborn in its policy toward Pakistan. Yes, Pakistanis are unquestionably the most hospitable people in the world. However, diplomacy has its own peculiar requirements and if a state deviates too far from the well-established diplomatic practices, especially in a deeply acrimonious inter-state relationship, unilateral flexibility becomes burdensome rather than helpful.

Talking about hospitality and well-established diplomatic practices, I may mention here that I had stopped serving alcohol at the parties in my home from 1994 when I was posted from New York to Sana'a. That was in keeping with the Quranic injunction declaring the consumption of alcohol as satanic. My wife and I thought that, since we ourselves did not drink alcohol, why should we serve others? However, diplomats would still come to our parties. The entrenched notion that diplomatic parties are incomplete without alcohol is clearly misplaced.

Our first dinner at the Pakistan House in New Delhi, without alcohol, was thus a huge surprise for our Indian guests. They were curious to know why the decades-old practice had been discontinued. My response to them was that the high commissioner's residence was Pakistani territory. How could a thing that was proscribed and illegal in Pakistan be allowed at the Pakistan House. I never faced any issue, even in Geneva, London or Berlin, of invited guests not turning up at our place.

After my retirement, I had suggested to Prime Minister Imran Khan on one of my TV talk shows that all Pakistan diplomats abroad, especially ambassadors, be instructed to not serve alcohol even in their private parties in line with our constitution. Nevertheless, I do not see that happening in the foreseeable future for a majority of Foreign Service Officers do not find the suggestion either palatable or enforceable.

I would, nevertheless, advise our young diplomats not to be swayed by stereotypes. Diplomatic practices, though well-established, are not static. They also undergo a metamorphosis in tandem with the rapidly changing dynamics of international relations. We must take pride in our religious and cultural ethos and this becomes all the more important when we are representing our state abroad. Diplomats and local guests would come to your parties not because you serve alcohol but because of the importance they attach to Pakistan, how actively you move around, and how effectively you cultivate people and consolidate your friendships. Our warm hospitality and the way we serve and look after our guests are our strengths, not serving expensive alcoholic drinks.

Interestingly, some Indian states like Gujarat and Bihar are legally dry states where alcohol is banned. Ironically, Kashmir, where Muslims are in a majority, remains open to alcohol despite their resentment and the consistent demand to ban it.

******

As the Indian government and media would not allow the focus on the Pathankot incident to peter out, it was necessary from our standpoint to not let the Kashmir dispute be seen as losing its primacy. I therefore thought that I should continue meeting Kashmiri leaders. This was also needed to convey to the Indian side that Pakistan would not buckle under the pressure of Pathankot and stop raising its voice in support of Kashmiris. I met Syed Geelani, Mirwaiz Umar Farooq, and Nayeem Ahmad Khan in early February and the Indian media, as always, kept shouting at the top of their lungs against my interaction with the Hurriyat leaders.

Syed Geelani was particularly concerned about the way Pakistan was trying to reach out to India. He was of the view that Pakistan should talk to India only if the latter agreed that the Jammu & Kashmir issue was the core dispute and that Kashmir was not an integral part of India. Syed Geelani would always emphasize that Pakistan must understand the BJP/RSS's long-term agenda; they were working to split the state and turn Jammu & Kashmir into a Hindu majority state. Nevertheless, he always stressed that a weak and unstable Pakistan would never be able to talk to India from a position of strength. He would worry that a weak Pakistan might come under gradual pressure to keep diluting its position on Kashmir and making unilateral concessions without even realizing the damage being done to the Kashmir cause.

Syed Geelani fell critically ill in early March. I made a point to visit him in the hospital in New Delhi on 11 March. We also offered special prayers for him in the high commission after the Friday congregation. These were widely reported in the Indian media. With the blessings of Allah, Syed Geelani recovered and was able to attend the Pakistan Day Reception on 23 March.

The Mirwaiz, Abdul Ghani Bhat, Yasin Malik and Agha Hassan Mousavi also had serious concerns and suggested many ideas for managing the Kashmir dispute. I would faithfully report my conversations to Islamabad with practical proposals but it seemed there was no appetite left back home to even read my recommendations related to Kashmir, much less consider them and respond to me.

My meeting with the head of "Dukhtaran-e-Millat", Asiya Andrabi, in the Pakistan House on 9 March was also covered widely by the Indian media with the usual venom against me and Pakistan. So much so that Arnab Goswami, then with the Times Now TV channel initiated a campaign to boycott the upcoming Pakistan Day Reception. However, his campaign failed miserably as the reception was a huge success as always. As for Ms Andrabi, she is a woman of steel nerves and her commitment to the Kashmir cause is non-negotiable. Her husband, Dr Qasim Faktoo's long imprisonment of 27 years and the long years of Indian repression against her could not weaken her determination. She is presently being kept at the notorious Tihar jail but I am sure that, despite the fact that she is ill, her iron will can never be suppressed.

I proposed to Islamabad umpteen times that, while we would immediately summon an official of the Indian high commission in Islamabad to protest against the ceasefire violations on the LoC, we would not do so on Kashmir. Why didn't we summon the Indian high commissioner every now and then to lodge an official protest against the arrest of Hurriyat leaders and innocent Kashmiris? Islamabad would never respond.

I would often discuss this with my team in New Delhi. I decided to write to the ministry that, if they had no objection, I would like to raise this issue with Jaishankar and put our views across. Though, speaking from the diplomatic point of view, this should have been done in Islamabad and not by the high commission in New Delhi. I had thought that my pushing the envelope might help but Islamabad seemed to be sulking and had no time for Kashmir. Lo and behold they did not object to my suggestion. Accordingly, I sought a meeting with Jaishankar conveying that the high commissioner would discuss matters related to Kashmir.

I met Jaishankar on 18 February. I began by mentioning Kashmir-related CBMs which were also to be discussed within the agreed framework of the 2015 "comprehensive bilateral dialogue." I added that it was good to read a news report in the Indian press that day that New Delhi was considering removing AFSPA from Srinagar and Kathua to begin with. After the death of Chief Minister Mufti Mohammad Sayeed, his daughter Mehbooba Mufti was negotiating anew the terms and conditions for the PDP-BJP coalition government in Kashmir. I said, should this happen, it would be a step in the right direction and help improve the overall bilateral environment. I added that, hopefully, the Hurriyat leaders would also get some relief including offering Friday prayers and traveling abroad.

Jaishankar was visibly upset and refused to engage with me on this subject saying that he could not discuss issues on the basis of media reports and especially when these issues were India's internal matters in which Pakistan had no locus standi. When I responded to him that Kashmir-related CBMs were under bilateral discussion for many years, he said those were restricted only to cross-LoC CBMs, including trade, tourism and ceasefire. India would never talk to Pakistan on what was happening or not happening inside Jammu & Kashmir. In my response, I insisted that Kashmir was the core dispute and Pakistan could not stay indifferent to the plight of Kashmiris.

To my question on whether he had any dates for his impending visit to Pakistan, he ruled out both February and March adding that we should wait and see the outcome of the visit of SIT from Pakistan. This was a clear indication that

India was linking bilateral talks with developments related to Pathankot. I still find it difficult to believe that we could be so naïve diplomatically to play into the Indian hands and promote a narrative to their advantage rather than being in tune with our interests.

On the other hand, Ajit Doval, who was visiting Washington DC, had briefly met our Ambassador there at a party on 2 April and indicated his interest in visiting Pakistan in the near future subject to Islamabad's amenability. Ambassador Jilani sent the gist of his conversation to Islamabad recommending that Islamabad might respond positively as his visit would possibly help break the deadlock. When Islamabad asked for my views, I strongly opposed the idea on the ground that we must not fall into the Indian trap. The two NSAs had had many conversations on terrorism and it was time the Indian side suggested dates for the foreign-secretary level talks. Their intentions were thus clear.

Moreover, Ajit Doval's visit would also, besides Mumbai and Pathankot, discuss the arrest of R&AW agent, Commander Jadhav. While Islamabad might not have an issue with his visit to Pakistan on principle, we could not ignore Kashmir and other bilateral issues for long. Kashmiris were watching and we should avoid welcoming Ajit Doval before a visit by Jaishankar to Islamabad.

Interestingly, Doval never called me after returning from the US to even informally suggest his interest in visiting Pakistan. I also do not know if this was ever raised by the Indian high commissioner in Islamabad. The matter, however, never came up for discussion again.

As I mentioned earlier, our official reception on Pakistan Day (23 March) was hugely successful and went smoothly without engendering any controversy unlike the previous year when the chief guest, Minister of State V. K. Singh, had uploaded a distasteful tweet indicating his uneasiness at attending the Pakistan Day Reception in the performance of his official duty. By then, the arrest of Commander Kulbhushan Jadhav had not been made public by us. This time India nominated Prakash Javadekar, Minister of State for Environment, Forests and Climate Change, to represent the government of India.

At the Pakistan Day Reception, I would, in deference to the presence of the chief guest, avoid mentioning Kashmir explicitly. I would make brief remarks to welcome and thank our guests and usually pick up a specific theme related to Pakistan such as women's empowerment or democracy. My remarks, however, would be brief, not more than 5 to 7 minutes. This year, I decided to talk about what Pakistan was doing on the economic front. By doing so, I also mentioned the China-Pakistan Economic Corridor (CPEC) and how it would be a game-changer for Pakistan. Though some Indian newspapers picked up this point in the context of India's claims on Pakistan Administered Kashmir and Gilgit-Baltistan, the event by-and-large concluded positively, the usual hullaballoo created by the likes of Arnab Goswami notwithstanding.

Throughout this period, including that of my visit to Jaipur in the first week of March, I had been very consistent and forceful in conveying three messages to my host government. First, talks were not a favor by India to Pakistan. If we were to move from conflict management to conflict resolution, comprehensive and sustained talks were unavoidable. Setting unnecessary preconditions would not work. Second, Jammu & Kashmir remained the core dispute. Without finding a fair solution to this protracted dispute, there was no possibility that the two countries could ever achieve a lasting peace. Third, on the Pathankot attack, India must avoid jumping the gun and drawing premature and possibly off-the-mark conclusions. No country in the world would execute its citizens on the basis of hearsay or questionable evidence, adding that Pakistan had moved very quickly and even put Maulana Azhar in protective custody but, to initiate a criminal case against him under terrorism laws, we would need India's full cooperation. India should help, not pressure Pakistan, moving beyond its domestic political compulsions and foreign policy considerations.

However, the messaging from Pakistan was sadly not consistent. For instance, Sartaj Aziz, in an interview with Karan Thapar, said that Maulana Azhar had been in protective custody since 14 January while Fatemi, in an interview with a Pakistani television channel on 28 February, denied any knowledge of what Sartaj Aziz said. They were working under the same roof but issuing divergent statements. The inconsistency sadly did not end there.

Barkha Dutt was one of those 17 Indians who had attended the Karachi Literature Festival, where her book, *This Unquiet Land* was also launched. She wanted to be issued a visa for Islamabad in addition to Karachi and Lahore as, she told Manzoor Memon, she might call on Prime Minister Sharif. However, as per visa rules specific to Indian nationals and in the absence of instructions from Islamabad, we issued her visa for Lahore and Karachi only. We had also informed Islamabad about this, emphasizing that she had not been issued a journalistic visa and that she must not be obliged with a call on the prime minister as, in all likelihood, she would use the meeting to create some controversy to Pakistan's embarrassment. But the prime minister, perhaps, had already committed to see her in Islamabad as she was in direct touch with the prime minister's office, if not the prime minster himself. She was brought to Islamabad from Karachi and received by the prime minister which she herself confirmed on her TV talk show.

On 11 February, she asserted that top Pakistan government sources confirmed to her that the JeM chief was not in preventive custody and that he "is on the run and may even be hiding in Afghanistan". Mohammad Zubair, then a minister in the Sharif cabinet, appearing on Barkha Dutt's program, "The Buck Stops Here", confirmed Barkha's assertion. (NDTV program "The Buck Stops Here", 11 February 2016.) Barkha's story was never denied by Islamabad.

Pakistan then had three foreign ministers; Prime Minister Sharif himself who retained the portfolio of foreign minister; Advisor Sartaj Aziz and Special Assistant Tariq Fatemi. When such was the situation, how could sanity prevail? Or perhaps there was too much cumulative sanity to handle for the pedestrian people like myself and many other Pakistanis.

Following this, the debate started in India that, while, Nawaz Sharif was very keen to move against the JeM and Maulan Azhar, General Raheel Sharif, the Pakistan Army Chief, was the biggest impediment, implying that "the deep state" in Pakistan would never allow the prime minister to take any meaningful action against the alleged Pathankot attack perpetrators.

It is such inconsistencies at the top level which often put countries like Pakistan in a cleft stick. While India was quick to accuse JeM without any concrete evidence, we helped reinforce the Indian narrative by our institutional inabilities to counter India's fabricated stories in an effective and sustained manner.

There is also another serious problem with our politicians. When in government, no matter whether it is the prime minister or ministers, they are all accessible to Indian journalists. Barkha's meeting with Prime Minister Sharif in

Islamabad is just one example. I can cite many more. But the question is how many Pakistani journalists would be able to meet the Indian prime minister and ministers and interview them? I remember that Saleem Safi, a well-known Pakistani journalist, was invited to attend a conclave in New Delhi. He asked the high commission if we could arrange an interview with either Swaraj or Jaishankar. We formally requested the MEA on his behalf but there was no positive response. Even the foreign office spokesperson had expressed his inability to oblige. Safi was definitely disappointed but such was, unfortunately, the case. We would hardly see Indian government officials on Pakistani TV talk shows but Indian journalists can always approach even Pakistani ministers directly and we often see them on their shows and that, too, without preparing to speak on the subject.

There is, inherently, no harm in putting across your views and positions and engaging in public diplomacy. But there is a difference between doing things individually and institutionally. The latter is what counts and makes a difference. Public diplomacy done for personal aggrandizement is usually hazardous for the state. This is especially true when we are operating in an environment of hostility.

On their part, Indians had launched a systematic campaign through the media that the SIT was fully facilitated as per the mutually agreed Terms of Reference, and that the visit was a success and now the ball was in Pakistan's court. The Indian opposition, however, was taking the government to task for allowing, for the first time, Pakistan's security and intelligence officers to visit a sensitive security facility like the Pathankot airbase without achieving anything substantive. The government was also being chided for not being able to get a reciprocal visit of the NIA team to Pakistan. In short, the BJP government was under immense domestic pressure for its dilly-dallying on Pakistan and, in the process, messing up India's Pakistan policy.

******

I was not in favor of the foreign secretary's visit to New Delhi to attend a Senior Officials' Meeting (SOM) of the HoA Ministerial Conference to be held on 26 April. The annual ministerial conference was scheduled for later in the year in Amritsar. I had three basic issues and concerns. Firstly, India was feeling the heat after my remarks that it was India which had suspended the bilateral talks by linking them with progress on the Pathankot issue, a self-serving and myopic stance. That India had now itself proposed a meeting between the two foreign secretaries was indicative of their angst. In diplomacy, keeping good optics and a façade of rationality is also significant. The New Delhi meeting would be used by India to continue delaying formal, structured bilateral talks on issues other than terrorism. There was no point in Pakistan providing a pretext to India on a platter.

Secondly, the foreign secretary, I believed, would have to meet the Hurriyat leaders as per the tradition and skipping it would amount to abandoning our principled position. Kashmiris would not like it.

Thirdly, India had attended the SOM in Pakistan last year at the level of joint secretary. Pakistan should observe reciprocity. There was no need to upgrade our participation just for the sake of a meeting between the foreign secretaries which, in any case, as per my assessment, would achieve nothing from our standpoint. It would be another meeting between the two sides to repeat their well-known respective positions on issues without reaching any agreement.

Aizaz conveyed to me that the summary had been submitted to the prime minister giving all the pros and cons and it was for him to take a decision. I later learnt that the foreign office, in its final recommendation, did suggest attending the New Delhi meeting by the foreign secretary. As for a meeting with the Hurriyat leadership, it was argued that, since the foreign secretary would be visiting New Delhi for a multilateral meeting and only for a day, not meeting the Hurriyat could be justified. I had in turn contended that the argument that the SOM was a multilateral conclave was untenable. I reminded Islamabad that a former foreign secretary who had visited New Delhi on 13 November 2013 to attend the SOM of Asia-Europe Meeting (ASEM) had met the Hurriyat leadership.

It seemed that Islamabad had already made up its mind and for me to go on arguing against our participation at the foreign-secretary level would make no difference. Perhaps, the prime minister had thought that a foreign secretary meeting might help make some headway. But I had no plausible reason to be optimistic.

The foreign secretary arrived in New Delhi by a special aircraft for a day trip. He was received by Jaishankar for a bilateral meeting but did not offer to host a lunch lest that be misinterpreted as more than a meeting on the margins. The meeting as I feared, achieved nothing and, as expected, ended in mutual recriminations. Both sides reiterated their respective positions on bilateral issues. Jaishankar made the significant remark that India could not "de-prioritize" Pathankot. When he talked about a reciprocal visit by a team of the NIA, I interjected to emphasize my earlier argument that, if India were interested in results, it should focus more on active cooperation than one-time reciprocity. Aizaz, reading throughout from his brief, put forth Pakistan's position on all issues including Kashmir.

As we left the meeting, the Indian media was making its jingoistic and bombastic claims that Pakistan had been told in absolute terms that talks and terror could not go together. Whereas the Pakistan media was asserting that the Indian side had been told without pulling punches that the Kashmir dispute was the core issue and that foreign-secretary level talks should resume without further ado so that the peace process could be brought back on rails in a comprehensive manner.

After the visit, I had shared my assessment with Islamabad once again underlining that every step of ours should be well-calibrated. We must be patient; the more we talk about bilateral talks the more we come under pressure. I was, nevertheless, cognizant of Islamabad's restlessness as India could stymie the 19th SAARC Summit scheduled to be held in Islamabad in November though, at Ufa, Prime Minister Modi had agreed, in principle, to attend the summit as was also contained in the Ufa joint statement. Be that as it may, I would consistently advise Islamabad to be patient; and keep in mind an age-old Chinese adage: "more haste, less speed".

At the Kathmandu SAARC Summit in 2015, Pakistan was the only country that had blocked two important agreements, namely, motor vehicles and regional railways, aimed at enhancing regional connectivity. The Pakistan delegation had asked for more time to complete its internal processes for these proposed pacts would have obliged Pakistan to allow India overland access to Afghanistan through the Wagah border. It was, therefore, necessary that we should have completed our internal processes before the Islamabad summit as blocking the agreements again was not what Prime Minister Sharif had in mind.

On the other hand, it was encouraging that India had not cancelled the sixth meeting of the India-Pakistan Joint

Business Forum to be held in New Delhi on 3 May. I kept my address to the Forum confined to bilateral economic issues, especially the importance of having a level-playing field to create interdependencies, regional connectivity and economic integration. But the Indian participants were clearly upset at the delay on the part of Pakistan to grant NDMA to India. I briefed them on how things had been during the last two years. I stressed that, given the nature of our relationship, every bilateral activity was intertwined. Even the bilateral trade was no exception as demonstrated by India's stringent tariff and non-tariff barriers on imports from Pakistan that were least helpful.

I would often argue that India had granted the Most Favored Nation (MFN) status to Pakistan in 1996 but, interestingly, the balance of trade had been growing steadily in India's favor. Doubtless, there were other factors too, including India's large economic base and infrastructure, but imposing cumbersome sanitary and phytosanitary measures on Pakistani imports through Wagah was one of the major reasons that kept the volume of Pakistani exports hovering between US$300 to 400 million. It took weeks if not months to clear consignments from Pakistan and, in the case of perishable items, it became well-nigh impossible for Pakistani exporters to do business with India.

Taking advantage of some respite, I visited Chandigarh and Shimla on 9-11 May. I addressed think tanks and visited educational institutions for interaction with the youth. Another interesting visit was to Nagpur on 2-4 June, the third largest city in the state of Maharashtra after Mumbai and Pune. It is now more famous for being the headquarters of the RSS. I was invited by India's fourth largest media group, Lokmat, for a panel discussion on Pakistan-India relations. Other panelists were Sheshadri Chari, a BJP spokesperson, Ambassador Vivek Katju (retd.), a Congress party spokesperson, Priyanka Chaturvedi (she has since joined Shiv Sena), and a journalist, Jatin Desai.

It was a well-attended event, close to five hundred people, where RSS members/supporters were also present. Full credit to them that they listened to me patiently and did not create any ruckus as could be expected on such occasions. I was also extra careful in my remarks and, after the conclusion of the event, I was approached by many of them to congratulate me on my frank assessment of the relationship and how the two countries could move forward. One of them even asked why previous Pakistan high commissioners had not visited Nagpur and that "after listening to you I may say that Pakistanis are not as bad and vicious as we are routinely told." I thought this was a huge compliment and also underlined how important it was to reach out to people even in an unfriendly milieu. Many people may be hidebound in their views and unwilling to listen to reasoning but there are always some people who, with a little effort, are able to understand and respond constructively. Hence, I have always put a premium on public diplomacy.

I wanted to have more engagements in Nagpur but, unfortunately, there was much pressure from New Delhi and RSS on local institutions not to oblige me. For instance, I was disinvited by the Nagpur College of Engineering where I was to address the opening ceremony of the UN Model Conference. On the positive side, this gave me some extra time for sightseeing which I utilized to the fullest.

Putting pressure on institutions/organizations to not invite or disinvite me had now become a routine matter. I was disinvited twice by the Aligarh Muslim University and many other universities and colleges under pressure from the Indian authorities. I still greatly regret not being able to visit Aligarh. The then Vice-Chancellor, Lt Gen. Zameer Uddin Shah, had also called me once to personally apologize. Though I remember telling him there was always a next time, we both knew that, in the case of Aligarh, there was none at least for the incumbent high commissioner.

Unbeknownst to me, the two NSAs met in Moscow on 24 May on the sidelines of an international meeting of high-ranking officials dealing with security matters. I had subsequently come to know that Ajit Doval was not happy with the progress being made on Pathankot. He even alleged that some ISI officials were behind the attack without, however, corroborating his assertion. He also sought cooperation on capturing the Indian fugitive, Dawood Ibrahim, as well as on the Khalistan issue, admonishing Pakistan that it must realize that the cost of enmity with India was too high for Pakistan. Nasser Janjua, on his part, while reiterating Pakistan's position on the above, also discussed the possibility of providing India overland access to Afghanistan as well as to Gwadar. They also agreed to meet periodically.

On 19 June, Sushma Swaraj, in her annual press conference, made an effort to keep the deceitful notion alive (which I tried to puncture in my April media talk) that the bilateral talks had not been called off. Articulating India's policy, she said: "India was following a three-pronged policy on Pakistan. "First, we want to resolve every issue through talks. Second, talks will be between India and Pakistan and no third country or party will be a part. Third, terror and talks will not go hand-in-hand." (*The Times of India*, New Delhi, 20 June 2016.) She also tried to keep Pakistan under pressure on Pathankot by saying that Pakistan was not denying a reciprocal NIA visit but had only asked for some extra time. She also mentioned the good personal relationship between the two prime ministers in a bid to keep Pakistan guessing whether Modi would or would not attend the SAARC Summit in Islamabad in the coming November.

Meanwhile, I went ahead with my annual Iftar party on 25 June despite an attack in Pampore near Srinagar early in the day in which eight personnel of the Central Reserve Police Force (CRPF) were killed. The party was attended by Kashmiri and Indian Muslim representatives including Syed Ahmed Bukhari, Shahi Imam of Delhi's Jama Masjid and former foreign secretary, Salam Haider. The former was also kind enough to lead the Maghrib prayers after Iftar. In my address at the party, I stressed that both Pakistan and India must work together to have a tension-free and cooperative relationship. I also mentioned the centrality of the Jammu & Kashmir dispute hoping that, when talks resumed, a solution in line with the political aspirations of the people of Jammu & Kashmir would be found.

However, as we were proceeding towards the prayer room, some Indian journalists kept asking me for comments on the Pampore attack and the killing of CRPF personnel. Let me here confess that I did lose my calm a bit, and my response to them, despite their being importunate, could have been better worded. I was still polite but said: "I have already said what I had to say, I request you that this is an Iftar party. Let us enjoy ourselves." (*Hindustan Times*, New Delhi, 26 June 2016.) The word "enjoy" that I used in my response was indeed not in good taste; I was quite upset with myself. Not that Indians express grief when Kashmiris are martyred. But I should not have been insensitive to the families of those killed. I mentioned this to my colleague, Manzoor Memon, and, as usual, he was supportive and said that, "Sir, these things do happen in media interactions. You still did not say anything terribly wrong."

As expected, the Indian TV channels started running the story in no time and the next day Indian papers had headlines castigating me for my insensitive remarks. That was the only time during my entire stay in India when I felt really bad. But it was a good lesson in public diplomacy that never ever again should I lose my cool-headedness no matter how intense the pressure.

As a result, I was disinvited to an Iftar party being hosted by the Muslim Rashtriya Manch (MRM) on 2 July. Interestingly, MRM is headed by a national executive member of the RSS, Indresh Kumar. Another interesting aspect to this event was that, when I had learnt through my sources that I would be invited to the MRM's Iftar party, I had already written to Islamabad on 24 June that I would not attend as my participation would not go down well with Kashmiris and Indian Muslims. The fact of the matter was that, when I received the invite, my office had already regretted. But MRM/ RSS played it out differently in line with its own narrative. However, I did attend the Iftar party by a leader of the Janata Dal (United), JD (U), Sharad Yadav on 29 June where there were many opposition leaders including Sonia Gandhi, Vice President Mohammad Hamid Ansari, the chief minister of Bihar and president of the JD (U), Nitish Kumar. The media would not let me enjoy the party and meet people. Therefore, I had to leave early but the media people chased me relentlessly right up to my official car which, in a commotion-like situation, also got a few scratches. I felt bad about that.

******

8 July 2016 would always be remembered in the history of the struggle of Kashmiris for their right to self-determination.

On this day, Burhan Muzaffar Wani, commander of Hizbul Mujahideen (HuM) in Kashmir, was martyred in an operation by the Indian security forces triggering months-long unrest in the Kashmir Valley.

The handsome 22-year-old cricket-loving Kashmiri freedom fighter was fast changing the meaning of resistance by regularly posting videos on the social media. Soon, he became the epitome of Kashmiri resistance against the Indian occupation. "He was seen as a hero, for taking the fight to the Army and fighting for his homeland. He regularly posted videos, the recent ones being his assurance of not attacking the Amarnath yatra pilgrims, asking Kashmiri Pandits to return to their homeland as long as it doesn't turn into an Israel-like situation; and also threatening the army colonies." (Ravi Handa, "If Burhan Wani was a terrorist why does he have so many followers?", 14 July 2016, quora.com.)

Burhan left his family and home in Tral in Pulwama district of south Kashmir at the age of fifteen in October 2010.

Burhan's elder brother, Khalid Wani, was pursuing a master's in political science from the Indira Gandhi National Open University. He was also martyred by Indian security forces on 13 April 2015. The Indian army claimed that Khalid had been operating as an over-ground worker for the HuM and was killed in an encounter. Twenty months later, in contradiction of their own story, Khalid's name appeared on a public notice released by the office of the deputy high commissioner of Pulwama. The notice listed the names of 106 victims of death, injury, and damage to property. Ex-gratia relief was announced for the families of 70 of them including Khalid Wani's. One of the key conditions for granting compensation was that the dead person should not be a militant. However, his father, Muzaffar Wani, refused to take the money (Rs 4 lakh) for his son's killing. He, however, was open to accepting a job for his youngest son who was then studying in class 12 as also allowed under the compensation rules. ("Has the Kashmir government contradicted army's claim about Burhan Wani's brother?", Moazum Mohammad, 13 December 2016, Scroll.in)

Burhan Wani's funeral was attended by over 2 lakh people on 9 July. "Nearly 22 prayers had been held for him, a first, in the history of any such funeral. He was buried next to his brother Khalid Wani. On that day alone, in clashes across the Valley, 16 Kashmiris were killed by the Indian security forces. ("The Funeral of Burhan Wani and the Unrest that Followed", by Qadri Inzamam and Haziq Qadri, 10 July 2016, *The Caravan Journal of Politics and Culture.*)

Over the next six months, the situation in Kashmir remained extremely tense and Pakistan-India hostility at the peak. Despite the difficult circumstances, the valiant people of Jammu & Kashmir were not to give up. Every day there were peaceful demonstrations across Kashmir even in the Kargil region of Ladakh. They pelted stones at the security forces and the latter, in return, rained Kashmiris with pellet gun bullets.

Strict curfew remained in effect for over three months. Local businesses and the Kashmir economy had literally come to a halt. But Kashmiris yet again demonstrated that their political aspirations could not be crushed no matter what. They were determined to fight to the end.

It is quite painful to see that most Indian journalists and civil society organizations are hardly vocal when it comes to Kashmir. They talk about democracy day in and day out but I often say that the Indian democracy ends where the borders of Jammu & Kashmir begin. Though I know many Indian journalists whose credentials are beyond reproach, they would still hesitate to write anything beyond winning the hearts and minds of Kashmiris and none is willing to publicly admit that the Kashmir dispute is not about terrorism or territory but the right to self-determination.

******

At the envoys' conference in Islamabad on 1-3 August, I made a detailed presentation on how to deal with India without diluting our position on Kashmir. I also dwelt on how and when the Modi government would be dispensing with Article 370 stripping Kashmir of its special status. I was of the strong view that the time was now to ramp up our Kashmir diplomacy. When I suggested that, at the upcoming UNGA session, rather than make the traditional omnibus speech, Prime Minister Sharif should talk only and only about Kashmir and how its fair settlement was a prerequisite for a durable peace in South Asia, most of my colleagues disagreed. Rejecting the proposal, they argued that there were other important issues such as Afghanistan, Palestine and climate change that Pakistan could not ignore. However, there was agreement that Kashmir should be raised in strong terms as the worsening ground situation in Kashmir warranted.

I also discussed Mumbai, Pathankot and Doval's Offensive-Defense Doctrine and possible options for Pakistan. In general, my proposals sought to manage our relations with India in a coherent manner. I strongly discouraged taking unilateral steps or dealing with India through back channels at this stage.

As for the scheduled SAARC Summit in Islamabad, I had, even then, some apprehensions that it was not a shoo-in. A detailed discussion followed including on the pending Motor Vehicle and Railways agreements which Pakistan had blocked at the 2014 Kathmandu summit. The envoys agreed to submit favorable recommendations to the prime minister on these agreements as we were told that the prime minister was inclined to let the two agreements be adopted by SAARC in November with a caveat of national security implying that Pakistan would be within its rights to pend implementation of any provision in the agreements if it was in conflict with its national security interests. (Here I may mention that, on my way back to New Delhi, I called on Chief Minister Shahbaz Sharif. When I told him about this matter, his terse response was, "we should not sell ourselves cheaply.")

After the conference, I stayed in Islamabad for a couple of days as I had requested a call on the prime minister which, despite my repeated reminders, did not come through. I found it strange and disappointing that the prime minister had the time to see our ambassadors in New York and Manama, but not the one in New Delhi. I could, therefore, easily infer that the prime minister was not happy with my performance and, perhaps, had also been swayed by the Indian propaganda that I was the establishment guy. Utterly dosh as it was and, after thinking long and hard about it, I contacted one of the top aides of the prime minister from New Delhi requesting him to explore if there was any possibility of my transfer from New Delhi.

The most disturbing thing from my professional viewpoint was that my own ministry would prefer to conduct relations with India through its high commissioner in Islamabad and would not even keep me posted. I thought that to continue serving in India in that unhelpful environment where I was being scuttled by my own colleagues for whatever reasons made no sense. This was not about me, but Pakistan. How could I serve my country effectively in such a jaundiced and unfavorable environment? However, my efforts to get myself transferred from New Delhi could not see the light of day. When it finally happened the following year, it was indeed on a sour note. I will talk about it in the next chapter.

Bilateral atmospherics continued to be tense and this was amply reflected in the SAARC interior ministers' meeting that took place in Islamabad on 4 August. Rajnath Singh and his Pakistani counterpart did not even shake hands at the conclave. Then, Pakistan's interior minister had to skip the ministerial lunch which he was supposed to host as he was called for an urgent meeting with the prime minister. Rajnath Singh also did not attend when he came to know that the host would not be there. Here, I thought India was right to react the way it did. Our interior minister should have been present at the lunch no matter what.

Earlier, at the opening session of the conference, while the Indian minister kept harping on the mantra of terrorism, Chaudhry Nisar Ali Khan put forth Pakistan's perspective both on terrorism and Kashmir. Rajnath Singh returned to India before his scheduled time, that is, without attending the concluding session of the conference. Rather than helping, the SAARC meeting had only betrayed how bilateral tensions were brewing forcing Indian finance minister, Arun Jaitley, to stay away from the SAARC finance ministers' conference in Islamabad on 25-26 August.

On the Independence Day of Pakistan, Prime Minister Sharif, in his message to the nation, declared that this year's Independence Day was dedicated to the people of Jammu & Kashmir and their freedom struggle. Addressing the flag hoisting ceremony at the high commission on 14 August, I repeated what Prime Minister Sharif had said in his message. While no Indian guests were present at the flag hoisting ceremony, the Indian media lost no time in attributing the dedication of the day to me. As expected, another controversy engendered. Barring one or two newspapers, the rest literally went crazy. For instance, *The Economic Times* of 15 August reported my remarks under the caption: "Basit, the Agent Provocateur". Articles were written against me, suggesting that the government declare me a persona non grata under. Article 9 of the 1961 Vienna Convention on Diplomatic Relations and expel me from India.

However, Prime Minster Sharif's message, reinforced by me, went down extremely well with the people of Kashmir. It was unprecedented that a Pakistan prime minister would dedicate Pakistan's Independence Day to Kashmir. On that day, I was inundated by messages from Kashmir congratulating and appreciating the prime minister and me for raising our voices for Kashmiris and standing firmly by their side.

The 15th of August is India's Independence Day and, as per tradition, the Indian prime minister addresses the nation from the ramparts of Delhi's iconic Red Fort. Heads of diplomatic mission are also invited and their enclosure is usually next to the podium from where the prime minister delivers the speech. I was also invited and attended though my Indian guests were not that welcoming on the day. Prime Minister Modi, as we all know, loves to make long speeches. On that day, he spoke for over 90 minutes. I was attentive as I had the feeling that he would say something about Pakistan which had not been said before.

And then he said the following: "Today, from the ramparts of Red Fort, I want to greet and express my thanks to some people. In the last few days, people of Balochistan, Gilgit, Pakistan-occupied Kashmir have thanked me, have expressed gratitude, and expressed good wishes for me. The people who are living far away, whom I have never seen, never met—such people have expressed appreciation for prime minister of India, for 125 crore countrymen". (*The Hindu*, Tuesday, 16 August 2016.) The prime minister also accused Pakistan of supporting cross-border terrorism and glorifying terrorism.

This was the first time that India would be talking about Balochistan in this manner and at the prime minister level. Pakistan reacted sharply. Sartaj Aziz, in a statement, said: "Prime Minister Modi's comments on Balochistan, which is an integral part of Pakistan, only proves Pakistan's contention that India through intelligence agency R&AW has been fomenting terrorism in Balochistan." (*The Hindu*, Tuesday, 16 August 2016.)

I was slightly concerned at the way we had formulated our reaction to Modi's provocative remarks. In my view, there was no need to mention that Balochistan was an integral part of Pakistan as India would invariably say the same about Kashmir. The two situations were not comparable. There was no dispute or issue on the fact that Balochistan was an integral part of Pakistan like other provinces of Pakistan. Nuances cannot be given short shrift; they even become more important in an adversarial relationship. I conveyed my views to Islamabad. I don't know how Sartaj Aziz must have reacted to my contention but that was not my concern.

Modi's remarks on Balochistan were followed by a request to India by Brahamdagh Bugti, a Baloch nationalist and grandson of Nawab Akbar Bugti who was killed in an operation by Pakistan security forces on 26 August 2006, for political asylum in India. However, I doubted that New Delhi would oblige Bugti for a host of reasons. The foremost was that it did not suit India to be seen as supporting the insurgency in Balochistan. And I was right. Brahamdagh Bugti now lives in

Switzerland and operates from there. Pakistan's efforts to get him back have so far been unsuccessful.

Maharaja Krishna Rasgotra, former Indian foreign secretary, an illustrious diplomat and recipient of the Padma Bhushan award, India's third highest civilian award, invited me for a lunch on 8 September. I had a detailed discussion with him on the prevailing situation. I also sought his advice on a possible way forward. He agreed with me that Kashmir had to be resolved if the two countries were to live in peace and he thought that a solution could be worked out along Musharraf's four-point formula. It was important to break the ice and the upcoming SAARC Summit would be a good opportunity. He also suggested that a telephone call from our prime minister to Modi saying that he was looking forward to meeting him in Islamabad would be helpful. I thought the suggestion was worthwhile. Accordingly, I advised Islamabad that the prime minister might consider calling all SAARC leaders rather than only Modi. However, that was not to happen. Nor could we salvage the SAARC Summit.

As the annual UNGA session was fast approaching, and India was drawing international flak on the use of pellet guns in Kashmir (UN Human Rights Commissioner also suggested sending a fact-finding mission to Kashmir which India rejected), it was desperate to shift the focus on so-called "cross-border terrorism".

On 18 September, only three days before Prime Minister Sharif was to address the UNGA, an attack on an Indian army garrison at Uri in Kashmir took place killing 19 Indian soldiers and wounding over 20.

Pakistan immediately offered an international investigation into the attack but, as expected, India did not respond. I was summoned by Jaishankar on 21 September at 6 pm. I was accompanied by deputy high commissioner, Syed Haider Ali Shah. Jaishankar, accusing Pakistan of its links to the Uri attack, said that, if Pakistan wished to probe the attack, India was ready to provide fingerprints and DNA samples of the terrorists killed in Uri. He also alleged that the terrorist attack in Uri only underlined that the infrastructure of terrorism in Pakistan remained active. He also reminded me of Pakistan's commitment of 6 January 2004 that Pakistan would not allow its soil to be used for terrorism against India.

I listened to him patiently but had to respond to his allegations. I said that, if India was so confident of Pakistan's hand in the attack, it should have responded positively to Pakistan's call for an international investigation. It was unhelpful to accuse Pakistan without any credible investigation and jump the gun. I undertook to convey his demarche to Islamabad hoping that diplomacy would help contain the situation.

The next day, Prime Minister Modi chaired a meeting reportedly on the Indus Waters Treaty (IWT) of 1960 between India and Pakistan. The treaty was mediated by the World Bank, allocating the waters of the three western rivers of Indus, Chenab and Jhelum to Pakistan and, of the three eastern rivers, namely, Ravi, Sutlej and Bias to India. The Indian media, quoting reliable sources, reported that the prime minister had tasked his team to consider options apropos IWT as the flow of water and terrorism could not go together. This was a veiled threat to Pakistan that, if Pakistan did not behave, India, being the upper riparian could create problems for Pakistan. As for the IWT itself, it cannot be terminated unilaterally. Overall, the treaty is working well and, barring a few violations by India, it has survived many a crisis including the 1965 and 1971 wars and the 1999 conflict in Kargil. Pakistan continues to get around 133 million-acre feet (MAF) of water annually. Under the IWT, India is entitled to store and use 3.6 MAF from the eastern rivers and produce power of up to 18569 MW through run-of-river projects and irrigate 13.4 lakh acres of land in Kashmir.

In the backdrop of continuing heavy exchange of firing on the LoC, Jaishankar summoned me again on 27 September. He handed over to me a three-page document containing, according to him, actionable information on the perpetrators of the Uri attack. He claimed that the local villagers in the Uri sector had got hold of two Pakistan nationals, Faisal Hassan Nawaz, 21, and Yasir Khursheed, 19, who acted as guides for the terrorists. According to him, the two guides who were accompanying the infiltrators in the Uri attack belonged to Muzaffarabad. They also came up with the names and their coordinates in Pakistan asserting that they had all undergone training at a LeT camp for three weeks. Jaishankar also offered to provide consular access to these individuals apprehended in connection with the terrorist attacks in India.

Interestingly, *Hindustan Times*, in a story published on 23 September (four days before Jaishankar summoned me), had already reported on these two young Pakistanis who had reportedly strayed into the Indian side of the LoC. On the basis of this report, the high commission had already written to India's MEA to confirm the report and, if true, provide consular access under the May 2008 consular access agreement. The consular access was eventually provided on 29 November and the two boys subsequently travelled back to Pakistan and joined their families.

I reported all the details provided by India to Islamabad. As it turned out, India's so-called facts were all fictional. While Pakistan was willing to cooperate, there was no "actionable information" provided by India as claimed by Jaishankar. In retrospect, that was all being done to prepare grounds to create yet another fictional story this time of a surgical strike against Pakistan on 29 September.

Let us return for a while to 21 September, that is, to Prime Minister Sharif's address at the UN General Assembly. His words on Kashmir were strong and most appropriate doing full justice to what was happening on the ground. He also mentioned Burhan Wani who, he said, had emerged as the symbol of the latest Kashmiri Intifada. The prime minister said all the right things on Kashmir and in strong terms but his address became controversial not for what he said but for what he refrained to say. Back home, the opposition lambasted him for not mentioning the arrest of Commander Kulbhushan Jadhav and India's involvement in terrorism in Pakistan especially in Balochistan, Karachi and the tribal areas.

The impact of the prime minister's remarks on Kashmir was somewhat diluted not only because of the domestic controversy on Jadhav but also due to a gaffe by our permanent mission to the UN in New York. Pakistan Permanent Representative Dr Maleeha Lodhi, while exercising the right of reply to Sushma Swaraj's allegations against Pakistan on terrorism, showed a picture of a "Kashmiri" girl whose face bore the marks of pellet gun wounds. As the picture was of a Palestinian girl and not a Kashmiri, India did not lose a moment to make fun of Pakistan's response. The focus thus shifted from the substance to the faux pas. In my media interaction with the Indian media, I stressed that a human error should not be overplayed as that could not hide what was happening with Kashmiris adding that, if the Indian media was willing to publish, I could supply them with hundreds of pictures of Kashmiri pellet gun victims.

I am not privy to the discussions that must have taken place in New York on what should be included and not included in the prime minister's speech. However, it is clear that the prime minister was not fully convinced on Jadhav. No wonder Sartaj Aziz, addressing the Pakistan Senate on 7 December, reportedly said that the dossier on Kulbhushan Jadhav contained mere statements and no conclusive evidence. As the statement made instant headlines in India, our foreign office immediately denied it saying that the statement attributed to Sartaj Aziz was "absolutely incorrect," and that he had informed the Senate that the investigations into Jadhav's network were ongoing and the dossier shall be completed upon the conclusion of the investigation. (*Hindustan Times*, 7 December 2016.)

It was in the first week of January 2017 that Dr Maleeha Lodhi, handed over a dossier on Jadhav to the UN Secretary General. But the damage had already been caused by Sartaj Aziz by making a loose statement in the Senate on such an important issue. Moreover, I had thought the dossier should have been handed over to the UN Secretary General by Sartaj Aziz rather than our permanent representative. These small steps do make a huge difference in conveying how much importance is attached to a particular issue and how high the stakes are.

Perhaps, given the long and complex history of civil-military relations in Pakistan, Prime Minister Sharif had never believed in what was being said by the establishment. During those days he was also under pressure on the Panama leaks and stories of his family's involvement in illegal off-shore investments and money laundering. The Kargil conflict would also remain with him as he would not tire of mentioning the 1999 Lahore Declaration and how, according to him, it was sabotaged by General Musharraf. I could imagine his state of mind. He must have been thinking that the establishment was not comfortable with his reaching out to Modi and that Pathankot and Kulbhushan Jadhav were part of the same machinations to stymie his initiatives and rapprochement between the two countries.

Details of the civil-military officials meeting, chaired by the prime minister on 4 October, were leaked to the daily *Dawn* and published on 6 October. These gave the impression that it was the establishment that would not let the civilian leadership move against the militant non-state actors and betrayed the serious tensions prevailing between the two. Though a statement issued by the prime minister's office refuted the *Dawn* report, a committee was formed to investigate the matter. Subsequently, both Senator Pervaiz Rashid, Information Minister, and Fatemi had to step down. The *Dawn* leaks thus became another thorny issue between the civilian and military leaderships which led Modi to conclude that Sharif was not in a position to deliver. All doors for joint engagement were now firmly shut and finding a way out of the prevailing gridlock looked increasingly elusive.

India was also hostage to its own domestic political considerations. State elections were to take place in India's largest state, Uttar Pradesh, early next year. Taking a tough stand against Pakistan was a convenient and tested recipe for the BJP to win elections. I was, therefore, not very hopeful that things could be turned around easily. Rather, I could see more tension building up. However, an occasion would come up in November which I thought could be utilized to at least try for some improvment in the bilateral environment if not resumption of joint talks. However, all hopes dashed when the time came.

On 28 September, the Indian media reported that Prime Minister Modi would not travel to Pakistan to attend the 19th

SAARC Summit in November. The decision was reportedly taken in line with India's new policy of isolating Pakistan in the region and beyond. Following this, most of the other SAARC countries including Bangladesh, Afghanistan, Bhutan, Sri Lanka and the Maldives had also decided to stay away. Thus, the Islamabad SAARC Summit had to be postponed.

I do not see the summit taking place in the foreseeable future unless the venue is shifted from Islamabad to another SAARC capital such as Kathmandu or Colombo. However, Modi may still decide to stay away and India will be represented by its president or someone else.

For the record, it is India which has always been a factor in some way or the other in the postponement of the SAARC Summits. The organization was established in 1985. According to its charter, the summit is to be held annually. However, so far only 18 summits have taken place. This organization, despite its huge potential, has never been able to function smoothly let alone evolve organically into a meaningful organization for regional cooperation and integration. I would always argue that effective multilateral frameworks cannot be built on rickety and unpredictable bilateral relations.

The date 29 September became another tension-ridden date in the hostile Pakistan-India relationship. India claimed that it had carried out a surgical strike across the LoC destroying many terror launch pads and killing many. Our side immediately denied that any such action had taken place on the Pakistan side of the LoC. Islamabad-based foreign and local journalists were also taken to the site where India had claimed to have taken the action to show to the world that India was making up and the drama of surgical strike was staged primarily for the consumption of the Indian people to convince them that Modi was indeed a strong leader and that only he had the nerves to take action beyond mere threats as used to be the case with the successive Congress governments.

It was also an attempt to see how the international community would react to an action which was projected to have been taken in self-defense. And sadly, while the international community did show its concerns for the inherent risk of escalation in a nuclear environment, there was hardly a mention of the need to resolve the Kashmir dispute. Some disparate and meek voices were also heard criticizing the continuing violations of human rights in Kashmir but made no impact. At the end of the day, both parties were asked to contain the situation which, in any case, was immaterial as Pakistan had already denied that any surgical strikes took place as being claimed by India.

Domestically, the Congress party criticized Modi for going public as this was not the first time India had taken such an action. Congress leaders argued that both sides had been crossing the LoC, taking action and returning but neither side would ever claim to have crossed the LoC. They also demanded video evidence to substantiate the government claim that it had destroyed several terror-launch pads on the other side of the LoC.

The government counterattacked the opposition for raising unpatriotic questions and putting the credibility of its armed forces in doubt. The Congress party soon came under pressure saying that they were not doubting what the Indian military was claiming but the matter should not have been made public for political gains as such operations had been part of India's strategy for long and, by doing so, India was also openly giving Pakistan the right to carry out operations on the Indian side of the LoC.

I went all out to expose India's false claim by actively interacting with the electronic and print media. In over a dozen of my media interactions over a week including interviews with Karan Thapar and Rajdeep Sardesai, my line of argument was succinct and to the point. I termed the surgical strikes by the Indian Army as fictional; it was another firing across the LoC and a ceasefire violation by India as also given in the official statement by India's Director General Military Operations that the action was "along the LoC". Pakistan responded to this ceasefire immediately and proportionately; had there been any surgical strike, Pakistan would have responded in kind; Pakistan did not need time for preparation and while Pakistan wanted good and normal relations with India, this could only happen on the basis of mutual respect.

On 7 October, a joint statement was issued by the leaders of the parliamentary parties after a meeting chaired by Prime Minister Sharif. The statement, inter alia, averred that the people, the government, the political parties and the armed forces of Pakistan were firmly united in supporting the Kashmiri people's right to self-determination; expressed solidarity with the people of Jammu & Kashmir; condemned "India's documented interference in Balochistan; and the attempts by India to destabilize Pakistan as substantiated by the capture and confession of serving Indian naval officer Jadhav; regretted Indian refusal to engage bilaterally and at the SAARC forum; condemned the stated intent by India to use water as a weapon and any Indian attempts at unilateral revocation (of IWT) shall be taken as an act of aggression; and rejected the ludicrous claims by India of carrying out surgical strikes as blatantly false and brazen attempts at diverting international attention away from its atrocities in Kashmir."

The statement came just a day after the *Dawn* story of 6

October as discussed earlier. But it was a good move, at least in the context of the obtaining situation between the two nuclear neighbors, and helped convey that, when it came to India, Pakistan stood united.

Following the so-called surgical strikes by India, one of our diplomatic missions in one of the most important capitals suggested that Pakistan should propose a special OIC meeting. I vehemently opposed the idea simply on the ground that, when there was no surgical strike, why should Pakistan be doing anything that lent credence to India's preposterous claim? It appeared Islamabad was in agreement with me as I did not see any further discussion on the proposal.

******

It goes without saying that effective diplomacy is all about realizing foreign policy objectives through the maze of challenges and opportunities. To this end, diplomacy needs clarity, direction and sophistication. And it loathes policy vacuums, baroque abstractions and last but not the least its own passive practitioners.

After the US elections and Trump's victory, I wrote to Islamabad that the Trump administration may throw up more challenges for us at all levels. We were facing an intricate cobweb of variables involving India, Afghanistan and our strategic partnership with China. Needless to say, only through a holistic approach could Pakistan navigate through the Byzantine labyrinth. Diplomacy no longer had the luxury to work and deliver in silos. In short, more of the same would not work.

Unfortunately, we could not dispense with our usual casual approach to diplomacy. Firefighting remained the hallmark of our strategy. We were not attuned to anticipating scenarios and possible policy options for Pakistan. It saddens me to see that more-of-the-same approach continues to this day.

******

My eyes were now on the HoA conference to be held in Amritsar on 3-4 December. We had already agreed to attend and our delegation was to be led by Sartaj Aziz although my recommendation to Islamabad was to attend at the foreign-secretary level since Sushma Swaraj had a kidney transplant and would not be in Amritsar. Should the foreign secretary come, we would suggest a bilateral meeting. Let India decline but it would help create good optics for Pakistan.

Diplomats look for opportunities to break logjams and pave the way for smooth bilateral relations. However, in a bilateral environment that is perennially hostage to countless sub-systemic and systemic factors anchored in the dynamics of the zero-sum game, the possibilities for a genuine breakthrough are rare. Moreover, unilateralism also has its limitations and cannot be sustained for too long without reciprocity. India is a difficult neighbor immersed in enigmatic complexes. On the other hand, Pakistan has its own serious difficulties. Thus, finding a middle ground on any bilateral issue is the holy grail of Pakistani and Indian diplomats.

Before I talk about the HoA, let me briefly dilate upon another unhelpful episode. On 27 October, Jaishankar summoned me to protest against the activities of an official of the high commission and declared him a persona non grata. He was asked to leave India in two days.

The official was detained for many hours at a police station on 26 October in total violation of the Vienna Convention. Under pressure, he also mentioned the names of six officials of the high commission which, in total violation of the well-established diplomatic practices, were made public by India along with their photographs. We were left with no option but to quietly withdraw them. They were all sent to Pakistan by a PIA flight to Lahore on 2 November.

In a tit-for-tat move, Pakistan declared not one but two officials of the Indian high commission in Islamabad persona non grata. India then recalled the total of 8 officials from Islamabad. This episode created a further chill in bilateral relations and, coming a month before the HoA, was not a good omen.

I and a few other officials of the high commission were already in Amritsar to receive Sartaj Aziz and his delegation for the Heart of Asia Conference on Afghanistan. Previously, our side had thought that Sartaj would make a day trip and would not attend the dinner being hosted by Modi. However, he arrived a day earlier to also attend the dinner.

In the run-up to the conference, I was throwing positive feelers about a possible bilateral meeting on the margins of the conference. I gave many electronic and print interviews and also spoke at the annual Patrika Conclave in Lucknow on 14 November. My basic talking point was that Pakistan was open to a bilateral meeting in Amritsar. It was for our hosts to suggest if such a meeting was possible keeping in view the schedule of the conference. However, India did not seem interested in breaking the gridlock. In the event, no meeting took place between the two sides.

Since Sushma Swaraj was not attending the conference, India might have thought that a meeting between Sartaj Aziz and Ajit Doval would be of no use as the former was no longer the NSA. And behind-the-scene engagement between the two NSAs was not delivering much either from India's perspective on issues such as Mumbai, Pathankot and now Uri.

At the conference itself, both Modi and President Ashraf Ghani of Afghanistan in their inaugural speeches were very critical of Pakistan and censured it for providing safe havens to terrorists without, however, mentioning Pakistan by name. Going one step further, Ashraf Ghani also said: "We need to identify cross-border terrorism and a fund to combat terrorism. Pakistan has generously pledged US$500 million for the reconstruction of Afghanistan. This fund, Mr Aziz, could very well be used for containing extremism because, without peace, any amount of assistance will not meet the needs of our people. We have to balance the opportunities and the threats". (*The Economic Times*, New Delhi, 5 December 2016.)

Sitting behind Sartaj Aziz, I immediately asked him if we should respond to them, using our right of reply. I drafted a paragraph responding both to Modi and Ashraf Ghani's jibes at Pakistan and passed it on to him. He, however, preferred to not include the proposed paragraph in his speech. He later told me that he did not want to engage in a slanging match with Afghanistan in particular as that would have been further exploited by India. I thought he was making a valid point. He was, however, appalled at Ashraf Ghani's diatribe as the two had met in the morning and Sartaj Aziz had thought that, although the meeting was not very cordial, there was simply no justification for Ashraf Ghani to use the HoA forum to abuse Pakistan the way he did.

It was the Russian delegation, led by Zamir Kabulov, Special Representative for Afghanistan, who came to our rescue. In his address, he discouraged the tendency to single out any one country and bring up bilateral issues at the forum which he thought would negatively affect the work of this 40-member body. He added that the HoA was not the platform for India and Pakistan to score brownie points. He also said it was wrong to criticize Pakistan. As expected, the Indian media went all out to upbraid him for his remarks but he was not to come under pressure and reiterated the same in his later interactions with the Indian media.

I had known Zamir Kabulov from my days as additional foreign secretary and met him at different multilateral forums on Afghanistan including the Bonn process. I thanked Zamir for his helpful remarks. His remarks were also indicative of the Russian position on the Taliban going through a metamorphosis to be more in line with Pakistan's. Zamir knows Afghanistan extremely well and speaks Dari impeccably.

Two other incidents also marred the conference from our viewpoint. First, Sartaj Aziz was not allowed to visit the Golden Temple at Amritsar on security grounds. The Indian side knew very well that the Sikh community would accord him a very warm welcome, especially in the backdrop of their long-held demand for building the Kartarpur corridor so that they could travel to Gurdwara Darbar Sahib Kartarpur throughout the year without visas. Gurdwara Durbar Sahib Kartarpur was of great importance to Sikhs as the founder of the Sikh religion, Guru Baba Nanak, had spent the last 17 years of his life and died there. It is only 4 kilometers from the international border. Guru Nanak's place of birth, Nankana Sahib, is also in Pakistan and is about 90 kilometers from Lahore.

Second, the Indian side did not allow Sartaj Aziz to interact with Pakistani journalists who had travelled from Pakistan to cover the event. Despite our repeated requests, India would come up with one pretext or another to prevent the meeting. So much so that some of our journalists were not even provided local SIMs to carry out their journalistic duties. Even when I went to see them in the premises of the hotel where our delegation was staying, an Indian security guard tried to stop me from meeting them. Usually I am very calm but, on that day, I did somewhat angrily but still civilly tell the guard that nobody can stop the Pakistan high commissioner from meeting his own people. He eventually relented but the video clip of my arguments with him went viral and the Indian media went all-out to criticize me for violating the security regime laid out for the conference. In Pakistan, however, I was admired for standing up for the Pakistani journalists and not succumbing to Indian pressure.

Though there was no bilateral meeting, Sartaj Aziz and Doval did get a chance to walk together for about 10 minutes as we were leaving the dinner venue and going towards our cars. During that informal conversation, Doval repeated the mantra that talks and terror could not go together and that Pakistan must walk the talk on terrorism otherwise there was no point in talking for the sake of talks. Sartaj Aziz reiterated Pakistan's position stressing how serious the prime minister was in making progress on all fronts and resuming the dialogue process would be helpful and must be done without preconditions.

Some TV channels in India started reporting that, in a conversation with Sartaj Aziz, Ajit Doval had told him clearly that Pakistan should not expect India to engage with Pakistan while the latter did not take any conclusive measures on terrorism. I immediately briefed the Pakistani journalists to counter India's propaganda. First, there was no bilateral, formal meeting between the two. Secondly, it was an informal conversation and that Sartaj Aziz had clearly told Ajit Doval that Kashmir was the root cause of all our problems and, unless the two sides engaged formally, the issues that continued to bedevil the bilateral relations would never be resolved. My briefing to the Pakistani media was telecast in Pakistan which was necessary to counter the one-sided Indian story. Between Pakistan and India, no matter is a small matter.

I and Afghanistan Ambassador to India, Shaida Mohammad Abdali, were onboard the same flight from Amritsar to New Delhi on 5 December and, by coincidence, we were seated beside each other. During the conversation, I told him that his president's remarks on Pakistan and that, too, in India were unfortunate. There was no denying the fact that our two countries did have serious differences but, as two brotherly countries, we should not be bringing up these issues at such multilateral forums. I emphasized that the conference was on Afghanistan. Therefore, we were kind of caught off-guard as we could never reckon that Afghanistan, as the co-chair, would itself mar the proceedings of the conference. I also told him that I advised Sartaj Aziz to give a rebuttal but he demurred saying that Pakistan and Afghanistan could differ on many issues like twin brothers but altercating in public, especially in India, was not appropriate. Ambassador Abdali did not have much to say beyond giving Pavlovian responses and indulging in whataboutery.

The year 2016 was unquestionably a bad year for the two countries. Had Sushma Swaraj attended the HoA, we might have been able to clinch a meeting and one could have expected some amelioration in atmospherics. The Uri attack, real or a false flag had brought the relationship to a nadir. On 20 December, in yet another propagandistic move, India filed a charge sheet in the Pathankot case before a special court in Mohali, Punjab. The charge-sheet named Maulana Azhar, his brother Rauf Asghar and allegedly Pakistani handlers of the attack Shahid Latif and Kashif Jan.

On 29 December, India set up a high-level inter-ministerial committee task force, headed by Principal Secretary to the Prime

Minister, Nripendra Mishra, on the IWT. It included, among others, both Ajit Doval and Jaishankar, and was mandated to take all important strategic and policy decisions regarding the IWT. On the other hand, the World Bank announced halting the two simultaneous processes of Neutral Expert and Court of Arbitration as dispute-settlement mechanisms provided for under the IWT. It was a set-back for Pakistan, for India had been using the bilateral Indus waters commission's meetings to indulge in dilatory tactics and present Pakistan with faits accompli on several hydro-power projects on the western rivers with specifications in violation of the IWT.

Pakistan, it seems, never took the water issue seriously. The relevant institutions have never been up to the task. From the construction of dams to efficient use of water, Pakistan does not have much to show and take pride in. We, as a nation, must be concerned the way we waste the precious commodity and do so with criminal indifference. We can blame India for building dams and stealing our water but that would not help. First, we ourselves are to blame for the intricate mess we have created and, second, there is simply no national strategy on how to deal with the developing water crisis.

I agree that India's intentions are mala fide but this should prompt us to take concrete, strategic measures. Issuing statements and holding India responsible for all our problems has become blasé and would take us nowhere. Pakistan needs to dispense with this self-destructive attitude; it is high time to stop playing possum.

Pakistan should get serious; it must go back to the drawing board and review the available options. It may be worthwhile to consider separating technical from the legal issues and instead of insisting on the World Bank to initiate the two dispute settlement mechanisms simultaneously, we may propose a sequential process. Let us first settle legal issues through the Court of Arbitration and then the technical differences by appointing a Neutral Expert. I am not sure if this works but there is no harm to think of new approaches. We must also keep countries like UK, Germany, Canada, Australia and New Zealand posted as these countries had contributed significantly to the Indus Basin Development Fund as per the IWT.

5

2017

"If you are not bringing anything to the table, give up your seat."

Anonymous

As alluded to earlier, I was no more in the good books of Prime Minister Sharif. Some of my colleagues in the foreign office, including a few who had already retired, should be having, I guess, a sense of malicious pleasure at my uncomfortable situation. Not that I was expecting to become foreign secretary but I still could not believe that a senior officer could be treated in such an insulting manner. I had realized, even a year before, that it would be better if I were transferred from New Delhi. However, that could not happen for some reasons which I would refrain from discussing publicly.

During the envoys' conference last year, Tehmina Janjua, who had come from Geneva, was taken by Fatemi to the prime minister for an interview though the two had already met at the Davos World Economic Forum. I was told by one of the prime minister's aides that though he was not convinced, the prime minister could not say no to her elevation because of a close friend who also happened to be a cousin of Janjua. So I knew even then that there was no chance for me to be elevated especially when I was being seen as a man of the establishment. Moreover, less than two years were left to my retirement. All said and done, I had no big "*sifarish*" and, even if I had, I would never ask for any favor. Yes, there were some well-wishers who did try on my behalf, and I am grateful to them, but the die had already been cast.

On my wedding anniversary, that is, 13 February, a formal announcement was made that Janjua had been appointed as the new foreign secretary. I had no qualms on principle as anyone in Grade 22 was eligible to be given that position and it was the prime minister's prerogative to appoint anyone whom he thought would be best suitable for the job.

The problem for me was the decision to transfer me back to Islamabad. It was impossible for me to serve under my junior. In bureaucracy, this is considered to be a harsh comeuppance. *Faute de mieux*, the next day, 14 February, I wrote to Islamabad that I had decided to take early retirement adding that "May Allah give me strength to continue serving my beloved Pakistan with honesty and courage."

It was now the Indian media's turn to poke fun at me. An article from *The Times of India* (17 February 2017) explained: "Basit was said to be a certainty for the position of Pakistan's foreign secretary, it was pipped by Tehmina Janjua. The fact that Basit was seen as taking a hawkish position on most contentious issues with India is said to have gone against him in Islamabad's choice of foreign secretary. Sharif in the past few months, or more specifically since the retirement of General Raheel Sharif, has been keen to reach out to India, the fact that Sharif could conveniently ignore Basit's claim to the foreign secretary's post only shows his growing clout after the departure of Raheel Sharif. Basit was seen as the army's man and his presence in New Delhi is being seen as an impediment to any breakthrough in bilateral ties. The fact that the new army chief, Qamar Bajwa, doesn't seem inclined to intervene in political issues has also gone in favor of Sharif."

How easy it was to blame the Pakistan high commissioner for everything as if I was calling the shots and Islamabad would always go by my advice. It was primarily India, which had become totally unreasonable, and was using all the possible tricks to avoid talks with Pakistan and to mislead the world on terrorism. If I was the big barrier, then things should have been improved after I had left New Delhi. In fact, the later events vindicated what I had been saying and writing to Islamabad.

It was correct that I knew General Raheel Sharif and had never met General Bajwa. However, despite being the senior most, I would know that my chances of becoming foreign secretary were remote as I was to retire next year. Secondly, I was aware of the fact that Sharif had lost trust in me for my steadfast position on Kashmir and on other bilateral issues from the issuance of visas to cultural relations. As a diplomat, I could never be an impediment to enhancing inter-state relations but, when it came to India, Pakistan could not afford to be oblivious to certain fundamentals. The irony of the fact was that Sharif was overly inclined to pander to India unilaterally and unconditionally and, as the high commissioner in New Delhi, I could easily assess that this approach was untenable as India was not prepared to have talks on Kashmir.

I remember writing to Islamabad in December last year that it would beggar belief that India under Modi would ever budge on Kashmir. Nor was New Delhi likely to give up its policy of destabilizing Pakistan. Modi simply wanted us to revisit our Kashmir policy, convince ourselves of its futility and accept the status quo.

I was also of the view that, post-Pathankot, India succeeded in inveigling Pakistan into taking the public position for months that the two sides were in touch with each other to finalize the dates for a foreign secretary-level meeting. My view was that we would be well-advised to avoid such a situation again and must continue raising our voice for Kashmiris in stronger terms even if it meant further delays in the resumption of bilateral dialogue. I had thought that, after the state elections in Uttar Pradesh, India might be willing to consider talks about talks and that too only with the deceitful intention of building pressure on Mumbai and Pathankot.

Somehow I could see that Sharif had an emotional attachment to India and Indians which, at times, and if I my say so, went beyond his stature as the prime minister. I am reminded of another episode here.

There was a young Indian gentleman who approached my office saying that he wanted to see the high commissioner. He introduced himself as a journalist who, according to him, had recently joined a certain TV channel. After consulting Manzoor Memon, I agreed to see him. During the very first meeting, Manzoor and I could evaluate that he was an intelligence guy and had nothing to do with journalism. Interestingly, he also claimed that he was very close to Prime Minister Sharif and used to meet him during his exile in Saudi Arabia and that they were friends. This was quite a revelation because, as a journalist, he did not have any credentials to show. At least I had never heard his name.

Now knowing where he had come from, we treated him accordingly. Every time we met, he would unfailingly mention Prime Minister Sharif. On one occasion, he expressed his desire to visit Pakistan and meet the prime minister. I explained to him the visa procedure for Indian journalists but he appeared too confident that those procedures were not meant for him. Lo and behold, one fine morning we would receive visa instructions from Islamabad not only for him but also for his family. That was unbelievable, to say the least.

I tried my best to block him from visiting Pakistan but failed. Not only did he visit Pakistan, but he was also given state protocol by the government. He also called on the prime minister. I could not believe that this could happen in our state. On his return, two very damaging stories were done by his TV channel with his inputs. That was too much to digest and I made every effort to blacklist his name and stop him from visiting Pakistan again. I was sure that it was not to the liking of the prime minister but I was very clear that the man had to be blacklisted no matter how the prime minister took it. His easy access to the prime minister was mind-boggling. No one can dispute that it is good to be courteous and humble but, when we lose the capacity to draw a line between our personal relations and state interests, things usually go awry. The problem with Prime Minister Sharif was that he was too easily accessible to Indian journalists and refused to follow the established protocols. Even during his visit to New Delhi in 2014, he saw many Indian journalists without consulting the high commission. And I could hardly find any member in his team who would say anything which Sharif did not want to hear.

I also remember going to see the then Interior Minister Chaudhry Nisar Ali Khan during my visit to Islamabad from New Delhi. I briefed him about my meeting with the prime minister and my frank submissions to him on some critical issues. The minister was visibly surprised at me speaking my mind to the prime minister so frankly as, according to him, most people around him did not speak their minds and avoided being seen as having differing views from him. I could never be thankful enough to Allah for giving me the courage to express my views without fear of repercussions for myself.

It may be pertinent to talk here briefly about the much talked-about Sharif family business interests in India. As mentioned elsewhere in the book, Prime Minister Sharif wanted trade and economic relations with India to be enhanced. I would on and off receive calls from his nephew, Salman Shahbaz to issue visas to Indian engineers for the maintenance of their sugar mills. They were also planning to establish a new state-of-the-art sugar mill in Pakistan to be imported from India.

Prime Minister Sharif was also encouraging Jindal to invest in a mine mouth lignite coal power project in Thar. However, the latter was reluctant given the element of enormous unpredictability in the bilateral relationship.

I am not aware of any other business interests beyond these. It is also a fact that most Pakistani and Indian industrialists and businessmen would not mind seeing bilateral economic and trade relations improving in leaps and bounds and being kept separate from the politics of Kashmir and terrorism. The usual argument given in Pakistan is that, if we can get consumer and capital goods from India at the most competitive prices, it makes no economic sense to import, especially machinery, chemicals, etc., from the West as, at the end of the day, it is the consumer who bears the burden of costly imports.

From a purely economic point of view, this line of argument cannot be dismissed easily. However, one would wish economic relations between states could be insulated from politics in a neat and clean manner. The ongoing tariffs war between China and the US, and India's banning of 59 Chinese mobile applications following the skirmishes in the Ladakh region in May-June 2020 are cases in point.

In my considered view, there are serious limitations to what can be done between Pakistan and India. For instance, the two countries were almost close to concluding an agreement on India's supply of electricity to Pakistan in 2011-12. However, all the laborious work done on this came to naught when bilateral tensions soared in the years to come on Kashmir and the issues related to terrorism. It needs to be remembered that Pakistan-India relations are unique in many respects in which shared history and several commonalities become serious issues instead of being helpful. For example, for many in India, Pakistan was a historical aberration and the result of Britain's divide-and-rule conspiracy. Therefore, Pakistan should reunite with India.

However, people in Pakistan have a different worldview. No wonder then that, when Prime Minister Sharif remarked, in a speech, that there were no cultural differences between Pakistan and India and that we were the same people, he was taken to task by all and sundry in Pakistan. There is nothing apolitical in this relationship. People on both sides of the border with good intentions may have ideas and grand proposals for the two countries to live as normal neighbors but these will remain elusive until the two countries are able to sort out the fundamental issues instead of just managing this abundantly conflictual relationship.

******

Although I was to leave India soon, I continued my activities with full verve and vigor. Accordingly, I agreed to attend *India Today's* annual conclave in Mumbai on 18 March. There was a session on Pakistan-India relations and the co-panelist was a former Indian high commissioner to Pakistan, G. Parthasarathy. A public discussion on Pakistan-India relations is always tense and more so in Mumbai. I faced a barrage of provocative questions on terrorism and the Mumbai trial but maintained my cool. It is always very satisfying to see that, when you respond to questions sensibly and with humility, the audience, however hostile, does end up appreciating you. I was lucky in that sense. Never in India was I booed by the audience except on one occasion in New Delhi where the entire audience was from the RSS and Hindu Mahasabha. But even there, I could not be provoked and let them know that I was not someone who would leave the venue or stop participating in the discussion. This helped me significantly throughout my stay in India and gave me the inner strength to handle many untoward situations.

Writing in *Hindustan Times* on 22 March, Bobby Ghosh, in a column titled "Modi's new envoy to Islamabad", wrote: "Abdul Basit could help Pakistanis understand that it's not just Narendra Modi: ordinary Indians don't want renewed dialogue either.

"Basit's spell in Delhi has coincided neatly with that of the Modi administration, so he has watched the Indian Prime Minister more closely than any other Pakistani official. It's a fair bet that the question Basit will be asked at every gathering, private or public, will be: 'What does Narendra Modi really want?' The curiosity about—and concern over—Modi has grown exponentially since his triumph in the state elections, and his appointment of a Pakistani-baiting hardliner as chief minister of Uttar Pradesh. This means Basit will very likely have the opportunity to speak to a large audience of the Pakistani elites, beyond the tiny circle that has had access to his dispatches. Having failed to move the needle for Pakistan forward in

Delhi, Basit might better serve his country by becoming, after a fashion, Modi's envoy to Islamabad."

Ghosh concluded: "In short, Basit can provide Pakistanis with a much-needed reality check on their expectations from Modi's India. It is, of course, possible he will not find a receptive audience back home: the Pakistan ruling elite has a history of freezing out former envoys who speak inconvenient truths. But then Basit is already used to people not listening to him, and it's never stopped him before."

I must commend Ghosh for his far-sightedness. My advice was barely heeded to when I was in New Delhi. And on return to Islamabad, I was hardly consulted with a few exceptions notwithstanding. I will dilate on this later in this chapter and in the Epilogue.

This year was my last Pakistan Day in New Delhi. The day started with the flag-hoisting ceremony and then a formal reception in the evening. In my address at the flag-hoisting ceremony, I reiterated Pakistan's full support to the Kashmiri struggle saying that history was witness that freedom movements could not be suppressed forever. I did not have the slightest of doubt that Kashmiris would eventually succeed in winning their right to self-determination. I also expressed the hope that Pakistan and India are able to resolve the Kashmir dispute and other bilateral issues through dialogue so that this region can also benefit from regional cooperation and integration. I also emphasized that urging India to have a dialogue was our strength and not our weakness as Pakistan's position on all bilateral issues including Kashmir, terrorism, Siachen and Sir Creek was based on internationally recognized principles. Therefore, Pakistan would never shy away from a dialogue or set unnecessary preconditions which only served to complicate matters. As a bigger country, India must show magnanimity and reach out to Pakistan in the interest of its own people. However, if India was not willing to engage, Pakistan would not beg for engagement.

As expected, the Indian foreign office strongly reacted to my remarks. Spokesperson Gopal Baglay, who was India's deputy high commissioner in Pakistan before taking up this assignment, said that the high commissioner's remarks were not in keeping with diplomatic niceties and were tantamount to interference in India's internal affairs.

At the evening reception, India was represented by M.J. Akbar, Minister of State for External Affairs. In my short speech I welcomed the MoS and thanked him for gracing the occasion. Focusing on Pakistan's efforts to put its economy back on rails, I said in a light vein that Pakistan might not be the richest country in South Asia but, according to a recently published UN report, Pakistan was the happiest country in the region. This was indeed testimony to the resilience of Pakistanis who, despite having myriad internal and external challenges, kept their spirits high while tirelessly fighting against terrorism. M.J. Akbar did not make any remarks.

For a change and to show solidarity with Kashmiris, I had asked my team to also add the famous Kashmiri dish *gushtaba* to the menu. Our Kashmiri guests were delightfully surprised and the message to the Indians was loud and clear that Pakistan and Kashmir could not be separated. I don't know if the new menu was repeated next year or thereafter.

As per the tradition, I also met the Hurriyat leadership the next day in the high commission. We all agreed that Modi's designs on Kashmir were aggressive and that his government appeared hell-bent on realizing the long-held agenda of the RSS to trifurcate the state. Abdul Ghani Bhat put forth some useful suggestions aimed at countering India's mischievous agenda on different fronts. The Hurriyat leaders also thanked me for keeping the Kashmir issue alive and hoped that I would continue contributing effectively to the Kashmir cause even after my return to Pakistan. I assured them that the Kashmiri struggle was very close to my heart and that they would not find me wanting in this regard. Back in Pakistan, I think I am keeping my promise to the people of Jammu & Kashmir.

I feel absolutely great to be staying in touch with my Kashmiri friends, old and young, from all walks of life. I genuinely feel their pain. While their resolve cannot be doubted, I am growing somewhat pessimistic about Pakistan's commitment. I wish freedom could be won through bloviating alone.

******

On 10 April, my birthday, Commander Kulbhushan Sudhir Jadhav, 50, was sentenced to death by a Field General Court Martial under the Pakistan Army Act of 1952. He was tried for espionage and subversive activities aimed at destabilizing Pakistan and was provided with defense counsel as per legal provisions. When he was caught, he was in possession of two Indian passports, one in the fictitious name of Hussein Mubarak Patel.

Indians refuted the claims made in his confessional video which, New Delhi asserted, had no legal value as it was made under duress. According to the Indian version, Jadhav was retired from the Indian Navy in 2003 and had illegally obtained a passport in Pune, Maharashtra, in the pseudonym of Patel. After retirement, he moved to Chabahar and set up a private business to service dhows and ships operating out of the Chabahar port. Moreover, he was not arrested in Balochistan but kidnapped from Iran by the ISI.

The Indian media speculated that he was kidnapped to

exchange him for a retired Pakistan military officer, Lt Col. Mohammad Habib Zahir who disappeared from Lumbini, Nepal. It was suspected that Zahir, a former ISI officer, was lured by Indian intelligence services and was in their custody. (Pakistan also made a formal request to India, besides Nepal, to help locate him but India never responded. We still don't know where the ex-army officer is.)

Whereas India had made several formal requests for consular access since 25 March 2016, Pakistan had also written to India to provide some information about Jadhav as required by his defense counsel. India never responded to our request. From their point of view, they were right as cooperating with Pakistan in the Jadhav matter without consular access would have been interpreted as accepting the legitimacy of the trial. They were also aware that the crimes committed by Jadhav would definitely lead to conviction. Thus, cooperating with Pakistan would have weakened their position of subsequently regarding the trial as "farcical".

India also formally conveyed to Pakistan a request by Jadhav's parents and wife for a visit to Pakistan to see him. I was in favor of allowing the visit and had conveyed so to Islamabad weighing the pros and cons from Pakistan's standpoint. And the mother and wife of Jadhav did eventually come to Islamabad and meet him on 25 December, but that meeting generated its own controversies ranging from the behind-the-glass screen meeting to not allowing an official of the Indian high commission to speak or listen in on the conversation Jadhav had with his family. When inter-state relations are fed on mutual hostility and distrust, there is little room for even small things to proceed smoothly and it becomes impossible for both to not find faults in everything; allow things to play out in the open and then become hostage to their own propaganda.

I was summoned by Jaishankar on the same day, that is, 10 April. In his demarche, he termed the proceedings that had led to the sentence as "farcical" in the absence of any credible evidence, consular access and a neutral defending officer. Jaishankar stressed that, if the sentence was carried out, the government and people of India would regard it as a case of "premeditated murder". He also told me one-on-one that the development related to Jadhav was very serious and would have serious consequences for bilateral relations.

In my response I undertook to convey his demarche to Islamabad adding that Jadhav was tried under the law of the land and that he would have the legal recourse available to appeal against the verdict and, if his conviction was upheld, he would have the right to submit a mercy petition first to the Army Chief and then, finally, to the President of Pakistan.

As for the consular access, I reminded Jaishankar of the 21 May 2008 Consular Access Agreement (Annex VI) between the two countries and its Clause 6 which clearly stipulated that, in such security related cases, access would be decided on merit. I also told him that a military court was not established especially for Jadhav and that hundreds of Pakistanis had also been tried in military courts for subversion and terrorism. Pakistan's parliament had allowed those courts for a limited period to deal with such cases expeditiously as the country had been going through very difficult times. In any case, given the nature of his offenses, he could not be tried in a civil court. Moreover, following the arrest of Jadhav, our security forces had been able to arrest over 200 operatives in Pakistan on the basis of information provided by him. I insisted that Jadhav was working for R&AW and his involvement in subversion had been proven beyond any doubt.

Sushma Swaraj, speaking in both Houses of Parliament on 11 April, said that the government and the people of India were taking the Jadhav issue very seriously and cautioned Pakistan to consider the consequences for the bilateral relationship if they went ahead and executed Jadhav. She also asserted that the government would go out of the way to ensure justice for "son of India Jadhav".

On the other hand, Prime Minister Sharif said in a statement that Pakistan was a peace-loving country but we could not remain oblivious to defending its sovereignty, protecting its independence and that the nation had full trust in Pakistan's armed forces.

Given the history and nature of Pakistan-India relations, it was impossible that the versions emanating from the two capitals would ever match. As soon the death sentence was handed down, my office was literally flooded with requests for interviews by several Indian newspapers and TV channels and I obliged many defending the trial and the verdict forcefully.

While the Pakistani electronic news media was also keen to get me on the phone especially to know about the Indian protest and what my response was, I had deliberately avoided that front as it was for the foreign office to handle. I still do not know how it happened but one of the Pakistani TV channels reporting on my meeting with Jaishankar said that I had told him in very clear terms that Jadhav was a terrorist. This suddenly became breaking news in India on 10 April. Not surprisingly, I was chided and ridiculed by the Indian media in the strongest words possible. In my interviews to the Indian media when I was asked about this, I would deflect the question by saying that my response to the Indian demarche was not for the public to know. I had told Jaishankar what I had to tell him. Therefore, I would not indulge in disclosing the details of our meeting but willing to answer any question related to Jadhav's trial and the verdict against him.

It so happened that I had already agreed to a seminar on Pakistan-India relations by the Centre for Peace and Progress (CPP) on 11 April. Our former foreign minister, Khurshid Mahmud Kasuri, was also one of the speakers along with Congress leaders Mani Shankar Aiyar and Saifuddin Soz, well-known lawyer Ram Jethmalani and Sudheendra Kulkarni. I could anticipate what was awaiting me at the conference, especially in the backdrop of the remarks attributed to me on a Pakistani TV channel. I had already sent First Secretary, Mohammad Adeel Pervaiz, and Press Attaché, Khawaja Maaz Tariq, to the venue to let me know about the atmosphere there and whether it was advisable for me to attend. However, I was personally disinclined to skip. I had always stood my ground and there was no reason for the Pakistan high commissioner to be defensive about the Jadhav affair. The two officers reported to me that the conference had begun and the Indian media present there in large number was eagerly waiting for me. They were all well-prepared to grill me with their hard-hitting questions and beam it live.

However, that could not deter me. I was confident that I could handle the unfriendly media so long as they did not get rowdy and physical. Accordingly, I asked my security guards to be alert. I also asked my officers at the conference venue to spread the news that I was not coming. The intention was to get into the venue without creating any ruckus and disturbing the conference proceedings which were already underway. But I must give credit to the Indian media for their resourcefulness. To my surprise, I found over a score of reporters at the entrance. As soon I alighted from the car, they bombarded me with their tough questions. I told them that I had come to attend the conference and they should let me say my piece there and we could perhaps interact after the conference, if necessary.

At the conference, I was seated next to Kasuri. I could feel the tense atmosphere pervading the hall. There was heated debate going on where Saifuddin Soz was being chastised for his rejoinder to Jethmalani's remarks that Pakistan was creating disturbances in Kashmir. Soz fired back with a salvo saying India was responsible for the problems in the Valley and that India could not suppress the Kashmiris.

In his remarks, Kasuri emphasized that India and Pakistan should cooperate with each other and should not stop the process of dialogue and let things drift. He added that it was in the national interest of Pakistan to have good relations with India but the latter's preconditions for talks were least helpful. In my terse comments, without mentioning Jadhav, I repeated my fundamental arguments that unless the Kashmir dispute was resolved, there was no realistic chance of peace between the two countries; bilateral issues could be resolved only through dialogue moving beyond stereotypes; talks were not a favor by one to either country but a necessity and, the sooner the dialogue process began, the better it would be not only for the two countries but also the entire region.

When the question-answer session started, the journalists present began raising their voices. Referring to my comments as reported by a Pakistani TV channel, they alleged that the organizers of the conference were Pakistani apologists and that the Pakistan high commissioner should have been dis-invited. In short, the conference ended on a bitter note. There was much pushing and shoving when I was leaving the venue as the reporters would not let me leave without answering their questions. I had decided to not utter a single word. It was to the credit of my officers and Indian security guards who ensured that I got to my car unhurt.

Somehow Prime Minister Modi was optimistic that, given his personal equation with Prime Minister Sharif and their mutual affection, he could get Jadhav out of Pakistan. Perhaps he also wanted to test whether Sharif, who had been considerably weakened by the Panama Leaks, could prevail upon the establishment and deliver Jadhav. Modi badly needed something big from Islamabad especially after the Uri episode and the fact he was under tremendous domestic pressure on the botched demonetization initiative of November last year that created serious financial chaos in India without achieving much against money laundering, terrorism or black-marketing. Modi thus made a last-ditch effort before ramping up the Jadhav issue internationally.

On 26 April, he dispatched Sajjan Jindal to Pakistan for a day trip. While the purpose of the visit was not shared publicly, I was told by a senior staff member of Jindal's that it was about Jadhav. We had already received instructions from Islamabad through the foreign office to issue him a visa immediately for Lahore and Islamabad. We complied and, as per our procedures, confirmed it to all concerned.

Jindal travelled to Islamabad by his private jet and, as soon he landed in Rawalpindi, he was taken to the Murree hill resort, about 45 kilometers from the capital city, for a meeting with the prime minister. There was massive speculation going on both in Pakistan and India as to the purpose of the visit. The high commission also started receiving frantic calls from Pakistani and Indian media. We would make a standard response that it was a private visit and that the high commission was not privy to details.

The Pakistani media somehow also got to know that Jindal and two of his staff members were issued visas only for Islamabad and Lahore, and thus they were taken to Murree illegally without visas. That, in itself, became a big issue. However, in our system, it was not a big deal. Jindal was the prime minister's friend and guest and the matter of visas or no visas becomes meaningless in such situations. After all, Prime Minister Modi and his delegation also made a stopover in Lahore in December 2015 and, while visas were still being stamped on their passports at the airport, they were already at the sprawling private residence of Prime Minister Sharif at Raiwind.

In my curiosity to know the details of the message from Modi to Sharif, I sent a WhatsApp message to Jindal. He did respond immediately but hardly shared anything except to say that he was very happy and satisfied with his meeting with the prime minister. A well-placed Indian journalist later told me that Prime Minister Sharif, in response to Modi's message, had given some assurances that Jadhav would not be executed but he was not ready to commit that he would be released. Whereas Modi wanted Jadhav to be given clemency and released on time for a possible meeting between the two prime ministers on the sidelines of the SCO summit in Astana in June. Since that did not happen, neither side suggested a meeting in Astana.

According to the same journalist, the Indian side had calculated that the Pakistan establishment was reluctant to expedite the appeal process for they did not want the matter of clemency to reach the president as then it would be any one's guess what the political leadership did or did not do. I thought this was far-fetched. Jadhav was not an ordinary Indian convict. Sharif was already being criticized domestically for not mentioning Jadhav in his UNGA address. The maximum Sharif could have done was to get his death sentence converted into a life sentence, and that was, therefore, what he could commit to Jindal in response to Modi's request. But even that was not easy to deliver.

While discussing Jadhav it must not be overlooked that, on 29 March 2017, that is, about ten days before the Jadhav verdict, Pakistan amended its Declaration of 12 September 1960 on accepting the jurisdiction of the ICJ also, inter alia, including the national security clause. That was the right move to make in anticipation of a favorable outcome of the Jadhav case because there was a possibility that, in case of Jadhav's conviction, India might refer the matter to the ICJ invoking the Vienna Convention on Consular Relations since both Pakistan and India were also party to the Convention's Optional Protocol which stipulated that any dispute arising out of the interpretation or application of the Vienna Convention "shall lie within ICJ's jurisdiction."

Our fresh Declaration was, therefore, timely and in order; the Declaration had provided us with the requisite legal space to counter India should it decide to approach the ICJ. Why did we not invoke the security reservations when push came to shove was somewhat intriguing. I am not aware if Jindal had also raised this with Sharif requesting him to let the ICJ decide on the issue of consular access. However, once we had agreed to the ICJ's jurisdiction in the matter, it was like a Pandora's box as nobody could then anticipate which way the ICJ judgement would go. And then, in case of non-compliance, the aggrieved party could also approach the UNSC under Article 94 of the UN Charter for recommendations and measures that could also mean sanctions.

I was summoned by Jaishankar again on 3 May. This time the protest was on the alleged killing of two Indian soldiers on the Indian side of the LoC on 1 May. According to Jaishankar, Pakistani soldiers had crossed the LoC and not only killed the two soldiers but also mutilated their bodies. He asked me to convey to Islamabad India's outrage and demanded that immediate action be taken against the soldiers and commanders responsible for the "heinous act" in violation of the Geneva Convention. In my polite response, I stressed that, as one of the most professional armies in the world, our soldiers could not ever mutilate dead bodies. Denying the Indian allegation, I told Jaishankar that I would convey to Islamabad the contents of his demarche and the sentiments he had expressed. I also asked him to share with us any concrete evidence if the Indian side had it as making claims in the media that India had the undeniable proof alone was not enough. He did not respond to my last point.

Following this, a prompted story was published in the *Sunday Times of India* on 7 May alleging that secret intelligence papers showed how ISI funded the Hurriyat and that the conduit had links with High Commissioner Basit. The next day, *The Times of India* came up with another write-up contending that the Pakistan army's aggression on the LoC and the beheading of the two soldiers were clear indications that it was hobbling Prime Minister Nawaz Sharif's efforts to reach out to New Delhi. "The Pakistan military is now openly driving policy with Sharif reduced to little more than a figurehead; his gestures like addressing the Hindu community on the occasion of Holi swept aside by a fresh wave of aggressive acts by the army under General Qamar Bajwa." The piece also conjectured that the beheading of the two Indian soldiers "was seen to serve the important purpose of encouraging separatists and Jihadis in the Kashmir Valley. The brutal acts were to indicate that the Indian Army is vulnerable and that violence in the Valley will be stoked to the maximum extent possible."

These stories were not without a reason. On 8 May, India submitted a formal petition to the International Court of Justice

(ICJ) in The Hague pleading that Pakistan be stopped from carrying out the death sentence on Jadhav primarily on the grounds that Pakistan had violated the 1963 Vienna Convention by denying consular access to Jadhav and that the trial in a military court was nothing but a sham as it did not fulfil the basic requirements of justice. The Indian move had surprised many in Pakistan as New Delhi would adamantly stick to its position that bilateral issues should be discussed and resolved only bilaterally. Moreover, India had never accepted the ICJ jurisdiction in disputes with the government of any state which was or had been a member of the London-based 53-member Commonwealth. But people, who were dealing with the issue had known quite well what India could do.

India must have calculated that Pakistan could be embarrassed internationally. They were obviously convinced of the correctness of their legal position. Besides, one of the 15 ICJ judges was an Indian national. His presence there must have given some confidence to India that it could clinch a favorable judgment. No doubt, Pakistan was put in a difficult situation.

On 9 May, the ICJ president, using his extraordinary powers under Article 74 of the ICJ Statute, wrote a letter to Prime Minister Sharif asking Pakistan in effect to not execute Jadhav till such time as the court was able to take a formal decision on India's petition. The court also asked the two countries to come with their respective arguments on 15 May. On 18 May, the ICJ provisionally ruled that Pakistan should not hang Jadhav till final orders were issued by the court after hearing both the sides in detailed proceedings under the 1963 Vienna Convention.

The provisional ICJ ruling was termed in India as a huge legal and diplomatic defeat for Pakistan. In an interview to *The*

Statesman on 20 May, I tried to set the record straight that, while Pakistan as a responsible member of the international community would comply with the ICJ ruling, this did not have any bearing on the merits or demerits of the Jadhav case as the ICJ was only looking into the consular access issue. In another interview to *The Times of India* published on 22 May, I stressed that, on Jadhav, Pakistan was on terra-firma as terrorism could not be condoned under any circumstances. I also underlined that, despite all the misplaced hype in India, it must be noted that Pakistan was not in a position to hang Jadhav before the entire legal process had been completed including an appeal to the appellate court and then mercy petitions. This would take months if not years. Hence, Pakistan was not worried at all. Rather we were looking forward to presenting our case on the consular access robustly and solidly before the ICJ.

Fast forward, the ICJ, after lengthy proceedings, announced its final judgement on 17 July, 2019. As there was no Pakistani judge in the ICJ, as per its statute, Pakistan had appointed its former chief justice, Tassaduq Hussain Jillani as the ad hoc judge.

The ICJ judgement, in its operative part, found Pakistan in violation of Article 36 of the 1963 Vienna Convention on the issue of consular access. ICJ came to the conclusion that the absence of consular access to Jadhav had implications on the principles of a fair trial. Accordingly, the court asked Pakistan to take steps towards providing effective review and reconsideration of the case. However, it was left to Pakistan to decide on the ways and means for this. The court also directed Pakistan to immediately inform Jadhav of his rights under Article 36, grant him consular access and suspend the death execution till it fulfilled the ICJ directives.

Justice Jillani, in his lone dissenting voice, wrote that the Vienna Convention was not applicable to the case of Jadhav as he was tried for the charges of espionage and subversion.

Be that as it may, India declared a great victory in The Hague. Pakistan, too, was content with the verdict, perhaps without realizing the matter could pan out to its disadvantage, arguing that it had even earlier agreed to provide consular access to Jadhav with some administrative restrictions; an offer that India had refused. Additionally, the ICJ rightly kept itself away from discussing the merits or otherwise of the trial in a military court. Pakistan immediately announced that it would fully abide by the verdict and, as a first step, an official of the Indian high commission was allowed to meet Jadhav on 2 September 2019. As contained in the judgment, Jadhav was also informed of his rights under Article 36, paragraph 1(b) of the Vienna Convention on Consular Relations.

Interestingly, Pakistan's human rights minister, Dr Shireen Mazari, who said in a tweet that, had the Pakistan foreign office in 2008 registered the bilateral 2008 Consular Access Agreement with the UN, the ICJ could not have ignored it and the trial might have had a different outcome. She also asked as to who should be held responsible for this negligence. I wish she had done her homework. The agreement was registered with the United Nations Secretariat under registration number 54471 on 17 May 2017. And the foreign minister of Pakistan in May 2008, too, was Shah Mahmood Qureshi.

At present, the mercy petition of Jadhav is pending with the Pakistan army chief. He had filed this after his review petition was rejected by the appellate court and before the 17 July 2019 ICJ judgment. At a press conference on 8 July 2020, Pakistan's Additional Attorney General Ahmed Irfan claimed that Jadhav was asked to submit a review petition against his verdict to the Islamabad High Court which he had refused and insisted that he would prefer to pursue his mercy petition. In a quick reaction, India accused Pakistan of coercion against Jadhav to not submit a petition. India also argued that, since Pakistan had not allowed a non-Pakistani lawyer to be engaged in the Jadhav case, the ICJ ruling for an effective review had already been flouted by Pakistan.

Meanwhile, Pakistan also issued a Presidential ordinance in May to make it legally possible for Jadhav to file a review petition to the Islamabad High Court as was also advised in the ICJ judgment. This, too, became a controversy in Pakistan with the opposition taking exception to the government move and alleging that the stage had been set by the government to free Jadhav.

The second consular access was provided to the Indian high commission officials on 16 July which also immediately became controversial. India claimed the access was meaningless in the close presence of Pakistan security and diplomatic officials. Moreover, the proceedings were also being recorded with the aim of keeping Jadhav under pressure not to sign papers for a review petition. Under these circumstances, the Indian officials protested against not providing "unhindered, unimpeded and unconditional access". After concluding that "the access being offered by Pakistan was neither meaningful nor credible" they lodged a protest and left the venue. (Press release issued by India's MEA on 16 July 2020.)

Shockingly, Qureshi immediately tweeted conveying Pakistan's readiness to provide a third consular access in accordance with India's demands and officially conveyed this through a note sent to the Indian high commission. However, the Indian side did not respond. In the event, Pakistan itself filed a review petition though the Indian side also subsequently hired a Pakistani lawyer to represent Jadhav.

The entire episode yet again reflected so poorly on the working of our systems. One fails to understand why details of the second consular access could not have been worked out and agreed with the Indian side beforehand and that, too, in writing. Immediately agreeing to the Indian demands and offering a third consular access implied that Pakistan had come under pressure. In diplomacy, when a country is faced with such a situation, every facet of the situation is deeply analyzed, redlines are defined and then moves are made accordingly. I will give my take on options for Pakistan and what Pakistan and India are up to in the Epilogue.

Here I may briefly touch upon the case of Hamid Nihal Ansari, an Indian national, who entered Pakistan sometime in 2012 through Afghanistan without a Pakistan visa apparently to meet a girl he had befriended online. At the time of his arrest in Kohat city, he was also in possession of a fake Pakistan national identity card. Hamid, 33, was a lecturer at an educational institute. He had told his parents that he was going to Afghanistan for an interview with an airline company. His father, Nihal Ansari, was a banker and his mother vice principal of a college in Mumbai.

Hamid was tried in 2015 in a military court for espionage and was sentenced to three years' imprisonment. His parents, particularly his mother, made many petitions to Pakistan but to no positive outcome. I also met them once in the high commission to console them as I could feel their pain and the trauma they were going through. I also deputed a lady officer in the high commission to be available to his mother as and when she wanted to get in touch with us. Pakistan also refused to provide consular access to Hamid Ansari invoking the 2008 bilateral agreement.

In my personal assessment, which could be totally wrong,

after meeting the parents of Hamid, I concluded that the story of his falling in love with a Pakistani girl could be true. I therefore wrote to Islamabad to take a lenient view of the case and consider releasing him on humanitarian, compassionate grounds as, according his mother, besides some other health complications, he was also fast losing his eye sight. I also made a point that, since he was arrested in 2012 and convicted in 2015, his sentence could be deemed to have begun from the time of his arrest. After consulting a few lawyers in Pakistan on my own, I tried to persuade Pakistani authorities both from New Delhi and during my visits to Islamabad but I did not find them amenable to my recommendation. My suggestion to at least allow the parents to meet him in jail also did not meet their approval.

Hamid's release on 18 December 2018 and when he crossed the Wagah border somehow came as a relief to me as well. I am sure our authorities had valid security reasons to be dispassionate in his case. But I am still of the view that we would not have lost much by releasing him in 2015 or the next year after accepting his mercy petition. There was no doubt Hamid had committed a serious crime but releasing him earlier instead of 2018 would have been a useful public relations exercise as well. But Islamabad was not in sync with my views. Hostility, when deep-rooted, manifests itself sometimes in bizarre and disquieting ways. Now that Hamid is free and living with his parents, I wish the family the best of times ahead.

******

My request for early retirement had been approved by the prime minister and I had planned to leave India on 2 August. Disgrace at its height, I started receiving frequent calls from the ministry as to when I would be relinquishing charge. My detractors must have been thinking that I might be up to something as a verdict on Prime Minister Sharif's corruption cases was expected to be announced in July. But I was not up to anything. Now that I had taken the decision of early retirement and that the prime minister had approved it, there was no turning back. My only problem was that my return to Islamabad, I did not want to be put up in a government accommodation as my own house was under construction. There was a furnished apartment that I had rented but it was not available before August. So, I had to plan my departure from India accordingly.

Despite pressures from Islamabad, I continued with my regular diplomatic activities and had meetings with influential people including former finance and foreign minister, Yashwant Sinha, former foreign secretary, Ambassador M. K. Rasgotra and retired Air Vice-Marshal Kapil Kak. I also hosted a lunch for the Indian high commissioner in Islamabad, Gautam Bambawale, who was in New Delhi to attend an envoys' conference.

I met Yashwant Sinha at his Noida residence on 1 May. Under his leadership, a 25-member Concerned Citizens Group (CCG) was formed in October 2016 to help bring peace to Kashmir. Some prominent members of the group are Kapil Kak, Sushobha Barve, Bharat Bhushan and Wajahat Habibullah.

Sinha, who has now quit the BJP, continues to be vociferously critical of Modi's Kashmir policy and openly expresses concerns about changing the demographic realities of Kashmir. However, it does not mean that Sinha or the members of the CCG are inclined to raising voice for giving the right to self-determination to Kashmiris as provided for in the relevant UN resolutions. What the group is seeking is a political solution within the framework of the Indian constitution. These people, however, are not averse to engaging the moderate Hurriyat leaders in the tradition of the late BJP Prime Minister Vajpayee.

Sinha told me that the Indian position on Kashmir under Modi was not only getting harder and harder but also untenable in the longer term. He was thus not at all sanguine about improvement in the overall situation in the Valley. He was also of the view that, should Modi win the Lok Sabha election in 2019, we would see him more resolute in terms of finding a unilateral solution. When I asked him what a unilateral solution could be, he referred me to the BJP election manifesto that talked about revoking Article 370 of the constitution and stripping Kashmir of its special status. In response to my question as to what Pakistan should be doing under the obtaining circumstances, he was hesitant to give any advice except to say that Pakistan knew well what was in its interests, which also included having normal relations with India but looked a difficult proposition under Modi. He also opined that the Jadhav issue would most certainly become an intractable irritant should Pakistan go ahead with his execution.

Another member of the CCG told me (I am not disclosing the name as most of our discussions were off the record) that the situation in Kashmir was dangerously volatile. He thought Ajit Doval's "intelligence-driven worldview compromised their ability to strategize effectively".

The luncheon meeting with High Commissioner Bambawale on 6 May was also instructive. I was left with no doubt that India had now made up its mind to move away from the structured bilateral talks as was agreed in December 2015. According to him, since Pakistan was dilly-dallying on Mumbai and Pathankot, the 9 December 2015 joint statement had lost its relevance. Moreover, the conviction of Jadhav had further complicated the bilateral scenario. He was of the view that, instead of waiting for the dialogue process to begin, it would make more sense to look for progress in areas such as trade and consular matters. Though I challenged him on every count, insisting that Pakistan could not be blamed for the current stalemate, I still thought of exploring if there was any possibility for a diplomatic opening. I told him that, as the high commissioners of our respective countries, we could not be fence-sitters. I was of the view that we could not, at least, give up being forward-looking. One possibility was around the corner. I did not have any instructions from Islamabad but I thought Prime Minister Sharif would welcome an opportunity to meet Prime Minister Modi at the SCO summit in Nur-Sultan (new name of Astana), capital of Kazakhstan, next month. (I intentionally avoided talking about Jindal's recent visit to Pakistan as I had still not heard anything about it from Islamabad.) I added that, instead of getting into the quotidian stuff of which side requested the meeting, we could perhaps manage things informally. I found Bambawale agreeable. However, in the final event, there was no meeting between the two prime ministers but the two leaders did exchange pleasantries. It was at the Nur-Sultan Summit that the two countries became full members of the SCO.

I was invited by Ambassador Rasgotra for a lunch on 7 May. I thoroughly enjoyed our conversation. His every word was a testament to his deep understanding of the art of diplomacy in creating opportunities even in most intractable of circumstances.

I wish our conversation was not off the record and I was in a position to share all the details of our long discussion. However, let me say this much that he was worried about the way Pakistan-India relations were being conducted and pushed to the precipice. He had thought "intelligent diplomacy" was required on both sides to avert an irredeemable situation. He was dismissive of the view that Musharraf's four-point formula on Kashmir could be revived or become the basis for a modus vivendi on Kashmir. He had also thought that seeking common grounds in Afghanistan could help improve the bilateral situation. However, that too was easier said than done.

Another former Indian diplomat who impressed me was Shyam Saran. He also served as India's foreign secretary between 2004 and 2006, and after retirement as the Prime Minister's Special Envoy for Nuclear Affairs and Climate Change and as chairman of the National Security Advisory Board. He invited me a couple of times for detailed discussions on bilateral relations over lunch. A thorough gentleman and a fecund source of ideas, talking to Saran was always useful as it helped me enrich my understanding of India's internal and external policies, especially what Modi was up to in Kashmir and toward Pakistan. He was always very candid and so was I. Generally speaking, his approach was one of incremental cooperative measures in areas such as climate change and water issues. He thought the political dynamics on both sides of the border could not allow a sudden breakthrough; it had to be earned through a long drawn-out process; the key was to keep the channels of communication open and keep exchanging ideas, for it made no sense for the two countries to waste more decades in mutual animosity.

On the other hand, a meeting was held between the two national security advisors in Moscow on 24 May. They were there to attend the 8th international meeting of high-ranking officials responsible for security matters. They discussed

Pathankot with Doval even alleging that the ISI was behind the attack. He also gave a veiled threat by saying that Pakistan must understand that the cost of enmity with India could be very high for Pakistan. He advised that Islamabad should cooperate in meeting Indian concerns. On his part, Janjua conveyed our positions on different issues. To my surprise, he also told Doval that Pakistan could provide India overland access to Afghanistan, Central Asia and Gwadar subject to improvement in bilateral environment and the resumption of bilateral talks. They agreed to meet periodically. I am not aware if they had met again after Moscow but they were definitely in touch on WhatsApp till the time Janjua remained NSA. He stepped down on 27 June 2018, that is, before the general elections in Pakistan the following month in which the PTI emerged as the largest party and Imran Khan became the next prime minister of Pakistan.

******

Diplomacy has many shades and, more so, in an adversarial inter-state relationship. Sometimes even an innocuous move by one state germinates unfounded apprehensions in the opposite side. But diplomats do wade into situations to test waters and explore possibilities for their respective states. Effective diplomacy is both about optics and substance. The 73-day face off between China and India in the Doklam plateau in the middle of 2017, I thought, was one such opportunity for Pakistan.

According to New Delhi's claim, the crisis began in June when Chinese troops came to the area with equipment to extend a road settlement in Doklam towards a road southward that is an integral part of the Bhutanese territory. It is closer to the Siliguri Corridor, also known as the Chicken's Neck, which is a narrow stretch of about 22 kilometers wide, located in the Indian state of West Bengal that connects India's northeastern states to the rest of India, with Nepal and Bangladesh lying on either side of the corridor. Under the Treaty of Friendship of 8 August 1949 between Bhutan and India, as claimed by the latter, the defense of Bhutan's territorial integrity is the responsibility of India and that it was at the request of Bhutan that India moved its troops to stop China from carrying out illegal construction in the Bhutanese territory. There are no diplomatic relations between China and Bhutan.

From India's viewpoint, China is a perennial threat to this corridor as, in a full-scale war, China can create a precarious situation for India by blocking or destroying the corridor.

I met the Chinese ambassador in New Delhi on 18 July to get a briefing on the situation and how it was being resolved. I had also requested a meeting with the Bhutanese ambassador and was to see him on 20 July. I informed the Chinese ambassador that I would be meeting our Bhutanese counterpart. China-Pakistan meetings at all levels, whether official or unofficial, are always suffused with mutual warmth and affection. This is a relationship which has been nurtured with great care on both sides and it is no exaggeration to say that the strategic partnership between the two countries would continue to move from strength to strength in their mutual interest. One cannot, however, rule out differences on some issues but the two countries have been able to develop over the decades inbuilt resilience to get to grips with such situations should they arise.

After my meeting with the ambassador of Bhutan, the Indian media literally went into a frenzy as to why the Pakistan high commissioner would meet the Bhutanese ambassador after meeting the Chinese ambassador two days earlier. Many journalists contacted me and my press attaché for details of the two meetings. However, we had decided to keep quiet and not respond to their queries. *The Times of India* of 21 July 2017 reported my meetings with the two ambassadors under the title, "Pak tries to poke its nose into Doklam". Though there was hardly anything substantive in the story, the heading spoke volumes of India's concerns and uneasiness.

The meeting with the Bhutanese ambassador was very educative. I could sense that Bhutan, strategically located, had now come to the point where it would like to be gradually moving away from India's strong hold. It would make no sense for Bhutan to continue to be at the mercy of India indefinitely and deprive itself of taking full advantage of China's growing economic footprint around the world. The first step in that direction would be to have diplomatic relations established between the two countries followed by China's resident diplomatic mission at Thimphu when deemed mutually appropriate. If China and India can build substantial economic ties to their mutual advantage despite their territorial disputes and strategic divergences, why should Bhutan be forced to remain India's satellite state? The people of Bhutan also deserve to make progress in all areas while retaining their supremacy when it comes to the Global Happiness Index.

Bhutan is also a SAARC member. Pakistan, too, should consider having a physical presence in Bhutan. Presently, the Pakistan high commission in Dhaka is concurrently accredited to Bhutan. Thimphu may not respond under pressure from New Delhi but Pakistan would lose nothing by making the move. At present, only Bangladesh, India and Kuwait maintain diplomatic missions at Thimphu. The Bhutanese nation represents and epitomizes the highest standards of moral values and, as peaceful and nature-loving people, deserve a far better life commensurate with their potential. It is time for India to let this great country develop as a neutral state and realize its enormous potential for the wellbeing of its people.

I cannot share full details of my discussions with both the Chinese and Bhutanese ambassadors and what I reported to Islamabad. Suffice to say it was not about "poking Pakistan's nose into Doklam" but more about building bridges of peace and harmony in the region.

******

I was now in the process of winding up and had requested farewell calls on the president, prime minister, speaker of Lok Sabha, minister for external affairs and NSA. However, there was no positive response except that Jaishankar hosted a farewell lunch for me, as per tradition, on 29 July and Ajit Doval received me on 31 July.

Discussions with both Jaishankar and Doval are part of the official record. We reviewed the state of bilateral relations; where did we stumble, what could be done to resume meaningful bilateral talks and resolve issues, how to preserve the existing CBMs and build on them and how to handle public pressures on both sides.

I told them that I was leaving India with mixed feelings. I wished official India were more forthcoming and had engaged more frequently and productively at the diplomatic level. As compared to my Indian counterpart in Islamabad, I was handicapped as I was denied access to the Indian leadership. I also told them that, as a diplomat, I always wanted and sincerely strived for a better relationship with India as that was in our mutual interest. I was portrayed by the Indian government as a hawk which I was not. I was realistic in my approach. I did not think that, by being evasive, we could achieve much; even CBMs had their limitations and could not be sustained in a protracted environment of hostility.

I told them that, even in retirement and whatever I was planning to do next, I would keep myself fully engaged with Pakistan-India relations. They could count on me as a person who was willing to listen patiently and respond positively to saner voices. We had fought wars vigorously but never worked for peace as perseveringly as necessary. I sincerely hoped that posterity would avoid the mistakes we had made and allow the prevailing mutual hostility to be replaced by peace and mutual affinity.

As far as I know, I am the only Pakistan high commissioner who got a farewell article published in India's largest English daily, *The Times of India*. In an op-ed article on 1 August, I wrote, "Pakistan and India must return to the negotiating table, without further ado and preconditions", I regretted that I was returning to Pakistan without seeing the two neighbors engaged irreversibly and productively. I emphasized that Pakistan was serious about resolving all the bilateral issues through peaceful means and the centrality of the Kashmir dispute could not be ignored, adding that effective diplomacy was not about glossing over or shelving seemingly intractable issues but addressing them conclusively and satisfactorily.

I also talked about terrorism and the need to address each other's concerns. Mentioning Mumbai and Pathankot, I reiterated Pakistan's readiness to move ahead but those matters needed constructive and uninterrupted cooperation. Those cases could not be concluded unless India shared concrete evidence with us. I also underscored the necessity of bringing the perpetrators of the Samjhauta Express blast of 18 February

2007 to justice. (Shockingly, in what could be seen as a travesty of justice, all the four accused were acquitted on 24 March 2019.)

I also suggested that, in order to move from conflict management to conflict resolution, we must return to the negotiating table without preconditions as talks were not a favor by one country to another. "Dialogue is unavoidable. Since it will happen sooner or later, why waste time?"

I remain grateful to the newspaper for publishing my article without making any major editorial changes. However, I wish they had also retained a reference to the Jadhav case as was given in the original draft. Deleting the reference altogether was, in my view, unnecessary as I could anticipate how that issue would become another serious irritant in the bilateral relationship.

In conclusion, I thanked "the people of India for their warmth and affection. These over three years have been very exciting. I and my wife Summiya have made many friends across India. We would always cherish their friendship and look forward to staying in touch with them."

As for the people of India, barring a couple of incidents, I was welcomed everywhere with immense affection and respect. I am perhaps Pakistan's only high commissioner who was given the honor thrice to deliver an address from the pulpits of Jama and Fatehpuri mosques in Delhi during the Holy month of Ramadan and on the occasion of Eid prayers attended by tens of thousands of people. It took me hours to leave as every other person present there wanted to embrace me and take a selfie. My thanks to both Syed Ahmed Bukhari and Mufti Mukarram Ahmad, Imams of the Jama and Fatehpuri Mosques, respectively, for those unforgettable experiences. I am beholden to them for all times to come.

I may add here as a footnote that most of the historical mosques in India do not represent a very happy state of affairs. Even those two great mosques in the capital city are being neglected; there is simply no maintenance. I often thought of discussing that with the two Imams and ascertain if Pakistan could be of any assistance in that regard but I kind of hesitated bringing up that issue in our conversations. I was sensitive to their position as any financial assistance from Islamabad could have been misconstrued by the Modi government as interference in India's internal affairs and even seen as an attempt on the part of Pakistan to provoke anti-India feelings among Indian Muslims. Such is the level of mutual hostility that, even positive ideas like that, could not find place in bilateral discourse.

I must also mention that I had also attended many Hindu and Sikh events as chief guest, and addressed huge congregations, including at Ramlila Maidan at New Delhi. My message had always been of peace and cooperation. Sometimes I felt strange that despite New Delhi's unrelenting media campaign against me, ordinary Indians had always embraced me with effusive affection and I, no matter what, would always remember the warmth and respect I got from the people of India at large. Perhaps, people, however inimical, do develop a soft corner for those who speak their mind and avoid to be pretentious. Yes, it is important to maintain diplomatic niceties. But a diplomat is well-regarded when he presents his country's policies openly but politely. Suaveness is like an arrow in the quiver of diplomacy; and if it comes naturally to the practitioner, diplomacy becomes far more interesting and rewarding even in a tension-ridden environment.

On 2 August, Summiya and I were onboard a PIA flight from New Delhi to Lahore. Before the aircraft took off, I tweeted: "Goodbye India and thanks for everything".

Our lovely dog, Oreo, was travelling by car to cross the Attari/Wagah border and joined us at Lahore for the onward journey to Islamabad by road.

6

Back in Pakistan

As our plane was taxiing to the gate, I tweeted: "Just landed at Lahore airport. Thanks, fellow Pakistanis, for your support and encouragement. I am indebted. Pakistan Zindabad."

I was returning to Pakistan in an unusual situation. I had retired prematurely and the general public impression was that my decision was in reaction to the government's decision regarding the appointment of the new foreign secretary. As I explained earlier, that was not the case because that was not unprecedented. My problem was that I was asked to return to Islamabad and work under a junior. That was unacceptable. I did talk to Sartaj Aziz from New Delhi and protested but he appeared to have been totally sidelined. I really fail to understand why people even of his age and stature would be reluctant to leave the power corridors when they know themselves that they are no more in a position to do justice with their position and work. That is one of many reasons for the continuing decay in our civilian institutions.

As soon I came out of the airport, I found the media

waiting for me. The proceedings were being telecast live. They asked me several provocative and pinching questions but I was not to be agitated. My responses, I think, were balanced and conciliatory. In a nutshell I told them I was feeling great to be back in my homeland; during my entire career I had tried to serve Pakistan with honor and dignity; I had no regrets that I had sought early retirement; I looked forward to continue serving Pakistan as a private citizen as my love for my country was unconditional.

While I was still in New Delhi, I was informally asked to take over as President of the Islamabad Policy and Research Institute (IPRI) that was founded in 1999 under the ministry of information and broadcasting. It was a well-established think tank that, till recently, was headed by my senior colleague, Ambassador Sohail Amin, who had passed away a couple of months earlier. I took over as the President of IPRI on 7 August.

Heading a think tank was a new vocation for me but I had a few ideas that I thought would not only help increase the visibility of IPRI and strengthen its credentials as a genuine think tank but also promote Pakistan's foreign policy narratives in important capitals around the world. I took five key initiatives, namely, (1) Ambassador Lecture Series; (2) fortnightly roundtables on topical issues; (3) annual media workshop; (4) IPRI Margalla Dialogue; and (5) reviving and establishing institutional links with major think tanks abroad. These were in addition to the routine national and international conferences held on different subjects. I would always be grateful to the IPRI team for their full support in realizing these ideas. Then Director IPRI, Brigadier Sohail Tirmizi (Retired), was indeed the man I had wanted as my number two. He had served in Moscow as Pakistan Defense Attaché and was well-versed in international issues and foreign policy challenges for Pakistan. I used to call him the pivot of IPRI and he always delivered effectively and to my full satisfaction.

While *IPRI Journal* was already being issued regularly, I also introduced the monthly four-page "IPRI Update" giving glimpses of the activities at IPRI. However, my affiliation with IPRI also came to an end earlier than the contractual three years.

There was too much interference from the parent department in the day-to-day running of the institute which was something I could not brook. If I was the president of the institute and had been working strictly in accordance with the IPRI byelaws, there was no question that I could be dictated on matters within my purview. I had started getting some vibes that the foreign office was not very comfortable with my presence at IPRI and wanted me out. When things became absolutely indigestible, I resigned and left IPRI in the first week of August 2018 whereas my three-year contract was to end in August 2020.

Leaving IPRI in itself was not a big deal but we had been working hard to hold the first Margalla Dialogue. I am glad the event was finally held in 2019 but not in the way I had envisaged. I was expecting an invitation from IPRI to speak at the event but was invited only to attend as a guest. I was utterly disappointed but knew well who the people still hatching conspiracies against me were and, it goes without saying, that most of them were my own former foreign office colleagues. I feel sad for them for nurturing so much hatred against me.

After I had left IPRI, it was no wonder that some researchers related to retired foreign office officers were employed by the institute. I wish our country could get rid of this culture of nepotism. Interestingly, we do not mind accommodating our friends, our kith and kin in breach of rules and then also never tire of complaining that our public institutions are not delivering. Institutions do not deliver when they become parking places for "recommendees".

While still in New Delhi, I had also contacted a few Pakistani TV channels to explore the possibility of hosting a talk show. I did get three offers but the first one was from "News One" and so I decided to work with them. The maiden show of "Awaz-e-Pakistan with Abdul Basit" went on air on 11 September 2017. I did over 400 episodes and the feedback was not that discouraging given the stiff competition in the news media industry. I would remain grateful to Tahir A. Khan, owner of "News One", for giving me the opportunity and believing in my ability to host a TV show.

Here I may briefly dwell on the letter which I wrote to Aizaz in July 2017 when he had already taken over in Washington DC as Pakistan ambassador. My letter was in response to his valedictory letter of 12 March 2017 which he wrote as foreign secretary to all the officers enumerating his accomplishments and thanking them for their support.

There is no doubt that the two of us enjoyed reasonably cordial relations. When I was additional foreign secretary in charge of Pakistan's relations with Europe, he would often call me from The Hague where he was our ambassador and discuss both official and unofficial matters.

As discussed in the first chapter of this book, my nomination as foreign secretary had come, even to me, as a huge surprise. At that point in time in my career, I could not even think that I was being considered for the top post. I still do not know why Aizaz ended up holding that against me. And when he became foreign secretary I sent him warm greetings from Berlin, assuring him of my full support and looking forward to working under his guidance. Unfortunately, throughout my stay in India, he did everything unworthy of a team leader and tried to scuttle me in every respect. Simply put, he never wanted me to replace him for a variety of reasons, mostly administrative, for he might have thought that I would be least obliging.

I am not an angel. Foreign secretaries and ambassadors come and go and all invariably claim to have conquered Mount K-2. I would have definitely taken his farewell letter in the same spirit if I were not hurt by his continuous unreasonableness. Frankly, while I did want to vent my spleen, I also genuinely believed that, as foreign secretary, his performance was just average. From Ufa to Islamabad, in the joint statements of 2015, he not only failed himself but also Pakistan and Kashmir. It was also under his leadership that, for the first time, Pakistan lost an election for the membership of the UN Human Rights Council. And then, after seeing him working at the two envoys' conferences in Islamabad, it was not difficult to fathom that he was not a person, at least in my humble view, to represent Pakistan in a difficult place like Washington DC. And it seems I was right. Some people are excellent to be in number two position but barely inspire and rise to the challenge when made captain of the ship.

By now I definitely know who had leaked the letter to the media but I will not disclose. There were people in our system who wanted to get rid of Aizaz in Washington DC and they used my letter, a copy of which I had endorsed to Director (Foreign Secretary's Office) for record, to reinforce their case that he was not being able to deliver.

He was replaced by a young banker, Ali Jahangir Siddiqui, in May 2018. On principle, I was against his nomination for a raft of reasons and openly expressed my views. But still, with no diplomatic experience whatsoever, he surprised many by his ability to grasp the fundamentals of Pakistan-US challenges and got engaged in robust diplomacy to overcome them. No wonder then that the PTI, which made so much noise over his nomination in the parliament, did not mind appointing him as Ambassador-at-Large for investment when it came to power.

At an informal dinner in Islamabad in early 2020, I could not avoid but shake hands with Aizaz. I have moved on, and now that both of us are retired, I carry no grudge against him. I hope he, too, has moved on or at least is trying to get over his hostility towards me.

Some of my retired senior colleagues have not been fair to me either. But I still give them due respect and can never be impolite. Favoritism is fast eroding the credibility and capacity of the foreign office. We cannot take the first line of our national defense lightly and complacently. This national security institution is in long need of massive overhauling. Must we indulge in procrastination at our own national peril?

******

After winning the general elections in 2018, Imran Khan, in his victory speech on 27 July, also talked about Pakistan's relations with India vowing that, if India took one step toward Pakistan, we would take two toward India. He earned encomiums from all and sundry for his bold and positive statement. He also mentioned the need to resolve the Jammu & Kashmir dispute and urged India to join hands in achieving peace and prosperity in the region. On his part, Modi called Imran Khan on 30 July and felicitated him on his victory. He hoped that democracy would take deeper roots in Pakistan and reiterated his vision of peace and development implying that, when there was terrorism and violence, a cooperative environment could not be developed and sustained.

So far so good. There were general elections in India in April/May 2019. Talking to journalists on 10 April 2019, Prime

Minister Imran Khan said that the chances for resolving the Kashmir dispute were better under Modi and the BJP than with the Congress party at the helm as the latter might be afraid to seek a settlement on Kashmir, fearing a backlash from the right.

To me this was an uncalled-for statement. Not only had the statement betrayed his lack of understanding of the long-term agenda of the BJP/RSS vis-à-vis Kashmir but also was considered by many as interference in India's internal affairs. Perhaps the statement was prompted by the assessment that Modi would, in all likelihood, win the elections so there was no harm in obliging and sort of pushing him towards meaningful talks.

On 14 February 2019, there was an attack in Pulwama in Jammu & Kashmir on a convoy of vehicles carrying security personnel. The attack by a local Kashmiri killed 40 of India's Central Reserve Police Force ratcheting up tension between the two countries to a dangerous level. There was nothing much to show on the economic front. In fact, India's economic growth had slowed down and unemployment was on the rise. Modi needed to once again show his much-bragged-about 56-inch chest to recover political ground. In India, nothing sells politically better than high-voltage jingoism against Pakistan. But this time, the Modi government went a step further that could have embroiled the region in an irredeemably messy situation had Pakistan, too, acted irresponsibly.

In the early hours of 26 February, Indian warplanes entered Pakistan airspace and flew all the way to Balakot in the KP province. India claimed to have destroyed a terror camp, killing hundreds of JeM operatives and successfully returning back. This surgical strike, as per the Indian version, was carried out to avenge the killing of 40 Indian security personnel in Pulwama.

Pakistan immediately denied the Indian claim of causing

large-scale destruction. It took the Islamabad-based defense attachés to the site to corroborate its claim. A bomb was indeed dropped by the Indian fighter planes but, barring a few trees, there was no destruction caused to any building structure in the area. Pakistan also claimed no one was killed in the Indian operation.

The next day, Pakistan Air Force conducted airstrikes at multiple locations on the other side of the LoC. Indian Air Force jets started pursuing Pakistani planes and, in the resulting dog fight, Pakistan claimed to have shot down two Indian jets and captured an Indian pilot, Wing Commander Abhinandan Varthaman, who was flying a MiG 21 Bison aircraft. Initially, India rejected these claims but subsequently acknowledged that an Indian jet was shot down on the Pakistan-side of the LoC. They also claimed to have shot down a Pakistani F-16 warplane. Pakistan rejected the claim and denied there were any losses suffered by Pakistan. But the Indian Air Force did shoot down its own Mi-17 chopper at Budgam near Srinagar on the same day that resulted in the death of six IAF personnel and a civilian.

Videos of handlebar-moustached Abhinandan's capture by the locals in Pakistan Administered Kashmir went viral immediately. Addressing a joint session of parliament on 28 February, Prime Minister Imran Khan announced that Pakistan would release Abhinandan the following day and, accordingly, he was handed over at the Wagah border the next day. Imran Khan also subsequently asked India to share actionable evidence of involvement of any Pakistani in the Pulwama attack and committed to proceed against those involved. He once again extended the hand of friendship inviting India to sit across the table and resolve all bilateral issues, including terrorism, through dialogue.

Indians projected the quick return of Abhinandan as Modi's diplomatic victory. The Indian media also went berserk, urging Pakistan to take action against JeM and its chief, Maulana Azhar. They also argued that, whereas India had taken action in self-defense and hit non-military facilities, Pakistan tried to target Indian military facilities, which was an act of war.

However, some saner voices in India also started raising questions about the authenticity of India's assertions that over 300 JeM operatives were killed at Balakot in India's swift operation. India's opposition parties also got together and asked the government to brief them on the developments. However, Modi, busy in his election campaign, preferred to ignore the opposition and continued claiming that Pakistan had been taught a lesson and, henceforth, it would not dare to perpetrate terror actions in India again and, if it did, it would not be spared of serious consequences.

While I had publicly expressed the view on 27 February that, freeing Abhinanadan under Article 70 of the 1949 Geneva Convention without any delay would be the right thing to do, there were concerns as to how the Indian warplanes had breached the Pakistan airspace and flown back unharmed. Though India could not cause any significant damage, the optics that it was no longer constrained by the nuclear deterrence and was capable of taking swift punitive actions against Pakistan without escalating the situation were working significantly to its advantage. Indian commentators were jubilant that the Cold Start Doctrine, as contained in the 2017 Joint Armed Forces Doctrine, had worked effectively and was the perfect response to Pakistan's "asymmetrical war" against India going on for years.

While Indian strategists must have calculated that Pakistan would be constrained for it could not hazard the risk of escalation, the latter was under enormous domestic pressure to not let the Indian misadventure go unpunished. The entire nation appeared to have been demoralized by the Indian action. Moreover, from a purely warfare point of view, Pakistan could ill-afford to forego any response as the credibility of its all-spectrum deterrence was at stake. Had Pakistan limited itself to condemnation alone, urging the international community to reprimand India for its highly dangerous move, the latter might have miscalculated. It was imperative to convey a clear message to India that Pakistan could never resign to violation of its sovereignty and would go to any extent to maintain the credibility of its deterrence.

At the end, Pakistan showed its resolve and both the countries were fortunate in the sense that an Indian aircraft was shot and its pilot got captured early in the game. If that had not happened, escalation would have been difficult to stave off. However, Modi seemed to have achieved what he had wanted despite the setback of Abhinandan and the government's failure to substantiate the destruction it claimed to have caused in Balakot by presenting solid evidence. Even India's air force command was visibly reluctant to back the government's hyperbole about the number of people killed on the ground. They confined themselves to saying, in the vaguest of terms, that whatever objectives were set for the mission had been accomplished.

In Pakistan, the national sentiment post-Balakot was suffused with jubilation and confidence. Whether or not Pakistan was able to restore the credibility of its deterrence, only the time would tell. One thing, however, that is clear beyond a shadow of doubt is that India is bent to plunge this region into a Sisyphean arms race. Obviously, Pakistan cannot be oblivious to its security requirements nor can it be ruining itself economically as maintaining invincible defense without a sustained economic growth is hardly possible. Though China is a strategic partner and Pakistan can count on its support, it is important for Islamabad to retain its sovereign independence and position itself in a way that its national interests are not undermined.

After the Pulwama attack, India ramped up its pressure on China to remove its objection to designating JeM chief Maulana Azhar as a global terrorist. China, under pressure also from other P-5 countries, finally succumbed and Azhar was put on the UN terrorist list on 1 May. Multiple-phased general elections in India, were started in April and were to be completed on 19 May. Modi was re-elected with a thumping majority winning 302 of the 542 seats up for grabs.

In a tweet on 23 May, Imran Khan greeted Modi on the BJP's electoral victory expressing the hope they would be able to work together for peace, progress and prosperity in South Asia. He also telephoned him three days later. According to media reports, Modi on his part, thanked Imran Khan for the greetings, and also stressed that, for creating trust and enhancing cooperation for peace, progress and prosperity in South Asia, an environment free of violence and terrorism was essential. However, bilateral relations were waiting to hit rock bottom and the mutual hostility touching new heights as Modi decided to execute the long-standing RSS agenda on Jammu & Kashmir as also contained in the election manifesto of the BJP.

7

Fine Words Butter No Parsnips

As part of the Reorganization of Jammu & Kashmir Bill, passed on 5/6 August came into effect on 31 October 2020, Article 35-A, which had ensured subject rights of the State only to Kashmiris as was the case prior to independence from the British Raj in August 1947, was also dispensed with.

The princely state of Jammu & Kashmir, occupied by India on 27 October 1947 through an instrument of accession signed by the then Maharajah Hari Singh, is the only state with almost 68 per cent Muslims. Hindus are around 30 per cent and are mostly concentrated in Jammu, and Ladakh's population is roughly equally divided between Buddhists and Muslims, most of whom are inhabitants of the Leh and Kargil Divisions, respectively.

With the passage of the Reorganization of Jammu & Kashmir Bill by the Indian parliament and the Act's coming into effect on 31 October, non-Kashmiris were allowed to purchase property and settle in Jammu & Kashmir.

Moreover, the Indian parliament, also in clear violation of the state constitution not only revoked its special status but also split it into two union territories separating Ladakh from Jammu & Kashmir. Under Article 3 of the constitution, the request for this should originate from the state legislative assembly. The Indian plea was that, since the state was under presidential rule and no assembly was in place, Indian parliament was eligible to take decisions on its behalf. Never in India's history since 1947 has a state been demoted and made a union territory. It has always been the other way round. This blatant exception was made exclusively for Jammu & Kashmir.

Moreover, Article 35-A of the Indian constitution duly recognized Article 6 of the constitution of the Jammu & Kashmir which had its foundation in the State Subject Notification of 27 April 1927. As it could be seen that, even before the partition of the subcontinent and the idea of Pakistan was yet to be born, Kashmir, even under the Dogra rule, was sensitive about preserving its demographic mosaic and its unique and harmoniously diverse culture rooted in mysticism of all hues.

Since this book is not about the history of Jammu & Kashmir, I am constrained not to dig deeper into what had happened immediately before and after the independence of the subcontinent. However, it would be pertinent to briefly deal with at least one or two arguments usually made by India in defense of its volte face on the dispute.

We all are aware that it was India which referred the Kashmir issue to the United Nations Security Council (UNSC). While many resolutions were unanimously adopted by the UNSC, India, citing one resolution passed by the United

Nations Commission for India and Pakistan (UNCIP) on 13 August 1948 (Annexure VII) argues that, since Pakistan had failed to withdraw all its troops from the territory of the State of Jammu & Kashmir as was required in terms of Part II–A of the resolution to hold a plebiscite, Pakistan should blame itself rather than India for not complying with the resolution.

However, the record of the discussions that took place after the adoption of this resolution cannot be set aside. Pakistan forcefully argued against the resolution underlining that India could not be trusted, given the way it had refused to accept the proposed Stand Still Agreement and got the so-called Instrument of Accession signed by Hari Singh under duress. India's intentions were mala fide from the very beginning. The then Indian leadership had never intended to honor its commitment.

Thus, after prolonged discussions, arguments and counterarguments, the UNSC itself, not the UNCIP, unanimously adopted resolution 98 on 23 December 1952 (Annex VIII) which, under paragraph 4, urged both Pakistan and India "to enter into immediate negotiations under the auspices of the United Nations Representative for India and Pakistan in order to reach agreement on the specific number of forces to remain on each side of the then ceasefire line at the end of the period of demilitarization. The number specified was between 3,000 and 6,000 armed forces on the Pakistan side of the ceasefire line and between 12,000 and 18,000 on the Indian side as suggested by the United Nations Representative in his proposal of 16 July 1952. Such specific numbers were arrived at bearing in mind the principles or criteria contained in paragraph 7 of the United Nations Representative's proposal of 4 September 1952." The resolution was accepted by both the warring sides.

In any case, the right to self-determination of Kashmiris is given to them by international law and the relevant UNSC resolution and is not predicated on what Pakistan did or did not do. For the sake of argument, why should the people of Jammu & Kashmir continue to suffer if Pakistan had not fulfilled its part of the commitments as claimed by India by picking up a single resolution but conveniently ignoring many others which it had also agreed to at the time of their adoption?

Many in India also question whether Pakistan is willing, as a first step, to withdraw its troops from Pakistan Administered Kashmir. This question is disingenuous, to say the least. Again, for the sake of argument, I think Pakistan should be able to consider the proposition provided India openly commits itself to holding a plebiscite in Jammu & Kashmir under UN supervision within a mutually agreed time frame. Is India ready to accept this proffer?

India also contends that much water has been flown under the bridge and the ground realities have also been altered by Pakistan by unilaterally entering into a boundary agreement with China on 2 March 1963 and ceding chunks of Kashmir territory to China (Annexure IX). India conveniently overlooks Article 6 of this agreement which states: "The two parties have agreed that after the settlement of the Kashmir dispute between Pakistan and India, the sovereign authority concerned will reopen negotiations with the Government of the People's Republic of China on the boundary as described in Article 2 of this agreement so as to sign a formal boundary treaty to replace the present agreement... ."

On the other hand, the constitution of Pakistan in its Article 257 also states: "When the people of the State of Jammu & Kashmir decided to accede to Pakistan, the relationship between Pakistan and the State shall be determined in accordance with the wishes of the people of the State." There cannot be a more explicit statement than this that Pakistan never wanted to usurp the Kashmiri land but would respect the political aspirations of the people of Jammu & Kashmir.

It is not only about the UN resolutions. From the Tashkent Declaration (1966) to the Simla Agreement (1972) and to the Lahore Declaration (1999), India had agreed to settle the Kashmir dispute through peaceful means. Also, the Composite Dialogue between the two countries that started in 2004 was many years after the Indian parliament resolution of 22 February 1994 in which India declared that it would wrest Pakistan Administered Kashmir from Pakistan and merge it into Kashmir. It is a fair question as to why India had then engaged with Pakistan on the back channel for almost four years to work out a settlement along the lines of Musharraf's four-point formula.

India also claims that the international community has forgotten about Kashmir and even the UN resolutions have been rendered irrelevant. That is again far removed from the truth. In this regard, India must refer to UNSC resolution 1172 of 6 June 1998 (adopted after the nuclear tests by India and then Pakistan in May 1998) and its paragraph 5 which "urges India and Pakistan to resume the bilateral dialogue between them on all outstanding issues, particularly on all matters pertaining to peace and security, in order to remove the tensions between them and encouraging them to find mutually acceptable solutions that address the root cause of tensions, including Kashmir" (Annexure X).

After 9/11 and the Mumbai attacks of 26 November 2008 in which 166 people were killed including a few foreigners, India clearly saw an opportunity to malign the legitimate Kashmiri struggle as terrorism. Its mantra that "talks and terror cannot go together'" is nothing but an attempt to avoid meaningful and result-oriented talks on Kashmir. It is now using both Mumbai and Pathankot as alibis for not engaging with Pakistan. India's Reorganization of Jammu & Kashmir Act has now created a dangerous situation not only between Pakistan and India but also China and India as changes made by the latter to the status of Ladakh also involve China. In 1834, the Dogra rulers had invaded Ladakh and conquered it. Subsequently, Britons took control and made it a part of Jammu & Kashmir under the control of the Maharajah of Kashmir. China considers Ladakh as a part of Tibet.

I am of the firm view that India would not, for the foreseeable future, like the Mumbai attack trial to conclude. It would want the case to drag on so that it keeps Pakistan under pressure on the issue of terrorism as well as to continue portraying the Kashmir struggle as terrorism. And I am not saying this on the basis of my assessment alone, the facts speak for themselves.

India has been slow in granting permission to the Pakistan Judicial Commission on Mumbai to visit India to record statements of prosecution witnesses and no cross-examination was allowed despite Pakistan's insistence. The first visit could take place only in March 2012, and the second and last visit over a year later in September 2013. Intriguingly, India also demonstrated undue haste in executing Ajmal Kasab, the lone survivor of the 10 attackers, so as to deny any possibility to the Pakistan commission of recording his statement or cross-examining him. He was hanged in Pune on 21 November 2012.

Moreover, it is also a matter of record that India never handed over to Pakistan the material allegedly used in the Mumbai attacks. It also took India a year to respond in September

2016 to Pakistan's formal request made in September 2015. It is also showing reluctance to allow 24 or so Indian witnesses to appear before the relevant court in Pakistan. Instead, India is insisting that Pakistan should send a commission as was done earlier to record their statements in India. It is anyone's guess how many more years India will take to allow this and under what conditions. If India is so serious, then it should be insisting on Pakistan making suitable arrangements for the Indian witnesses to appear before the court. But we have been witnessing stubborn hesitation on the part of India to be forthcoming and cooperative in the matter.

On the other hand, India has been forcefully suggesting to Pakistan to include the testimony of one David Coleman Headley (a US national of Pakistan origin whose original name was Dawood Gillani), who was sentenced to 35 years imprisonment by a US court in 2013 for his role in plotting the Mumbai attacks. India has requested the US for his extradition to India but, so far, there has been no progress on this count despite the extradition treaty between the two countries signed in June 1997.

Headley pleaded guilty and the circumstances under which he confessed to his crime remain largely dubious. Moreover, he was a drug peddler and had been involved in many other crimes. Hence his statements, as recorded by the US prosecution, might not be legally acceptable in Pakistan.

******

Not that Pakistan was caught unawares on 5 August 2019. Both from New Delhi and then after retirement in August 2017, I have been relentlessly urging the government that Pakistan must already be thinking of how it can prevent India from going down that road and, in case of failure of our efforts, what strategy Pakistan should be adopting to counter the Indian move. It pains me to say that we, as a nation and state, displayed our collective nonchalance and cluelessness. The Imran Khan government was visibly in a blue funk. Pakistan simply did not know how to go about the perilous Indian action beyond making bombastic statements.

Some steps were indeed taken after the meeting of the National Security Committee on 7 August but those, too, had barely impressed New Delhi. Pakistan downgraded the diplomatic relations asking the Indian high commissioner to leave the country. The high commissioner-designate of Pakistan, who was in Islamabad and was scheduled to join his post in New Delhi in a couple of days, was sent back to Paris where he was earlier stationed. It was also decided to mark 15 August, the Independence Day of India, as the Black Day.

Pakistan also decided to halt, with immediate effect, all bilateral trade with India as well as close its airspace to India for all its commercial flights. It was also decided to launch a massive diplomatic campaign and rally international support. A Kashmir Cell was established at the ministry of foreign affairs to devise a comprehensive diplomatic strategy. The Pakistan parliament also adopted a unanimous resolution condemning India and reiterating Pakistan's full support to the struggle of the Kashmiris.

Foreign Minister Shah Mahmood Qureshi, who was in Saudi Arabia for Hajj, had to return to Islamabad immediately. However, before leaving for Islamabad, he attended an urgent meeting of the OIC Contact Group on Kashmir (Pakistan, Turkey, Saudi Arabia, Niger and Azerbaijan). The group, in its outcome document, condemned the unconstitutional Indian move and urged it to restore Kashmir's autonomous status forthwith. It also asked India to allow the OIC Human Rights Commission to visit Kashmir to assess the situation as there was a complete blackout in Kashmir and the people there were totally cut-off from the outside world including India. A curfew was imposed and even pro-India Kashmiri leaders, including three former chief ministers, namely, Farooq Abdullah, Omar Abdullah and Mehbooba Mufti were put under protective custody.

New Delhi was so scared of severe reaction by the people in Kashmir that it had even closed mosques for prayers. It also did not allow opposition politicians or well-known members of Indian civil society to visit the Kashmir Valley. The international media, too, was banned from visiting the state and reporting from there. However, India, true to its characteristic hubris, did not budge an inch as showing even minimum flexibility at this stage would have signaled its readiness to revisit its decision. This is not how the ideological parties' work. With the political opposition already in disarray and a majority of Indians, including Muslims, commending the government for ending the long-held constitutional and political anomaly, there was no real pressure on Modi to reconsider the decision much less to rescind it.

The international community, too, appeared least bothered about the political aspect of the Indian move. Some noises were raised initially about the worsening human rights situation but to no big effect. India was confident that diplomacy driven by interests was on its side. India's increasing economic clout was its biggest asset. Countries around the world were not ready to publicly inveigh against India. Adding insult to injury, most countries, including a number of OIC members, in their statements considered the matter internal to India. Pakistan had almost lost the diplomatic battle before it could even gather itself to come out of the initial shock to stitch together a workable strategy and begin pursuing it. At best, the international community was mostly concerned about possible military escalation between the two countries leading to a full-scale war.

Pakistan has a tendency to work in haste and, more often than not, whimsically; the foreign policy domain is no exception. This is, however, not to imply that every diplomatic step is visceral but, in crisis situations, the relevant institutions find it difficult to step up to the plate. For instance, it was clearly improvident to convene the OIC Contact Group in a hurry because the foreign minister happened to be in Saudi Arabia at that given time. And then, in our typical fashion, we created such a hype around the statement issued by the group as if the entire OIC was standing by Pakistan and would be ready to chide India's unilateral action with no reservation. Since Pakistan was happy to be fobbed off with the meaningless outcome of the Contact Group, there was hardly any appetite even in the "brotherly" Gulf countries to oblige Pakistan beyond the Contact Group meeting. In the event, Pakistan failed to get a special session of the OIC on Kashmir.

Even Pakistan's request to shift a regular annual meeting of the OIC Council of Ministers scheduled to be held in Niamey in April 2020 to Islamabad could not get the necessary traction. We requested Niger, also a member of the Contact Group, to swap as the 2021 meeting was to be held in Islamabad but failed to get a positive response. India's Foreign Minister Jaishankar, visited Niamey in January 2020 and inaugurated one of the largest convention centers in Africa built by India in fourteen months. More Indian assistance was announced for Niger during the visit thus effectively foreclosing any possibility for Niger to offend India.

Having failed in the OIC, no sensible person could wager on Pakistan's success in the 47-member Human Rights Council in Geneva. Its session was held in September before the UNGA session in New York. Pakistan needed only 16 votes in the Council for a special session on Kashmir. Even eight other OIC members in the Council, namely, Afghanistan, Bangladesh, Bahrain, Cameroon, Somalia, Egypt, Iraq, Nigeria, Qatar, Saudi Arabia and Senegal showed no enthusiasm for coming to Pakistan's diplomatic rescue. Except in the official Pakistan statement at the plenary, no member country referred to the brazen human rights violations in Kashmir by the Indian security forces.

Disturbingly, one could not find coherence in Pakistan's diplomacy. Every step was taken in fits and starts and thus failed to generate the desired momentum. It had made eminent sense for Foreign Minister Qureshi to dash to Beijing for consultations but it was equally incomprehensible why he did not visit other P-5 capitals. Pakistan's diplomacy had literally come to such a nadir that the French could not be contacted till after the conclusion of the UNSC informal consultations on Kashmir held on 16 August. This was a clear indication that Pakistan had already been losing ground to India around the world. When diplomacy is conducted episodically and as an event and not a process, then such outcomes should not be surprising at all. Simply put, diplomacy is a continuum and usually fails to respond if called to service intermittently.

As for the informal consultations in New York, those were also a diplomatic blunder made in haste. In a letter addressed to the UNSC President for the month of August who was the Polish permanent representative to the UN, Qureshi requested an emergency meeting of the UNSC to consider India's unilateral action in violation of the UN Charter and its own several resolutions on Jammu & Kashmir. Pakistan sought the meeting under Rule 37 of the provisional rules of procedure of the UNSC so that it could also attend the meeting as a non-member of the UNSC.

In my view, the three-page letter by Pakistan was poorly drafted. In its final shape, it was pleonastic and thus became unwieldy and lost the desired impact. It included almost everything but failed to generate any sense of urgency. The letter should have focused on the serious specter of war looming in the region as Pakistan could not be a silent spectator in the newly created situation. It was not primarily a matter of self-defense but about defending Kashmiris against India's actions. The letter also left the impression that Pakistan could live with the revocation of Articles 370 and 35A so long as India did not ratchet up the situation on the LoC. Mentioning the 2003 ceasefire understanding was most inappropriate.

Ironically, the letter failed to refer to the first resolution (No.38 of 17 January 1948) of the UNSC on Kashmir which in its operative paragraph 2, "requests each of those governments to inform the Council immediately of any material change in the situation which occurs or appears to either of them to be about to occur while the matter is under consideration by the Council, and consult the Council thereon." The letter should have also mentioned the 27 July 1949 Karachi Agreement establishing a ceasefire line in Kashmir following the first war between the two countries in 1947. There is a saying in Malay, "When you lose your way, you must return to the beginning and start again."

The letter, unfortunately, also failed to mention UNSC resolution 1172 of 6 June 1998 which was adopted by the

Council after the serious security situation that had developed in the region as it had gone nuclear. The resolution in paragraph 6 explicitly mentioned the Kashmir issue as the root cause of instability in South Asia.

Then the letter in itself was not enough. Diplomacy seeking peace must be backed by the state's unflinching resolve and readiness to use force. We did not convey any such intention to India. Nor was this alluded to in Pakistan's letter to the UNSC. India as well as the international community soon realized that Pakistan was indulging in brouhaha only for domestic reasons. Pakistan did not have any plan of escalating the situation on the LoC in a managed way which, in my view, was then essential to get the international community involved in the tension-riven situation which had the potential of flaring up into even a nuclear war.

As the UNSC seemed to be prevaricating, Pakistan requested China for help. In the end, most UNSC members thought the matter did not require an emergency meeting right away; it would be prudent to first hold informal consultations and then, if the Council considered it necessary, a formal meeting of the UNSC could be convened.

Most ironically, Qureshi, at a press interaction in Muzaffarabad on 15 August, asked the people of Pakistan to not in live in "fool's paradise" and expect the UNSC to "wait with garlands" to support Pakistan on Kashmir. The statement came when Pakistanis and Kashmiris around the world were marking India's Independence Day as Black Day. This was indeed to lower the domestic expectations of UNSC informal consultations the next day. Surely, inadvertently, Pakistan also ended up conveying to the UNSC that it was not expecting a major outcome and that was what exactly happened.

The informal consultations held under the title "India-Pakistan Question" failed to issue a press or presidential statement. As those were closed-door consultations with no record maintained, the entire exercise turned out to be inconsequential. Tactically speaking, it would have been far better for Pakistan to have escalated the situation militarily and waited for the UNSC to call a formal meeting itself as had happened in 1998.

And then it was not for Pakistan to term the informal consultative meeting as a historic accomplishment claiming that the UNSC met exclusively on Kashmir after a long hiatus of over 50 years. On 21 December 1971, the Council had adopted Resolution 307 following the Indo-Pakistan war that had resulted in the emergence of Bangladesh, formerly East Pakistan. Trumpeting about something inconsequential, as we had done in the case of the OIC Contact Group, had left the impression that Pakistan was content with the outcome. There was no reason left for the UNSC countries, especially the P-5, to oblige Pakistan further and put their important relations with India under unnecessary strain.

This time we could get the informal consultations only because of China as all the other four P-5 countries were disinclined. Also, since China was a party to the Kashmir dispute and had serious reservations about India's changing the status of the disputed Ladakh, it could not have completely ignored the legal and security situation created by India's unilateral decision.

Had Pakistan been able to get such informal consultations in 2016, it would have been considered a diplomatic achievement to be reckoned with. Following the killing of Burhan Wani, Commander of HuM, on 8 July 2016, the situation in Kashmir was tense. Even then, we never made serious diplomatic efforts beyond incoherent utterances. Had Pakistan started building some international pressure on India, things could have been slightly different this time round or at least would not come to this sorry pass.

Perhaps, the stresses of the political situation then prevailing in the country also worked, to some degree, to Pakistan's disadvantage. The Sharif government fighting for its survival was hardly paying attention to Kashmir. Even the recommendations prepared at the envoys' conference were put aside. There was no appetite for any serious work. Pakistan's Kashmir diplomacy was clearly on the wane. The only consolation was a report by the Office of the United Nations High Commissioner for Human Rights (OHCHR) on "the situation of human rights in Indian-Administered Kashmir and Pakistan-Administered Kashmir" released on 14 June 2018. However, this report was never endorsed by the Human Rights Council.

Moreover, Pakistan's refusal to allow an OHCHR delegation to visit the Pakistan side of Kashmir unless it could also visit the Indian side was, I think, nothing less than a serious diplomatic blunder. By doing this, Pakistan had, perhaps, unwittingly helped release pressure on India, if there was any. Pakistan had nothing to hide. By allowing the UN delegation to visit Pakistan Administered Kashmir, Pakistan would definitely have stood on a high moral ground, gaining some diplomatic space to build pressure on India. But it wasted the opportunity. The report was issued again in 2019 and, as expected, again went unnoticed by the world failing to cause any embarrassment to the pathologically brazen Modi government.

Of course, Prime Minister Imran Khan made a vociferous statement on Kashmir at the UNGA session on 27 September, striking all the right notes. But such statements had also been made by his predecessors from the same podium with little effect. Imran Khan's statement was no exception as there was no desire on the part of Islamabad to put its money where its mouth was. Rhetoric may earn one some genuine or inflated plaudits but that is not a substitute for a policy.

No other world leaders except President Recep Tayyip Erdogan of Turkey, President Hassan Rouhani of Iran and Prime Minister Mahathir bin Mohamad of Malaysia mentioned Kashmir in their statements at the UNGA session. No other OIC country, including Saudi Arabia, UAE or Qatar, bothered to make even an innocuous reference to Kashmir in their respective statements. So much for the OIC Contact Group's work on Kashmir.

Interestingly, in June 2019, the OIC Secretary General appointed Ambassador Yousef M. Aldobeay, a Saudi national, as his special envoy on Jammu & Kashmir. Later, Pakistan also established its Permanent Mission to the OIC in Jeddah in December 2019. In March 2020, the special envoy, instead of travelling around the world to rally support for Kashmiris, visited only Pakistan and with full trappings of official protocol. During his visit to Pakistan, he was also taken to the LoC. Pakistan should be grateful to him for at least agreeing to visit the LoC as the United Nations Secretary General, Antonio Guterres, who visited Pakistan earlier in February, had politely turned down the idea. He must have thought of India's ire raising questions about his neutrality as the secretary general of the apex intergovernmental multilateral forum.

It needs to be mentioned here that this is not the first time that the OIC Secretary General has appointed a special envoy on Kashmir. In 2009, too, the then OIC Secretary General had appointed Ambassador Abdullah Bin Abdul Rahman Al Bakr, also a Saudi national, as his Special Envoy on Kashmir. At least

I am not aware what actually he did to garner intra-OIC support on Kashmir. He had also enjoyed full protocol and privileges during his visits to Pakistan but never undertook, as far as I know, any systematic effort to galvanize the OIC members to stand fully behind the Kashmir cause.

Meanwhile scores of conferences and seminars were held in Pakistan in support of Kashmiris. The day 27 October, when India occupied Jammu & Kashmir in 1947, was also marked with rallies all over Pakistan and in some capitals abroad. This is what Pakistan does every year. Though the symbolic value of marking such occasions cannot be underestimated, such annual activities start losing their diplomatic utility if they become an end in themselves. This is what has happened over the years. So much so that Kashmiris living overseas do not turn up at such rallies in respectable numbers. In the end, such thin rallies in fact become embarrassing and counterproductive.

The level of seriousness of the Imran Khan government in respect of Kashmir could also be gauged from the fact that it took them almost a year to appoint a Chairman of the Kashmir parliamentary committee. Appointed in March 2019, Syed Fakhar Imam, 78, a well-known Pakistani politician, could hardly make any mark except presiding over tedious and meaningless conferences and conclaves. The government, despite its tall claims, was never able to send special envoys for lobbying in important capitals. And then in April 2020, Imam was suddenly changed and appointed as minister for national food security and research. It remains to be seen how Shehryar Khan Afridi, the new chairman of the committee—young, energetic and committed—is different from his two immediate predecessors. In any case, to expect the committee to perform miracles and deliver in the absence of a coherent, well thought-out Kashmir policy is hardly justifiable.

The government of Pakistan also established a Kashmir Cell in the ministry of foreign affairs in the wake of India's belligerent 5 August decision with the mandate of coming up with policy recommendations. The cell, working under the chairmanship of Foreign Minister Qureshi, started consulting the relevant people. He also gathered former Pakistan high commissioners to India but excluded the author of this book. That was no issue for me. I knew right from the word go that the cell would end up doing nothing but having meetings for domestic public consumption. (I may mention here that, when the PTI had won the election, I sent a congratulatory message to Qureshi and he responded by saying he looked forward to calling me for consultations on foreign policy matters but he never did perhaps under pressure from my senior foreign office colleagues.)

To be fair, I was subsequently invited to attend a meeting of the cell on 22 January 2020. I politely regretted saying that my participation might not be helpful at that late stage. I could assess that my hard-hitting criticism would not go down well with the foreign minister. So, it was better to stay clear of such meetings as I also did not want to compromise my freedom to express my views on foreign policy issues, especially on Kashmir, openly and freely.

However, I had always responded positively to the meetings convened by the prime minister of Pakistan Administered Kashmir, Raja Farooq Haider Khan. Our serious deliberations helped prepare several proposals but he would complain of imperviousness in Islamabad. I could feel his pain and desperation. He was willing to go to any length and would often tell me that the people in Pakistan Administered Kashmir were dying to move towards the LoC and ready to sacrifice their lives for their brethren in Kashmir and that he was finding it difficult to contain their emotions. He would add that, should Islamabad fail to take some concrete steps, it would become well-nigh impossible for the Pakistan Administered Kashmir government to control the situation. I could understand he was up against heavy odds. I would tell him he could not afford to lose hope and that he must persevere.

After a very successful visit of the prime minister to New York, as had always been the case before him, the government decided to appoint a new permanent representative in New York. Ambassador Munir Akram, who was posted from Geneva to New York in 2002, had retired in 2005 but was given three yearly extensions till 2008 and had since been living in the US. An experienced diplomat with an illustrious career mostly in multilateral diplomacy, he was brought in with high expectations.

I have worked with Ambassador Akram in Geneva as his number two and learnt a lot from him professionally. I would always respect him as my senior. Nevertheless, this does not take away from me my right to express my views frankly, and I know for a fact that he always takes constructive criticism positively.

Islamabad expected Ambassador Akram that, if not a formal UNSC session, he would at least be able to get another round of informal consultations on Kashmir and this time with at least a presidential or press statement so that there was something to at least convey to the people of Kashmir that the world had not forgotten about their unending woes and agonies. However, no such thing was to happen. In fact, Pakistan had to settle for discussion on Kashmir under the agenda item "Any Other Business" in informal consultations held on 15 January 2020. It was a setback, i.e. from exclusive informal consultations on Kashmir in August last year to a brief discussion initiated by China with no meaningful support from other members.

Pakistan was now looking forward to the Chinese presidency of the UNSC in March 2020. To provide a basis to China, Foreign Minister Qureshi wrote a letter to the UNSC president on 9 March requesting the UNSC to consider the Kashmir situation. This time we left the matter vague about the nature of the proposed meeting as both Pakistan and China were not sure if they could get something, even informal consultations were not a shoo-in. The prospects also dimmed because of the coronavirus pandemic that gripped the world exacting a very heavy toll and putting the world in an uncertain situation. The world's concerns on Kashmir, which had already become hostage to realpolitik, were fast dissipating. It was only on 27 March that Pakistan made the letter written to the UNSC president earlier in the month public. By then, Pakistan had almost lost the plot on Kashmir.

To coincide with the first anniversary of the abrogation of the special status of Jammu & Kashmir on 5 August, Pakistan tried again to have UNSC informal consultations exclusively on Kashmir. It failed again. The issue was discussed briefly under "Any Other Business" initiated by China but most other countries parroted their position that Kashmir should be resolved bilaterally between Pakistan and India. But, in Pakistan, the government claimed another victory saying that the UNSC had discussed Kashmir thrice since 5 August 2019, which was unprecedented and was a result of Pakistan's robust diplomacy.

As discussed earlier, Pakistan had failed to come up with an effective and sustainable plan of action following the Indian decision of 5 August. The pandemic worked to further hobble Pakistan's capacity to keep Kashmir on the world radar. It seems Pakistan has almost given up. We continue to make hortatory and didactic statements to jolt the world's conscience on Kashmir but the world appears to have stopped listening to what Islamabad is trying to convey. Even countries like Turkey and Malaysia have lost interest. When the major stakeholder itself is indecisive and lacks clarity on how far it can go in the pursuit of its national interest, others should not be expected to fight the diplomatic war at its behest.

In this context, it is pertinent to mention another case of waffling by Prime Minister Imran Khan. In a trilateral meeting of the president of Turkey and the prime ministers of Malaysia and Pakistan in New York where they were attending the UNGA session, the three leaders agreed to convene a summit in Kuala Lumpur on 18-20 December 2019 which would be attended by Muslim leaders to take stock of the Muslim world situation, the challenges it was facing internally and externally such as governance, development, terrorism and Islamophobia, and to suggest practical solutions. The three leaders also agreed to establish a global Muslim TV channel to counter anti-Islam narratives. Implicitly, this was an indictment of the 57-member OIC which had failed miserably to rise above narrow national and sectarian interests to think and act globally and had become almost dysfunctional. Indubitably, the intra-OIC rifts, especially the unbridgeable chasms between Saudi Arabia and Iran, had not allowed this Saudi-led organization to make its mark and pursue the ever-increasing challenges collectively.

As expected, the Kuala Lumpur initiative had raised eyebrows in Riyadh and was seen as an affront to the Saudi leadership at least of the Sunni Muslim world. There were apprehensions that those non-Arab countries including Iran might be up to something to further render the OIC irrelevant. Interestingly, Qatar, the only GCC country with serious problems with Saudi Arabia and UAE, was also on board the initiative.

A week before the Kuala Lumpur summit, Foreign Minister Qureshi paid a hurriedly-arranged day-long visit to Riyadh to assuage the Saudi concerns. That did not work. Pakistan could have quietly solicited Turkish and Malaysian understanding of its politico-economic considerations. But Pakistan's diplomatic history is replete with examples of going overboard and this time, too, it was more of the same.

Prime Minister Imran Khan dashed to Riyadh on 14 December hoping that he would be able to mollify and prevail upon the young and unpredictable Crown Prince, Mohammed bin Salman. He, too, failed and succumbed to the Saudi pressure as did the Indonesian President, Joko Widodo. The irony of the fact was that Pakistan's policy advisors had unnecessarily embarrassed the prime minister by advising him to personally visit Riyadh and talk to Mohammed bin Salman. The situation had unfortunately become so obvious that Pakistan did not even send its Kuala Lumpur-based high commissioner to the summit meeting let alone attend at least at the foreign-minister level. Although Prime Minister Imran Khan subsequently did pay a bilateral visit to Malaysia in February 2020, Pakistan had already tarnished its image as a sovereign country. Kashmiris and Pakistanis raised questions of how a country, which so quickly buckled under the Saudi pressure, would fight the long and difficult diplomatic battle for the cause of Kashmir. In diplomacy, flexibility is usually rewarded but indecisiveness is invariably punished.

There were two more aspects of Pakistan diplomacy which I, at least, found difficult to digest. First, immediately after 5 August, Prime Minister Khan started referring to Modi as a fascist in his tweets. I was astounded. We all know where Modi has come from but, at the highest level, even during conflicts, leaders do maintain some courtesy as that helps in breaking gridlocks when the time is right. This sort of language, however factual, should, in my considered view, have been avoided by the prime minister. Kashmir is not about scoring domestic political points. Such statements by the prime minister have also not gone down well with other world leaders.

This is not, however, to suggest that the realities of Modi should not be talked about in public. My only contention is that such things are not done at this level or even at the government level. After all, we all knew about Modi and what he was even before 5 August and, in fact, tried to reach out to him. Imran Khan, accompanied by Qureshi, also met him in New Delhi in December 2015 as the PTI Chairman and even invited him to visit Pakistan. Caustic tweets calling Modi names make no sense to me. I even find them in bad diplomatic taste. Whether we like it or not, Pakistan has to deal with Modi, and one does not know for how many more years to come.

Prime Minister Khan should have also avoided saying that war was no option between Pakistan and India. Practically speaking, he was right as a full-fledged war between the two countries would result in massive mutual destruction. However, in a diplomatic crisis situation, states do not take any option off the table. By announcing that Pakistan would not go to war with India had badly affected the efficacy of our diplomacy. A nuclear state must have kept all the options open to get the international community involved in the Kashmir dispute. Openly surrendering a war option was a huge diplomatic mistake in my view. If nothing else, it would have been better for the prime minister to have stayed quiet or formulated the remarks in neutral terms. I do not know who advised him to issue such a statement or was it his own idea?

******

In New Delhi, Sikh delegations would meet me now and then to request Pakistan to agree to constructing the Kartarpur Corridor that would connect the Gurdwara Darbar Sahib in Pakistan to the border with India. The founder of Sikhism, Guru Nanak, had spent the last 17 years of his life at Kartarpur and died there. This is one of the most sacred places for Sikhs and, every year, thousands of Sikh pilgrims visit Darbar Sahib to pay obeisance. The Darbar Sahib is only 4.7 kilometers from the Pakistan-India border. The visa-free corridor was first discussed between the then prime ministers Nawaz Sharif and Atal Bihari Vajpayee during their meeting in Lahore in February 1999. The 550th birth anniversary of Guru Nanak was on 12 November 2019 and the Indian Sikhs desperately wanted the corridor to be in place by then so that they could travel to Darbar Sahib freely all year round without getting involved in the tedious exercise of obtaining Pakistani visas.

The demand was legitimate and made perfect sense. I would tell the Sikh delegations to also approach their own government to get in touch with the high commission so that we could discuss this and consider possibilities. We were never contacted by the Indian government at least not since I took over as high commissioner in early 2014.

Be that as it may, I would keep writing to Islamabad favourably and also discuss the matter with the relevant authorities during my visits to Islamabad. Some stakeholders were not ready to agree for a variety of reasons including security. Some would also argue that this should not be discussed and pursued outside the bilateral dialogue process.

There were apprehensions that India would not be terribly keen to see this happening as the project, if materialized, would help generate massive goodwill for Pakistan amongst Indian Sikhs. India also carried some apprehensions that, using this religious corridor, Pakistan would also likely abet the Sikh separatist "Khalistan" movement.

However, I continued sending favourable missives from New Delhi as I was convinced that the Indian Sikh community should not be deprived of performing their religious rites freely. Moreover, creating a goodwill constituency was not a bad idea. Sikhs, though not more than 2 per cent of the Indian population, were still quite relevant for Pakistan. They were generally well-off economically and disproportionately represented in the Indian armed forces. Both the communities seemed to have erased bitter memories of Partition from their respective collective memories. At least, I found Sikhs very welcoming and full of affection for Pakistanis. During my stay in New Delhi, I was treated by them most honorably and continue to maintain contact with many of my Sikh friends.

It was a pleasant surprise for me when the Pakistan Army Chief had conveyed to Navjot Singh Sidhu, India's former cricket player, now a minister in the Punjab government, who was invited by prime minister-elect Imran Khan to attend his swearing-in ceremony in Islamabad on 17 August 2018, that Pakistan would immediately start working on the corridor so that it was ready by the 550th birth anniversary of Guru Baba Nanak. That was a big day for the Indian Sikhs and this news somewhat overshadowed the oath-taking ceremony of Imran Khan.

This sudden and unilateral decision had put the Indian government on the back foot especially as Prime Minister Modi was to seek re-election for another five-year term early next year. The fait accompli given to Modi could not be spurned by him in the election season. Thus, New Delhi had to come on board the initiative. On 22 November, the Indian cabinet formally approved the corridor on its side of the border from Dera Baba Nanak with Vice President M. Venkaiah Naidu laying the foundation stone on 26 November 2018. Prime Minister Imran Khan laid the foundation stone on the Pakistan side on 28 November.

Despite the Pulwama attack on 14 February and India's misadventure in Balakot, Pakistan, on 26 February 2019 just two months before the Lok Sabha elections in India, the work on building the corridor was not disrupted. Pakistan had made up its mind to give this priceless gift to the Indian Sikhs on their big religious occasion no matter what. Pakistan persevered despite India's aggression. Modi won the election and this time, instead of SAARC leaders, he invited six members of the Bay of Bengal Initiative for Multi-Sectoral Technical and Economic Cooperation (BIMSTEC)—the sub-regional South and Southeast Asia group that includes Nepal, Bhutan, Myanmar, Bangladesh, Thailand and Sri Lanka. Kyrgyzstan was invited as the then Chair of the Shanghai Cooperation Organization and Mauritius as a special guest.

As for Pakistan, Prime Minister Imran Khan called Modi to greet him on his re-election, reiterating his desire to open a new era of friendship with India. In the same spirit, Pakistan also endorsed India's candidature for the non-permanent member of the UNSC for the term 2021-22 in the 55-member Asia-Pacific Group meeting in June. Then came the 5 August Kashmir decision.

I think I was the only person in Pakistan who had openly suggested that, what India had done on 5 August, could not justify the Kartarpur Corridor and Pakistan should immediately suspend the construction work. But Pakistan should allow as many Indians as possible to attend the birth anniversary and make special arrangements for the pilgrims as had been the practice for decades in terms of the 1974 bilateral Protocol on Visits to Religious Shrines.

A clear message had to be sent to the Sikh community that it was the Modi government that was responsible for sabotaging the corridor and that they should build pressure on New Delhi to revoke its decision however difficult that might appear. Nevertheless, Islamabad had thought otherwise, deciding to keep the religious matter separate from politics. It was also argued that, making the corridor controversial, would also bring bad name to Pakistan internationally.

The corridor was thus inaugurated on 9 November and the first group of over 500 pilgrims led by Punjab Chief Minister Capt. Amarinder Singh visited the shrine the same day. The group also included former Prime Minister Manmohan Singh, and Union Cabinet Ministers Harsimrat Kaur and Hardeep Singh Puri.

I am still of the view that the work on the Kartarpur Corridor should have been stopped forthwith along with the other measures the government of Pakistan had taken. What New Delhi had done to Kashmir, the massive crackdown and arrests of thousands of young Kashmiris and putting the Kashmir Valley in an indefinite communication blackout were unprecedented. As discussed earlier, all this was in absolute violation not only of the relevant UN resolutions and the inalienable right of people to self-determination but also India's own constitution. How could Pakistan look the other way?

That was the time for Imran Khan to have demonstrated some courage and vision. There was no point in pandering to

Sikhs post 5 August. That was the time for Pakistan to have shown non-negotiable solidarity with Kashmiris as that would have helped build some pressure on the Modi government. Pakistan had lost another opportunity to register its anger, conveying in no uncertain terms that nothing was more critical for Pakistan than Kashmiris; the country was ready to give more sacrifices in the cause of Kashmir. Modi should not take Pakistan and Kashmiris for a ride.

******

The first anniversary of the draconian 5 August decision by India was marked by Pakistan with rallies and demonstrations, and by condemning India in philippics. 5 August will become another day in the Pakistan/Kashmir calendar a la 27 October, 13 July and 5 February. There is nothing wrong in marking these days and continuing to show solidarity with the people of Kashmir but freedom is not won by marking days, holding rallies, composing emotional songs, changing the names of main highways, and convening conferences alone. For instance, what difference would it make now that Islamabad has changed the name of the Kashmir Highway to Srinagar Highway? The intrinsic problem with such steps is that these not only make one complacent but also betray one's limitations. Such measures are important for creating good optics but meaningless on their own. Our every step related to Kashmir must flow from a comprehensive strategy. Stand-alone actions soon lose their optic value and become blasé and risible over time.

Pakistan also unveiled a new political map, as approved by the cabinet, on 4 August, trumpeting it as yet another big leap forward by the PTI government on Kashmir. The new map shows the entire Jammu & Kashmir region including Kashmir as part of Pakistan but also mentioning that this is a disputed territory waiting to be settled in terms of UNSC resolutions. Here Pakistan indeed indulged in self-contradiction. How could Pakistan claim a territory as its own that could also potentially go to India as a result of a plebiscite. Perhaps, this was done to avoid a constitutional amendment which would have created its own problems in view of Article 257 as discussed earlier.

Interestingly, Gilgit-Baltistan (GB) is also shown as a disputed area and a part of the Jammu & Kashmir region (reinforcing the Indian position on GB and making CPEC more controversial). Historically speaking, this may be right but GB is not being run by the Muzaffarabad government. It has its own Governor, Chief Minister and its own Assembly like the other four provinces of Pakistan. The people of GB strongly reacted to a resolution passed by the Pakistan Administered Kashmir Legislative Assembly on 14 January 2016 (the Legislative Assembly had passed similar resolutions earlier as well; there were also judgments by the Pakistan Administered Kashmir High and Supreme Courts) that condemned any possible change in the constitutional status of the GB region asserting that GB was an integral part of Kashmir and that any change would hurt the Kashmir cause. The people of GB, protesting against the resolution, said that Pakistan Administered Kashmir had no legal authority to speak on their behalf, especially in view of the Karachi Agreement of 28 April 1949 under which the Government of Pakistan Administered Kashmir had ceded to the Government of Pakistan complete control over GB, then called the "Northern Areas". It is also interesting to note that the new map retains Pakistan's claim on Ladakh, which is also claimed by China as a part of Tibet.

Patriotism of close to two million people of GB is commendable. However, this is not the time to fiddle with the legal status of the region, not even provisionally. In my assessment, this is what India is hankering after and, perhaps, the US is also pushing us in that direction to eventually find a status-quo based solution to the Kashmir dispute. What Islamabad needs to do is to invest in the socio-economic development of GB and implement the 2009 Empowerment and Self-Governance Order in letter and spirit.

It is also not yet clear as to what was the need of including Junagarh, now in the Indian state of Gujarat, in the new map. Junagarh was one of the princely states at the time of independence with a Muslim ruler but with a Hindu-majority population. The Muslim ruler acceded to Pakistan. However, a referendum in Junagarh in February 1948 was in favor of accession to India.

I do not know how reviving the issue of Junagarh at this stage would help the cause of Kashmir on the diplomatic front. It also beggars belief that Pakistan is willing to send its troops into Kashmir, capture it and hold a plebiscite on its own as was done by India in the case of Junagarh. Diluting focus on Kashmir by raising issues which Pakistan has long forgotten makes no sense whatsoever.

In my view, issuing a new political map, apparently for public consumption, was an unnecessary move with implications that may not be understandable in their entirety. This was indeed in reaction to the new political map issued by India on 2 November 2019 but that was done once the Reorganization of Jammu & Kashmir Act came into effect on 31 October 2019. Such measures not showing careful thought may make favorable headlines domestically and win plaudits for the government but they do not make sense and may backfire.

In another disquieting development, Foreign Minister Qureshi, in an interview to a private Pakistan TV channel, openly vented his spleen against Saudi Arabia's prevarication on supporting Kashmir especially in the context of convening a special ministerial session of the OIC. In a veiled threat to Saudi Arabia, he said that if there was no positive response from Riyadh and some other capitals, he would recommend to Prime Minister Imran Khan to consider convening a meeting of Muslim countries on Kashmir outside the OIC framework. (Source: https://www.dawn.com/news/1572857)

I do not know if these remarks were intended to be made or were made off the cuff. Whatever the case may be, these remarks only betrayed Pakistan's frustration on the diplomatic front and should have been avoided. If there were any possibility of an OIC meeting, though apparently there was none, the foreign minister had ruined even that possibility. Saudi Arabia would not like to be seen obliging Pakistan under pressure. This should have been discussed with Saudi Arabia offstage. Moreover, saying that Pakistan might call a meeting outside the OIC was most undiplomatic as, making such major emotional statements without carrying out the spade work would only bring more embarrassment and nothing else. Saudi Arabia, not on board, would go to any extent to ensure that any such initiative is doomed to failure as it did in the case of the Kuala Lumpur summit. Let us acknowledge that Pakistan does not, at present, have the capacity to take such an initiative.

Pakistan must be clear about every step it takes. Handling such sensitive diplomatic issues waywardly would create more challenges preventing Pakistan from exploiting emerging opportunities to its geostrategic and geo-economic advantages. It is a tough chess game that needs gravitas, the courage to make bold timely moves and, above all, the patience to endure the pressures that are inevitable when the game gets complicated and all the bets are off. It is simply bad diplomacy that instead, of solving its existing foreign policy problems, it is creating more. On Kashmir at least, Pakistan has no valid reason to blame Saudi Arabia. In the best of plans, even an OIC ministerial meeting would have barely achieved much. It is important that Pakistan should stop projecting Kashmir as an Islamic issue. Kashmir has never been our priority in the real sense of the word. Pakistan is itself to blame for the international indifference.

It is only by responding to the stimulus as correctly as possible and at the right time can diplomacy deliver. Once the time is lost in creating just optics, diplomacy also loses its momentum and goes haywire. That is what actually happened to Pakistan's Kashmir diplomacy. Simply put, the report card of the PTI government on Kashmir under Imran Khan is not very encouraging. Their failures on Kashmir will haunt Imran Khan for years to come.

Epilogue

"Here is my first principle of foreign policy: good governance at home."

William E. Gladstone

Pakistan is facing multiple and monumental internal and external challenges. Hopes for betterment were generated by PTI leader Imran Khan and people brought him to power in 2018. Throughout his political struggle, spanning over 23 years, he has been claiming that, should he come to power, he would bring about a whole new political culture that, instead of protecting the elite and rich of Pakistan, would look after the poor. He would fight against corruption and nepotism and change the destiny of Pakistan. Instead of borrowing from abroad, his government would turn Pakistan into a lender country.

On the external front, he committed himself to pursuing an independent foreign policy that would protect and promote Pakistan's interest. He would often tell us that those Pakistani politicians who maintained their assets and families abroad could never be independent in foreign policy matters. They would inevitably make bad compromises, for foreign powers know how to leverage and exploit them. Since he did not have any assets or bank accounts abroad, he could never come under external pressures.

In short, his internal and external policies would be markedly different from his predecessors who did nothing but plunder Pakistan. A new era was to begin after the July 2018 general elections in Pakistan.

It seems people are fast losing hope. I am, however, reluctant to jump the gun. We should be able to give our verdict at the next general election to be held in 2023 unless something dramatic happens and politics yet again get ugly and we are back to square one and start the democratic experience afresh after a hiatus of, I don't know, how many years. I would, nevertheless, like to believe nothing of that sort happens and the democratic process continues with all its anomalies notwithstanding.

Moreover, states' interests and foreign policies do not change overnight. They go through a metamorphosis of their own depending on systemic and sub-systemic changes. Yes, sometimes, indisputable leaders can be so dominant that radical policy shifts taken by them are not questioned though such situations are a rarity. Indisputable leaders are not born often. Pakistan has been particularly unlucky in this regard. Our entire politico-economic system is in the strong grip of influential people with deeply entrenched interests in maintaining the unjust status quo. The poor in Pakistan have no real prospects of socio-economic upward mobility. The country is in a deep mess and it will get messier if the privileged in this country are not willing to share their wealth and power with the downtrodden. I do not know if we will ever have a person of the stature of our founding father Mohammad Ali

Jinnah again as, without such a person who had the courage and conviction to take revolutionary decisions, there is little hope of any meaningful change in the country.

I am now increasingly convinced that the presidential form of government would be better for Pakistan given the nature of our political, economic and social issues. However, this must be achieved through national consensus and by amending the constitution accordingly though, in the prevailing extremely partisan and divisive politics, that looks hardly possible. However, in the longer term, there is no escape from reforming our political system as it has serious bearings on our internal and external policies. Let me return to the latter, especially how Islamabad is or is not doing in the context of Pakistan-India relations.

As in politics, the art of diplomacy also seeks to make the impossible, possible. Pursuing diplomatic objectives in an environment riven with deep and seemingly perpetual hostility is far more difficult, especially when the country is also facing endless turmoil of all kinds internally. When such is the case, much also depends on the quality of leadership. Though rhetoric is also a tool in the service of diplomacy, it must be in tune with the state's pivotal foreign policy objectives. But excessive rhetoric bordering on sterile verbosity usually turns out to be meaningless. Effective diplomacy needs consistency and must be rooted in clarity of vision and realistic assessment of variables relevant in any given situation. Diplomacy despises incoherence and fails to deliver when strategy and tactics do not fit together.

Nor can diplomatic goals be attained with good intentions alone. Mutual hostility stemming from bitter history cannot be ended in one go unless the state is ready to concede unilaterally. Diplomacy in an environment of conflict is a painstaking process warranting strong nerves and an iron will as well as the wherewithal to complement it. In hostility, states must be ready and able to even wage wars in order to achieve honorable and durable peace. There are no shortcuts in diplomacy.

******

From Berlin, where I was Pakistan ambassador, I had recommended to Islamabad in 2013 that, in view of Afghanistan's undeniably enormous significance, Pakistan should also appoint its own special envoy for Afghanistan. On a subsequent visit to Islamabad, I had learnt from one of my senior colleagues in the foreign office that the ministry's leadership had thought that a special envoy would take the limelight away from them; the Pakistan ambassador in Kabul was also not on board as he saw the proposal as an intrusion in his mandate. Moreover, creating an additional bureaucratic structure would make no sense especially when the Afghanistan affairs were, in any case, being handled mostly by the security establishment. I was appalled at this thinking. But I am glad that, almost seven years after I first floated the idea, the government finally appointed a special envoy for Afghanistan in June 2020.

Since I retired in 2017, I have been consistently pursuing appointment of a special envoy for Jammu & Kashmir. I am privy to the country's systemic limitations not only in the context of resources but also the institutional ability to sustain policies to their logical conclusions. The foreign office, in my view, has long lost its ability to think holistically and act coherently. There is a serious leadership crisis. I do not see people at the senior level who inspire. Diplomacy in the hands of typical bureaucrats is a recipe for unending failures. I am, therefore, least surprised the way Pakistan-India relations are being dealt with, especially Kashmir. Pakistan will likely suffer more setbacks should it remain adamantly oblivious to the criticality of the national stakes involved.

I am convinced that the government would eventually appoint a special envoy for Jammu & Kashmir because the coordination that the Kashmir diplomacy warrants, including mobilization of Kashmiris living around the world, cannot be done either at the level of foreign minister or foreign secretary; their platters are always full. They cannot humanly do justice in coordinating the multidimensional Kashmir diplomacy. Moreover, unless Pakistan itself raises the Kashmir diplomacy by appointing a special envoy, why would others stick their necks out for Pakistan? Thus, the sooner it is done the better it would be. Kashmiris, living under India's brutal occupation now for more than seven decades, desperately want Pakistan to put its house in order and take some practical steps beyond making statements that have become boringly monotonous. Pakistan urgently needs to break the crust of its unacceptable complacency to make a real difference on Kashmir. Even in this demoralizing situation, Pakistan is not without plausible options; the question remains whether the country is willing to piece them together in a strategic whole with tactical flexibility?

Besides appointing a special envoy and encouraging other countries to do the same as was done in the case of Afghanistan, the Pakistan Administered Kashmir government should also be consulted on the steps to be taken. In my view, and contrary to what many are suggesting, I do not subscribe to the idea of Kashmiris forming a government in exile with London as the right place for this. The first step the Pakistan Administered Kashmir government needs to take is to amend Article 2 of the Pakistan Administered Kashmir Interim Constitution of 1974.

Article 2, inter alia, states: "Azad Jammu & Kashmir means the territories of the State of Jammu & Kashmir which have been liberated by the people of that State and are, for the time being, under the administration of Government and such other territories as many hereafter come under its administration." Now that India has ended the special status of Kashmir and leaving the people of Jammu & Kashmir literally stateless, amending Article 2 to also include all the territories of the State of Jammu & Kashmir, as existed on 26 October 1947, must be done urgently. This would at least constitutionally strengthen the hands of the Pakistan Administered Kashmir government to speak on behalf of Kashmiris as well. Establishing a government in exile may appear to be an attractive idea but, in my view, it is unnecessary when the Pakistan Administered Kashmir government is there and a small amendment to the constitution can take care of the situation at hand.

The Pakistan Administered Kashmir president may also, as provided for in Article 11 of the Interim Constitution, "appoint a Plebiscite Advisor to advise the Government in relation to the holding of a plebiscite in the State of Jammu & Kashmir in terms of the UNCIP Resolutions." Here I must add, as mentioned earlier in the book, that UNSC resolution 98 of 23 December 1952 needs to be kept in view as this resolution allowed both Pakistan and India to retain certain numbers of troop on their respective sides of the LoC.

What else can or should Pakistan do? Can the two neighbors live in a stalemate forever? Should Pakistan restore the status quo ante without getting anything substantive in return from India on Kashmir. There are suggestions to bring the diplomatic relations back to the high-commissioner level, as well as resume bilateral trade as we reopened the airspace for India after about three months. I am not yet convinced that India is willing to concede anything to Pakistan on Kashmir or to the Kashmiris. Modi has a plan and his government is pursuing that though it is also clear that the resistance movement will continue for the foreseeable future. The recent issuance of domicile certificates to thousands of Indians to settle in Kashmir is a case in point.

I do not think Pakistan is at the stage yet where it should be trying to break the bilateral stalemate unilaterally. It has not been able to build any significant pressure on India and if it comes itself under pressure for no valid reason that would be too much to digest. Rather Pakistan should be doing things differently. For instance, what stops it from closing its airspace to Indian airlines at least once a week or fortnight? Let India approach the International Civil Aviation Organization and other relevant organizations but it must strike where it hurts. In my view, it will be a huge misstep to start moving towards normalizing everything with India without the latter showing any tangible and consequential flexibility on Kashmir.

Some are suggesting that Pakistan should in retaliation revoke the 1972 Simla agreement and free itself from the shackles of bilateralism on the Kashmir dispute. Once Pakistan had reverted to the pre-1971 war situation, converting the LoC into ceasefire line (CFL), the stakes for peace would heighten, and the international community might get involved into the potentially volatile situation between the two nuclear powers. There appears to be some merit in this suggestion, especially now that Pakistan has also issued a new political map as discussed earlier. Another view is that it does not matter whether it is the LoC or CFL. Once push comes to shove, even international borders become irrelevant.

It also needs to be emphasized that Kashmiris will never be able to win their right to self-determination only by counting on Pakistan's diplomatic and moral support. They must reorganize themselves to take their struggle to a higher level.

Their struggle has to be reinvigorated on both political and military fronts. Even in regard to armed struggle, international law is clearly on their side. The principle of "Erga Omnes" (towards all), that is, rights and obligations are toward all and therefore enforceable against anybody infringing that right. Considering this immutable legal principle, India's refusal to hold a plebiscite in Jammu & Kashmir cannot be condoned and it is incumbent upon the international community to force India to hold a plebiscite in Jammu & Kashmir as the right to self-determination is inalienable.

In this regard it is also useful to mention UNGA resolution 3314 adopted on 14 December 1974 on "Definition of Aggression". In outlawing all forms of aggression, the definition provides an exception for the right to armed struggle. It states: "Nothing in this definition of aggression could, in any way, prejudice the right to self-determination, freedom and independence of people forcibly deprived of that right, particularly people under colonial and racial regimes or other forms of alien domination; not the right of those people to struggle to that end and to seek and receive support."

This and many other UNGA and UNSC resolutions, as well as the United Nations Charter and the Universal Declaration of Human Rights are still valid and relevant and must be implemented. In fact, the above resolution binds the international community to respond positively if the people living under occupation seek their support and help in their struggle for their right to self-determination. And the world "struggle" here is all-encompassing to also include armed struggle. India also voted in favor of this resolution. It has thus no legal, political and moral ground to gripe about Pakistan's support to the Kashmiris.

Nor did the US have any right to proscribe HuM and term

it as a terrorist organization as it is engaged in a legitimate armed struggle against the Indian occupation and never targeted innocent civilians. US must revisit and redress the great injustice done to the legitimate Kashmir struggle. The people want nothing but freedom. This is their inalienable right; it raises serious questions about the credibility of liberal democracies when they themselves contribute towards sacrificing international legal norms and principles at the altar of their narrow interests and at the cost of endangering millions of lives. If they could all rally for the freedom of East Timor from Indonesia, or South Sudan, what stops them from openly supporting the Kashmir cause? Indeed they are being driven by their strategic and economic interests but, in the process, they are contributing also to endangering stability in the nuclearized South Asia.

Time is of the essence. India will go all out to further consolidate its iron hand in Kashmir. It would not mind working with those who have been playing on both sides of the field and can be won with favors and largesse. India would likely restore the status of State for Jammu & Kashmir. But that will not happen any time soon. This may coincide with holding elections whenever they are allowed to be held. The delimitation process will be extended and manipulated to suit evolving political and demographic ground realities. Splitting Jammu from Kashmir may not happen as it is the Jammu region where non-Kashmiris will be settled for now to steadily shift the demographic fulcrum in favor of Hindus. As for the Valley, Muslims belonging to the RSS (Muslim Rashtriya Manch) may be brought in to begin the process but in small numbers just to test waters and that, too, in relatively peaceful areas in the north.

India will also use all possible means to gradually shrink the space for the military resistance and may well succeed. It would not mind if some pocket close to the LoC remain manageably active to keep Pakistan under pressure on terrorism and the LoC hot. False-flag operations are also a part of India's strategy to avoid talking to Pakistan. India's objective of keeping Pakistan unstable and under international pressure on issues such as the Financial Action Task Force can best be achieved by improving the situation in the Valley significantly but short of full normalcy and keeping Afghanistan in turmoil.

As for Ladakh, it will remain a Union Territory and may be given the right to elect its own legislative assembly when the situation is conducive. The Kargil Muslim Shia population may not be terribly keen to resort to violence. They will accept whatever is given to them so long as they are treated at par. India may oblige them by making Kargil and Leh Union Territory headquarters alternately for six months each.

The China-India tension in Ladakh in the months of May-June 2020 resulting in the death of 20 Indian soldiers and also some unconfirmed causalities on the Chinese side was a reminder that India-China might be working to promote good working relations, the territorial disputes on the Line of Actual Control (LoAC) and India's strategic partnership with the US would continue making this relationship difficult to normalize. China is a party to the Kashmir dispute given its historical claim on Ladakh and India's claim on the Aksai Chin region. Claims and counter-claims could be explained and justified depending on how far one would like to go back into the history of this region.

******

As with Kashmir, Pakistan is also seemingly unsure about how to deal with the Jadhav issue. Right from the word go, Pakistan somehow could not succeed in sustaining its narrative.

It had good reason to deny him consular access in terms of the bilateral agreement. India went to the ICJ and Pakistan agreed to implement its judgment which had two primary parts. One, to provide consular access as provided for under the 1963 Vienna Consular Convention. Two, as suggested by our legal team itself, carry out an effective review and reconsideration of the case.

As for the latter, the ICJ, in paragraph 147 of its judgment, ruled: "To conclude, the Court finds that Pakistan is under an obligation to provide, by means of its own choosing, effective and review consideration of the conviction and sentence of Mr Jadhav so as to ensure that full weight is given to the effect of the violation of the rights set forth in Article 36 of the Vienna Convention, taking account of paragraphs 139, 145 and 146 of this Judgement."

Paragraph 146 of the judgment, while leaving the choice of means to Pakistan, stressed that "Pakistan shall take all measures to provide effective review and reconsideration including, if necessary, by enacting appropriate legislation." In paragraph 139, the Court remarked that "it is normally the judicial process which is suited to the task of review and reconsideration." This had effectively ruled out the military court in Pakistan to act as an appellate court.

Soon after the 10 April 2017 verdict against Jadhav, he filed a clemency appeal with the Military Appellate Court in Pakistan which was rejected on 16 April 2017. His mercy petition has now been pending with the Army Chief of Pakistan since 17 April 2017.

Keeping all this in view, what options are left for Pakistan and India. As far as Pakistan is concerned, it can neither free Jadhav, nor, it seems, hang him. For the army chief to approve his mercy petition would seriously damage the institution's reputation and credibility especially among the people of Pakistan. Not only that, it would also deal a severe blow to Pakistan's narrative of India's involvement in terrorism in Pakistan.

In case of the army chief's rejection of the mercy petition, one should not expect the PTI government or for that matter any government and the President of the country to decide differently as showing mercy to an Indian terror convict, who has been responsible for the death of countless innocent lives in Pakistan, would be politically suicidal.

Given the above, options left for Pakistan are limited. Hence, it may not be in a hurry to take the difficult decision of either hanging or freeing Jadhav. On the other hand, the Islamabad High Court, after reviewing the case, may decide that the trial was unfair and did not fulfil all the requirements of justice. Accordingly, the trial must start anew and be shifted from the military to a civilian court. This would be quite a damaging verdict on the military courts in Pakistan. On the other hand, it would be helpful in that it would not only cause further delays, but also strengthen the international credentials of Pakistan's judiciary. However, the people of Pakistan would look at it differently with serious apprehensions.

As for India, it knows full well that it cannot get Jadhav back unless the Islamabad High Court or then the Supreme Court of Pakistan changes the conviction to life imprisonment using the ICJ verdict as a basis in its broadest context. By creating a fuss around consular access and by attaching too many conditions, India, perhaps wanted the matter to be taken back to the ICJ or the UNSC under Article 94 of the UN Charter which says: "Each Member of the United Nations undertakes to comply with the decision of International Court of Justice in any case to which it is a party." It further says: "If any party to a case fails to perform the obligations incumbent upon it under a judgment rendered by the Court, the other party may have recourse to Security Council, which may, if it seems necessary, make recommendations or decide upon measures to be taken to give effect to the judgement."

While India's two-year term as non-permanent member of the UNSC will start from 1 January 2021, referring the matter to the UNSC may not be its preferred option. In all likelihood, it will return to the ICJ for a clearer judgment on consular access and "effective review and reconsideration" of the case. Prolonging the case also serves India's interests in that it keeps the bilateral tension at a certain level and the resumption of a structured dialogue an impossibility. Nor would India have any qualms if attention stays on Jadhav, especially when the ICJ judgment has provided them with some ammunition to reinforce their narrative.

Moreover, dragging the Jadhav case also helps India divert attention from what it is doing in Kashmir. Internationalizing Jadhav now makes perfect sense and the suggestion of approaching the UNSC leaves Pakistan guessing and somewhat under pressure. And in case India, despite the presence of China at the UNSC, is able to get a press or presidential statement, it would be a huge embarrassment for Pakistan given the setbacks it has faced in the UN on Kashmir. It is likely that India will make an effort in this direction under its own month-long presidency of the UNSC but may not succeed in getting a statement in the presence of China.

In short, it serves the interests of both Pakistan and India if the case gets complicated legally and drags on for years so that Pakistan is saved from taking the difficult decisions of freeing or hanging him, or converting his death sentence into life imprisonment. For Indians, keeping Jadhav alive would be their great victory and, frankly speaking, they may not be terribly keen on welcoming him back. Jadhav now serves India more if he remains in Pakistan custody rather than with his family in Sangli, Maharashtra.

******

The world is getting increasingly complex and, in many ways, paradoxical. It is integrating and fragmenting at the same time. While, on the one hand, the global challenges such as the ongoing Covid-19 pandemic demand active global cooperation, on the other hand, such issues are also pushing the world towards rethinking the very fundamentals of globalization. The West, led by the US, seems particularly worried at the way the world has evolved during the last 40 years that helped China become an economic giant and militarily assertive posing challenges to the interests of the West across the world.

How China takes all this would largely depend on the capability of its leadership to keep its growing domestic political dissension to a manageable level so that the hybrid system it has very efficiently created is not upended. Liberal democracies, big and small, are looking askance at China though a majority of the developing world is careful not to upset Beijing for their own respective economic interests. Unlike the US, China does not pursue creating regional and global blocs. It places emphasis on strengthening bilateral relations even with the US itself and its strategic partners.

The ideological cleavages covering all domains of life are the real challenges. The existing international system may not be to the liking of many including China but, so far, they have been playing ball. From the United Nations to the G-20, China is showing the will to accommodate. However, its internal politico-economic system does not tessellate with the international legal regime underpinned by liberal democratic values. For instance, differences on the interpretations of human rights do resurface time and again. Rooted in the communist philosophy, China sees the collective interests of its society rather than individual liberties as supreme.

Should the West become more protectionist and politically nonchalant, the post-Second World War order is likely to face major risks making the world more chaotic and unpredictable. Multilateralism, which is already under stress and struggling to deliver in crucial areas, would be further strained and effective only in those limited areas where the major powers find themselves on the same page. International relations are going through a significant transformation with the world moving towards amorphous multi-polarity and increasing reliance on bilateral engagement.

China is not the erstwhile Soviet Union which collapsed in 1990 under its own military weight. Contrarily, China has been pursuing a different route with a different social contract which, in a nutshell, is economic prosperity with limited and controlled democratic freedoms. Whether the Communist Party of China, under the leadership of Xi Jinping, is able to retain the present social contract against the onslaught of cataclysmic developments in information and communications technologies is a question difficult to answer. However, one can perhaps say that, as Western democracies are also undergoing changes that are not necessarily in sync with the well-established democratic traditions, internal pressures on China may not be as critical as was the case with the Soviet Union. Economic prosperity is a double-edged sword. In the case of China, it may help the autocratic system to sustain itself but, on the other hand, when people are prosperous, they do hanker after more political liberties as indeed they also do when there is unbearable economic deprivation and a country becomes plutocratic with no hope left for a peaceful change.

From issues in the South China Sea to Hong Kong and Taiwan, China has shown that it would never succumb to outside pressures. The West is on the decline but the game is not yet over. The world is bound to witness many a crisis in the decades to come. Jolts of tension would be felt everywhere. The world is interconnected and interdependent. The US should not be expected to give way to China's ascendency easily. It will do everything possible to ensure the Belt and Road Initiative (BRI) does not become a reality whereas, from China's perspective, BRI's success is the sine qua non to achieving its long-term objective and becoming a global power in all its aspects. Escape from the so-called Thucydides Trap may be possible but it is likely to manifest itself in ways short of causing irretrievable disruption.

Be that as it may, global and regional tensions are likely to ramp up in the months and years ahead but we cannot be certain whether the world moves towards more integration and connectivity or becomes more anarchic and chaotic. Though I would not like to wager on what would ultimately happen, it goes without saying that much will depend on how China and the US manage their relations because that, in turn, will determine whether the existing international system can be sustained. China will, no doubt, avoid conflicts as its economic agenda is critical for both its internal and external imperatives but it can be drawn into conflictual situations by the US if pushed too far, especially on Taiwan and Hong Kong.

Other important players like Russia and the European Union are watching closely but their influence around the globe has significantly waned. Russia, under Vladimir Putin, is trying to reassert itself as we have seen in Ukraine, Belarus,

Syria and Libya but its stagnant economic base may not allow it to leverage its influence effectively beyond certain peculiar situations. But it will be particularly concerned over any negative developments taking place at the country's "near abroad". Putin will also remain close to China avoiding taking unhelpful positions on issues of pivotal importance to the latter. Their internal political systems give them enough room to pursue foreign policies independent of domestic public opinion or political opposition.

Similarly, given Russia's close defense relations with India, it is careful about the latter's sensitivities but that does not prevent it from augmenting its relations with Pakistan as India is gradually diversifying its defense inventory. The supply of four gunship helicopters, Mi-35, to Pakistan in the recent years was an indication that Moscow is favorably inclined. However, it is Pakistan which has not been able to sustain the momentum created by the official visit of former President Asif Ali Zardari to Russia in May 2011. Among other things, Russia was also willing to help Pakistan in reviving the Karachi Steel Mills that was built with the Soviet help in the 1970s. A joint business forum was also established but all these initiatives failed to take off for a host of reasons including the inertia that permeates bureaucracies in both countries. Accordingly, President Vladimir Putin has still not been to Pakistan though he was once scheduled to visit Islamabad in September 2012 for a day trip but that was cancelled at the eleventh hour apparently under pressure from India.

However, Russia will stay engaged with Pakistan on Afghanistan. When it comes to the latter, most players in the region, including Pakistan, are still grappling with the question, whether the withdrawal of US forces from Afghanistan would be good or bad for them. The recent intelligence reports that

Russia has been paying bounties to some Taliban militants for killing US soldiers are ominous and further complicate matters in land-locked Afghanistan.

Afghanistan is unlikely to settle and, in my view, is gradually slipping into another long civil war. The intra-Afghan reconciliation process is likely to unravel for the Taliban, being an ideological movement, can ill-afford to play second fiddle to the Kabul government. As soon as the Taliban move away from their ideological moorings, their movement would come under unbearable pressure from within and may disintegrate. It also needs to be underscored that they draw their strength from the gun. Elections are not their strength. Their objectives seem to get into power; reestablish the Islamic Emirate of Afghanistan; provide peace to the people of Afghanistan; and unilaterally change the Afghanistan constitution while retaining the provisions related to women and freedom of expression with some changes. Should they come to power, their "Talibanization" of Afghanistan would be different and mild as compared to the extremist policies they adopted in 1996. This may help them get the necessary support from abroad, especially of the US and other Western countries, China, Russia, et al., to rebuild Afghanistan.

As for the European Union, the Brexit shock will take time to be absorbed. Britain as a P-5 country was a dominant voice within the EU especially on security and foreign policy matters. Some EU members are still struggling economically and some are drifting towards populist right-wing politics. The Covid-19 pandemic has exposed the inherent EU limitations. The member countries have not yet been able to integrate fully to conduct themselves as a single voice in international relations. The EU experiment, though, has withstood some serious economic challenges in the past but it remains to be seen if it is able to salvage itself from several policy and procedural maladies and difficulties confronting this pioneering regional organization. Should the right-wing forces in member countries continue expanding their political hold domestically and sending more and more of their members to the EU parliament, the EU's future will remain on tenterhooks raising more doubts about its sustainability. The EU will come under tremendous pressure if another big member country decides to quit. Who knows the next in line may be Italy or Spain.

Evolving alignments and realignments across the world are also being played out in South Asia. India, as a bigger country in the region, is still not clear whether it wants to fully align itself with the US strategic objectives or pursue a balanced if not a neutral policy. Whereas on the one hand it is concerned about the increasingly assertive China and its growing influence in the region, India cannot perhaps afford to alienate itself from China and Russia or be lukewarm to the SCO despite the presence of Pakistan there. However, in the longer term, India will come to a pass where it will have to either gradually move away from the US strategic objectives and focus more on strengthening bilateral relations without entangling itself in the complexities of evolving international relations. India is aware that it cannot achieve its regional and global aspirations without China's goodwill and US support. But these choices are not easy to make. The way India has so far positioned itself; it will be difficult for it to strengthen its bilateral relations with the US without sharing its strategic goals against China.

India is also sensitive to the Pakistan-China strategic partnership. Though India will keep trying to create problems between Pakistan and China, the latter will not readily oblige so long as India continues consolidating its strategic ties with the US against China. If India were to resort to subverting CPEC, that will be a huge blow to its relations with its big eastern neighbor. The time for India to have its cake and eat it too may come to an end sooner than expected. It will have to take some fundamental decisions including on its adversarial relations with Pakistan.

It needs to be underscored and understood that the Pakistan-India relations have come to such a pass where they cannot break the deadlock without some help from mutual friends. But the problem is that India has closed all doors for diplomacy on Kashmir and bilateral engagement sans meaningful negotiations on Kashmir will be another exercise in futility. Pakistan should not be bamboozled again into a dialogue process that leads to more logjams. The UNSC must give a suitable mandate to the UN Secretary General to help work out a tenable solution to the Kashmir dispute. Without some sort of international mediation, there is no possibility left for the two countries to find solutions to their problems and disputes bilaterally.

The next question that comes to mind is what kind of a solution for Kashmir is possible. Should Pakistan accept the Indian moves and move on subject to India's withdrawal of its claims on the Pakistan side of the LoC, including GB? Will Kashmiris be amenable to this solution, especially if the Muslim majority areas of the Jammu region are also made part of the Kashmir Valley and given a separate statehood within the Indian Union? Or, is there any possibility left to revert to the four-point formula? Obviously, all these and other possible options could be discussed between the two countries without giving up their respective stated positions. Eventually, the two sides would have to exhibit flexibility to arrive at a fair modus vivendi. And for that to happen, Pakistan and Kashmiris would need to build pressure on India both from within and without.

Prime Minister Imran Khan, after his first official visit to the US in July 2019, returned to Pakistan triumphantly announcing that President Donald Trump has offered to mediate on Kashmir. President Trump also avoided publicly slamming Pakistan during his visit to India in February 2020. Unexpectedly, he appreciated Pakistan's assistance in promoting reconciliation in Afghanistan. However, the joint statement issued at the end of the visit on 25 February did "call on Pakistan to ensure that no territory under its control is used to launch terrorist attacks, and to expeditiously bring to justice the perpetrators of such attacks, including 26/11 Mumbai and Pathankot." According to the joint statement, "President Trump welcomed India's role in continuing to provide development and security assistance to help stabilize and provide connectivity in Afghanistan."

Pakistan must stop harboring illusions about its relations with the US. There is no strategic convergence. US supports India in all matters ranging from its bid for a permanent seat on the UNSC to its membership of the NSG which are of direct security and political implications for Pakistan. Even on Afghanistan, I see problems lurking. India will do all it can to ensure Afghanistan remains mired in chaos at least till the time it is able to consolidate the 5th August measures in Jammu & Kashmir. Also, an unstable Balochistan also serves US interests as it continues to openly express its concerns over CPEC.

Ideally, Pakistan and India should live in peace to focus on multiple regional and global challenges. India has serious territorial disputes with at least four of its neighbors. The world is changing. India will only delude itself if it is thinking of realizing its regional and global aspirations without making peace particularly with China and Pakistan. Shenanigans apart, India is in need of early soul-searching. It must lead the way to regional stability by fixing the long-standing issues rather than compounding them by moving in the opposite direction and by clinging to the inherently retrogressive and divisive political philosophy of Hindutva as being promoted by the RSS that has been banned thrice since 1947 — the first time for killing India's indisputable leader, Mohandas Karamchand Gandhi in 1948.

The people of India, like the people of other South Asian countries, deserve far better. India has so far failed to provide leadership because of its blinkered vision rooted in arrogance and self-serving, banal narratives.

Let me underline again that the road to peace and prosperity in South Asia goes through Kashmir. I genuinely do not see any prospects for peace without the two major countries in the region reaching out to each other and settling the core dispute once and for all. That will require objectivity and flexibility. India will gain nothing by being delusional that it can win the hearts and minds of Kashmiris by suppressing them. It may also draw some satisfaction from the fact that the international community is mostly showing criminal indifference to the worsening plight of the Kashmiris. Pakistan's diplomatic failures cannot be India's success so long as Kashmiris are resolved to continue fighting for their freedom.

Meanwhile, Pakistan must pay more attention to fostering its relations with other South and Central Asian countries. And we must not see this exercise from the lens of zero-sum calculus of their relations with India. The telephone conversation between Prime Minister Imran Khan and Prime Minister Hasina Wajid on 22 July 2020 was a welcome initiative by Pakistan. We must not leave it at that now that the ice has been broken. One hopes the government has a concrete plan of action. It must, however, desist from the tendency of creating undue and premature hype around such initiatives. As I stressed earlier, diplomacy is not an event but a process and must be taken in that spirit. Nothing moves linearly; ups and downs are part of the diplomatic game; what is important is to be steadfast and never give up.

There is also a need to go back to the drawing board and look at our relations with Saudi Arabia, UAE and Iran afresh. Pakistan must disabuse itself of the notion that it has the capacity of mediating between Iran and Saudi Arabia and other key Arab countries. The tendency to punch above its weight brings nothing but entails frustration and embarrassment. We would need drastic changes in the way we formulate our foreign policy and conduct our diplomacy. Political systems, both in Iran and most of the Arab world despite the "Arab Spring", will likely come under pressure at some stage in the future. A more chaotic West Asia, as Israel is growing in power and annexing more and more Arab territories, is a foregone but worrying conclusion. Thus, it is not surprising if some important Arab countries, who consider Iran as their implacable and intolerant enemy, are reaching out to Israel. It will be interesting to see whether Saudi Arabia also recognizes Israel and establishes diplomatic relations with it without getting anything conclusive from Israel on Palestine. Ultimately, nothing is more important for Saudi Arabia than its own stability and the Kingdom's survival under Mohammed bin Salman and his lineage. Pakistan is an important Muslim country. It must position itself in a way that it can avoid being embroiled in extraneous issues but fully cognizant of its geo-strategic and geo-economic interests.

Of course, that is easier said than done. Saudi Arabia is still a strong US ally and, therefore, extremely careful in its engagement and relations with China. Saudi Arabia knows well how important its relations with Pakistan are. However, our strategic partnership with China does create issues. Saudi

Arabia would like us to also tread carefully. However, US policies in our region, especially in the context of India, are least helpful. Thus, it is not easy to maintain a balance without economic space. Pakistan will be gradually pushed away from the US and consequentially from Saudi Arabia and other Gulf countries, barring Qatar, in case of increasing economic stress and the lack of suitable responses from the US, Saudi Arabia and the UAE who not only have their own economic constraints but also political aversion to China's BRI and CPEC. The nub of the problem for Pakistan would remain as to how to preserve its relations with the US and Saudi Arabia without hurting its strategic partnership with China. If Pakistan somehow failed to play its cards deftly, it may end up losing on many fronts to India apart from Kashmir.

China is now making significant moves toward Iran, willing to invest billions of dollars in the country that is still under stringent sanctions. This should help Pakistan and Iran remove the mutual misgivings that exist despite several efforts made by Pakistan. Iran is obviously not very comfortable with India's growing partnership with the US. Now that China has jumped into the fray in a big way, it cannot be without some impact on India-Iran relations. India does not have the resources to match China nor does it have the will to strain its relations with the US that are unquestionably considered far more important. For Pakistan, there will be some opportunities arising out of these changing dynamics but it will have to ensure that CPEC does not face delays and all its linked projects complete on time. As mentioned earlier, both India and the US do have serious issues with the BRI and CPEC; it is not difficult to anticipate that they would continue creating problems for Pakistan and the CPEC.

In terms of realpolitik, Iran must not have any qualms

should Pakistan remain under pressure and CPEC become more controversial and thus faces delay to the dissatisfaction of China. I see huge challenges for Pakistan diplomacy in the region in the years ahead emanating from Afghanistan, Iran, and India. And all these situations are interlinked. Pakistan must start thinking of making several strategic and tactical moves to secure its flanks.

Also, Pakistan needs to fix its own internal problems urgently. Among other things, the lack of good governance and the perennial civil-military tension are not letting the country perform and deliver both internally and externally. Pakistan cannot afford to be complacent as the world is changing dizzyingly rapidly. And we must think ahead if Pakistan is to get its rightful position in the comity of nations.

However, our foreign policy objectives as I underscored earlier, would not be able to realize their full potential till MoFA is reorganized. For too long it has ignored the importance of economic diplomacy. We can learn from the experiences of other states and borrow from them mutatis mutandis. For instance, it now seems critical to have a separate Economic Diplomacy Division (EDD) within the MoFA headed by a secretary reporting directly to the foreign minister. The EDD, in general terms, must be responsible for enhancing Pakistan's economic clout and footprint across the world through trade and investments. No doubt, the EDD would face enormous resistance within the system but, appointing the right person as Secretary EDD for at least three years to begin with, would be essential for the new Division to overcome the teething problems and get off to a good start. Alternatively, the existing Economic Affairs Divison may be merged with MoFA with its own Secretary but this will likely face massive resistance from the powerful Pakistan Administrative Service.

Similarly, MoFA also needs, and needs it urgently, to revamp its spokesperson's office to make it a well-equipped Public Diplomacy Division. And I am sure our people know pretty well that public diplomacy is not about issuing press releases and statements only. It has now developed into a full-fledged area of expertise and specialization. This division must be headed by an additional foreign secretary to guide and coordinate activities both within Pakistan and its diplomatic and consular missions abroad to remove many misgivings about Pakistan and help burnish the country's international image. Needless to say that, without effective public diplomacy, Pakistan will continue finding it very difficult to bolster its interests and promote its foreign policy objectives including goals set for the EDD. It may also be worthwhile to reconsider the long-held proposal of taking the External Publicity Wing away from the Ministry of Information and Broadcasting and making it part of MoFA.

For both these initiatives to develop roots and deliver, the active involvement of overseas Pakistanis will be critical. It is sad to see our diaspora divided along political lines. Mobilizing the Pakistani community abroad in a sustained manner is an enormous task as every country where they live has its own peculiar circumstances and requirements. We have made many attempts in that direction in the past but have failed every time. Let us remember there is no substitute to planning and hard work. Haphazard, politically motivated steps do not yield positive results but end up driving more wedges among overseas Pakistanis. I have witnessed this myself in my own career in places from New York to London and Berlin.

In conclusion, may I refer to what Sun Tzu once said: "Opportunities multiply as they are seized." Pakistan and India must leave for their posterity a relationship cleansed of bitterness and conflict. As a Pakistani who has been part of the proud Foreign Service of Pakistan for over 35 years, I can say with full confidence that Pakistan is ready to extend the hand of friendship to India. Is India ready to reciprocate on the basis of mutual respect or will it get more belligerent and cause more disruptions leaving the region in conflicts and wretched poverty for generations to come?

As a former diplomat, I may still feign optimism but the way India is moving unapologetically away from its secular foundations and embracing the inherently parochial and ornery Hindutva, my hopes are fading. I hope I am wrong.

******

Annexures

Annex I - Fax message of 25 October 2014 by signed by Foreign Secretary Jilani.

25/10 2013 19:41 FAX 0092519207217 F S OFFICE ⌀001

H.E

FAX MESSAGE

From : Foreign Islamabad
To : Parep Berlin
No. : FSO)-1/2013
Dated : October 25, 2013

Foreign Secretary for Ambassador

Thanks you for your message of 23rd October 2013.

2. I plan to relinquish the charge of my current position on 1st December and after spending a couple of days with my parents will leave for Washington D.C. You may plan your arrival to Islamabad accordingly.

3. In the meanwhile, I have moved a summary to formalize your appointment as Foreign Secretary.

Best wishes + regards

(Jalil Abbas Jilani)
Foreign Secretary

25-OCT-2013 14:48 From: 0092519207217 ID:PAK EMB BERLIN Page:001 R=95%

Annex II - Sharm el Sheikh Joint Statement of 16 July 2009

"Prime Minister of India Dr Manmohan Singh and Prime Minister Syed Yousuf Raza Gilani met at Sharm El Sheikh on July 16, 2009. The two prime ministers had a cordial and constructive meeting.

"They considered entire gamut of bilateral relations with a view to charting the way forward in India-Pakistan relations. Both leaders agreed that terrorism was main threat to both the countries. The leaders affirmed their resolve to fight terrorism and to cooperate with each other to this end.

"Prime Minister Singh reiterated the need to bring the perpetrators of the Mumbai attack to justice.

"Prime Minister Gilani assured that Pakistan would do everything in its power in this regard. He said Pakistan had provided an updated status dossier on the investigation of the Mumbai attacks and had sought additional information/evidence. Prime Minister Singh said that dossier was being reviewed.

"Both leaders agreed that the two countries would share real time, credible and actionable information on any future terrorist threats.

"Prime Minister Gilani mentioned that Pakistan had some information on threats in Balochistan and other areas.

"Both prime ministers recognise that dialogue is the only way forward. Action on terrorism should not be linked to the Composite Dialogue process and these should not be bracketed.

"Prime Minister Singh said that India was ready to discuss all issues with Pakistan, including all outstanding issues. He reiterated India's interest in a stable, democratic Islamic Republic of Pakistan.

"Both leaders agreed that the real challenge was development and the elimination of poverty. They are resolved to eliminate those factors which prevent our countries from realising their full potential.

"Both agreed to work to create an atmosphere of mutual trust and confidence. Both leaders reaffirmed their intention to promote regional cooperation.

"Both foreign secretaries should meet as often as necessary and report to the two foreign ministers who will be meeting on the sidelines of the forthcoming UN General Assembly."—

Sharm el Sheikh

16 July 2009

Annex III - Joint Statement of 6 January 2004

JOINT PRESS STATEMENT

The President of Pakistan and the Prime Minister of India met during the SAARC Summit in Islamabad.

The Indian Prime Minister while expressing satisfaction over the successful conclusion of the SAARC Summit appreciated the excellent arrangements made by the host country.

Both leaders welcomed the recent steps towards normalization of relations between the two countries and expressed the hope that the positive trends set by the CBMs would be consolidated.

Prime Minister Vajpayee said that in order to take forward and sustain the dialogue process, violence, hostility and terrorism must be prevented. President Musharraf reassured Prime Minister Vajpayee that he will not permit any territory under Pakistan's control to be used to support terrorism in any manner. President Musharraf emphasized that a sustained and productive dialogue addressing all issues would lead to positive results.

To carry the process of normalisation forward the President of Pakistan and the Prime Minister of India agreed to commence the process of the composite dialogue in February 2004. The two leaders are confident that the resumption of the composite dialogue will lead to peaceful settlement of all bilateral issues, including Jammu and Kashmir, to the satisfaction of both sides.

The two leaders agreed that constructive dialogue would promote progress towards the common objective of peace, security and economic development for our peoples and for future generations.

Islamabad
January 06, 2004

Annex IV - Ufa Joint Statement of 10 July 2015

TEXT OF THE JOINT PRESS RELEASE BY FOREIGN SECRETARIES OF PAKISTAN AND INDIA AT THE JOINT PRESS CONFERENCE IN UFA, 10 JULY 2015

The Prime Ministers of Pakistan and India met today on the sidelines of the SCO Summit in Ufa. The meeting was held in a cordial atmosphere. The two leaders exchanged views on issues of bilateral and regional interest.

They agreed that India and Pakistan have a collective responsibility to ensure peace and promote development. To do so, they are prepared to discuss all outstanding issues.

Both leaders condemned terrorism in all its forms and agreed to cooperate with each other to eliminate this menace from South Asia.

They also agreed on the following steps to be taken by the two sides:

1. A meeting in New Delhi between the two NSAs to discuss all issues connected to terrorism.
2. Early meetings of DG BSF and DG Pakistan Rangers followed by that of DGMOs.
3. Decision for release of fishermen in each other's custody, along with their boats, within a period of 15 days.
4. Mechanism for facilitating religious tourism.
5. Both sides agreed to discuss ways and means to expedite the Mumbai case trial, including additional information like providing voice samples.

Prime Minister Nawaz Sharif reiterated his invitation to Prime Minister Modi to visit Pakistan for the SAARC Summit in 2016. Prime Minister Modi accepted the invitation.

Islamabad
10 July 2015

Annex V - Joint Statement of 9 December 2015

JOINT STATEMENT OF PAKISTAN AND INDIA - 9 DECEMBER 2015

The External Affairs Minister of India, Smt. Sushma Swaraj led the Indian delegation to the Fifth Ministerial Conference of the Heart of Asia-Istanbul Process in Islamabad on December 8-9, 2015. She called on the Prime Minister of Pakistan, Mr. Muhammad Nawaz Sharif and held discussions with Adviser to the Prime Minister on Foreign Affairs, Mr. Sartaj Aziz.

2. The EAM and the Adviser condemned terrorism and resolved to cooperate to eliminate it. They noted the successful talks on terrorism and security related issues in Bangkok by the two NSAs and decided that the NSAs will continue to address all issues connected to terrorism. The Indian side was assured of the steps being taken to expedite the early conclusion of the Mumbai trial.

3. Both sides, accordingly, agreed to a Comprehensive Bilateral Dialogue and directed the Foreign Secretaries to work out the modalities and schedule of the meetings under the Dialogue including Peace and Security, CBMs, Jammu & Kashmir, Siachen, Sir Creek, Wullar Barrage/Tulbul Navigation Project, Economic and Commercial Cooperation, Counterterrorism, Narcotics Control and Humanitarian Issues, People to People exchanges and Religious Tourism.

Islamabad
December 9, 2015

Annex VI Agreement on consular access between Pakistan-India on 21 May 2008

No. 54471*

Pakistan
and
India

Agreement on consular access between the Government of the Islamic Republic of Pakistan and the Government of the Republic of India. Islamabad, 21 May 2008

Entry into force: *21 May 2008 by signature, in accordance with its provisions*

Authentic text: *English*

Registration with the Secretariat of the United Nations: *Pakistan, 17 May 2017*

**No UNTS volume number has yet been determined for this record. The Text(s) reproduced below, if attached, are the authentic texts of the agreement /action attachment as submitted for registration and publication to the Secretariat. For ease of reference they were sequentially paginated. Translations, if attached, are not final and are provided for information only.*

Pakistan
et
Inde

Accord sur l'accès consulaire entre le Gouvernement de la République islamique du Pakistan et le Gouvernement de la République de l'Inde. Islamabad, 21 mai 2008

Entrée en vigueur : *21 mai 2008 par signature, conformément à ses dispositions*

Texte authentique : *anglais*

Enregistrement auprès du Secrétariat des Nations Unies : *Pakistan, 17 mai 2017*

**Aucun numéro de volume n'a encore été attribué à ce dossier. Les textes disponibles qui sont reproduits ci-dessous sont les textes originaux de l'accord ou de l'action tels que soumis pour enregistrement. Par souci de clarté, leurs pages ont été numérotées. Les traductions qui accompagnent ces textes ne sont pas définitives et sont fournies uniquement à titre d'information.*

I-54471

[ENGLISH TEXT – TEXTE ANGLAIS]

Agreement on Consular Access

The Government of Pakistan and the Government of India, desirous of furthering the objective of humane treatment of nationals of either country arrested, detained or imprisoned in the other country have agreed to reciprocal consular facilities as follows:

(i) Each Government shall maintain a comprehensive list of the nationals of the other country under its arrest, detention or imprisonment. The lists shall be exchanged on 1st January and 1st July each year.

(ii) Immediate notification of any arrest, detention or imprisonment of any person of the other country shall be provided to the respective High Commission.

(iii) Each Government undertakes to expeditiously inform the other of the sentences awarded to the convicted nationals of the other country.

(iv) Each Government shall provide consular access within three months to nationals of one country under arrest, detention or imprisonment in the other country.

(v) Both Governments agree to release and repatriate persons within one month of confirmation of their national status and completion of sentences.

(vi) In case of arrest, detention or sentence made on political or security grounds, each side may examine the case on its merits.

(vii) In special cases, which call for or require compassionate and humanitarian considerations, each side may exercise its discretion subject to its laws and regulation to allow early release and repatriation of persons.

This agreement shall come into force on the date of its signing.

Done at Islamabad on 21 May, 2008 in two originals, in English language, each text being equally authentic.

Satyabrata Pal
High Commissioner of India
For the Government of the
Republic of India

Shahid Malik
High Commissioner of Pakistan
For the Government of the
Islamic Republic of Pakistan

Annex VII - UNCIP Resolution of 13 August 1948

Resolution adopted by the United Nations Commission for India and Pakistan on 13 August 1948.
(Document No.1100, Para. 75, dated the 9th November, 1948).

THE UNITED NATIONS COMMISSION FOR INDIA AND PAKISTAN
Having given careful consideration to the points of view expressed by the Representatives, of India and Pakistan regarding the situation in the State of Jammu and Kashmir, and Being of the opinion that the prompt cessation of hostilities and the correction of conditions the continuance of which is likely to endanger international peace and security are essential to implementation of its endeavours to assist the Governments of India and Pakistan in effecting a final settlement of the situation,

Resolves to submit simultaneously to the Governments of India and Pakistan the following proposal:

PART I
CEASE-FIRE ORDER

[A] The Governments of India and Pakistan agree that their respective High Commands will issue separately and simultaneously a cease-fire order to apply to all forces under their control in the State of Jammu and Kashmir as of the earliest practicable date or dates to be mutually agreed upon within four days after these proposals have been accepted by both Governments.

[B] The High Commands of Indian and Pakistan forces agree to refrain from taking any measures that might augment the military potential of the forces under their control in the State of Jammu and Kashmir. (For the purpose of these proposals '-forces under their control" shall be considered to include all forces, organised and unorganised, fighting or participating in hostilities on their respective sides).

[C] The Commanders-in-Chief of the Forces of India and Pakistan shall promptly confer regarding any necessary local changes in present dispositions which may facilitate the cease-fire.

[D] In its discretion, and as the Commission may find practicable, the Commission will appoint military observers who under the authority of the Commission and with the co-operation of both Commands will supervise the observance of the cease-fire order.

[E] The Government of India and the Government of Pakistan agree to appeal to their respective peoples to assist in creating and maintaining an atmosphere favourable to the promotion of further negotiations.

PART II
TRUCE AGREEMENT

Simultaneously with the acceptance of the proposal for the immediate cessation of hostilities as outlined in Part I, both Governments accept the following principles as a basis for the formulation of a truce agreement, the details of which shall be worked out in discussion between their Representatives and the Commission.

A.

(1) As the presence of troops of Pakistan in the territory of the State of Jammu and Kashmir constitutes a material change in the situation since it was represented by the Government of Pakistan before the Security Council, the Government of Pakistan agrees to withdraw its troops from that State.

(2) The Government of Pakistan will use its best endeavour to secure the withdrawal from the State of Jammu and Kashmir of tribesmen and Pakistan nationals not normally resident therein who have entered the State for the purpose of fighting.

(3) Pending a final solution the territory evacuated by the Pakistan troops will be administered by the local authorities under the surveillance of the Commission.

B.

(1) When the Commission shall have notified the Government of India that the tribesmen and Pakistan nationals referred to in Part II A2 hereof have withdrawn, thereby terminating the situation which was represented by the Government of India to the Security Council as having occasioned the presence of Indian forces in the State of Jammu and Kashmir, and further, that the Pakistan forces are being withdrawn from the State of Jammu and Kashmir, the Government of India agrees to begin to withdraw the bulk of their forces from the State in stages to be agreed upon with the Commission.

(2) Pending the acceptance of the conditions for a final settlement of the situation in the State of Jammu and Kashmir, the Indian Government will maintain within the lines existing at the moment of cease-fire the minimum strength of its forces which in agreement with the Commission are considered necessary to assist local authorities in the observance of law and order. The Commission will have observers stationed where it deems necessary.

(3) The Government of India will undertake to ensure that the Government of the State of Jammu and Kashmir will take all measures within their power to make it publicly known that peace, law and order will be safeguarded and that all human and political rights will be guaranteed.

C.

(1) Upon signature, the full text of the Truce Agreement or communique containing the principles thereof as agreed upon between the two Governments and the Commission, will be made public.

PART III

The Government of India and the Government of Pakistan reaffirm their wish that the future status of the State of Jammu and Kashmir shall be determined in accordance with the will of the people and to that end, upon acceptance of the Truce Agreement both Governments agree to enter into consultations with the Commission to determine fair and equitable conditions whereby such free expression will be assured.

The UNCIP unanimously adopted this Resolution on 13-8-1948.
Members of the Commission: Argentina, Belgium, Colombia, Czechoslovakia and U.S.A.

Annex VIII - UNSC Resolution of 23 December 1952

RESOLUTIONS ADOPTED AND DECISIONS TAKEN BY THE SECURITY COUNCIL IN 1952

RÉSOLUTIONS ADOPTÉES ET DÉCISIONS PRISES PAR LE CONSEIL DE SÉCURITÉ EN 1952

Part I. Questions considered by the Security Council under its responsibility for the maintenance of international peace and security

THE INDIA PAKISTAN QUESTION[1]

98 (1952). Resolution of 23 December 1952

[S/2883]

The Security Council,

Recalling its resolution 91 (1951) of 30 March 1951, its decision of 30 April 1951 and its resolution 96 (1951) of 10 November 1951,

Further recalling the provisions of the United Nations Commission for India and Pakistan resolutions of 13 August 1948[2] and 5 January 1949[3] which were accepted by the Governments of India and Pakistan and which provided that the question of the accession of the State of Jammu and Kashmir to India or Pakistan would be decided through the democratic method of a free and impartial plebiscite conducted under the auspices of the United Nations,

Having received the third report, dated 22 April 1952,[4] and the fourth report, dated 16 September 1952,[5] of the United Nations Representative for India and Pakistan,

[1] Resolutions or decisions on this question were also adopted by the Council in 1948, 1949, 1950 and 1951.
[2] See *Official Records of the Security Council, Third Year, Supplement for November 1948*, document S/1100, para. 75.
[3] *Ibid., Fourth Year, Supplement for January 1949*, document S/1196, para. 15.
[4] *Ibid., Seventh Year, Special Supplement No. 2*, document S/2611 and Corr.1.
[5] *Ibid.*, document S/2783 and Corr.1.

Première partie. Questions examinées par le Conseil de sécurité en tant qu'organe responsable du maintien de la paix et de la sécurité internationales

LA QUESTION INDE-PAKISTAN[1]

98 (1952). Résolution du 23 décembre 1952

[S/2883]

Le Conseil de sécurité,

Rappelant sa résolution 91 (1951) du 30 mars 1951, sa décision du 30 avril 1951 et sa résolution 96 (1951) du 10 novembre 1951,

Rappelant en outre les dispositions qui figurent dans les résolutions de la Commission des Nations Unies pour l'Inde et le Pakistan en date du 13 août 1948[2] et du 5 janvier 1949[3], dispositions qui ont été acceptées par les Gouvernements de l'Inde et du Pakistan et qui prévoient que la question du rattachement de l'Etat de Jammu et Cachemire à l'Inde ou au Pakistan sera réglée par la voie démocratique d'un plébiscite libre et impartial, organisé sous les auspices de l'Organisation des Nations Unies,

Ayant reçu le troisième rapport du représentant des Nations Unies pour l'Inde et le Pakistan, en date du 22 avril 1952[4], ainsi que son quatrième rapport, en date du 16 septembre 1952[5],

[1] Question ayant fait l'objet de résolutions ou décisions de la part du Conseil en 1948, 1949, 1950 et 1951.
[2] Voir *Procès-verbaux officiels du Conseil de sécurité, troisième année, Supplément de novembre 1948*, document S/1100, par. 75.
[3] *Ibid., quatrième année, Supplément de janvier 1949*, document S/1196, par. 15.
[4] *Ibid., septième année, Supplément spécial n° 2*, document S/2611 et Corr.1.
[5] *Ibid.*, document S/2783.

1. *Endorses* the general principles on which the United Nations Representative has sought to bring about agreement between the Governments of India and Pakistan;

2. *Notes with gratification* that the United Nations Representative has reported that the Governments of India and Pakistan have accepted all but two of the paragraphs of his twelve-point proposals;[6]

3. *Notes* that agreement on a plan of demilitarization of the State of Jammu and Kashmir has not been reached because the Governments of India and Pakistan have not agreed on the whole of paragraph 7 of the twelve-point proposals;

4. *Urges* the Governments of India and Pakistan to enter into immediate negotiations under the auspices of the United Nations Representative for India and Pakistan in order to reach agreement on the specific number of forces to remain on each side of the cease-fire line at the end of the period of demilitarization, this number to be between 3,000 and 6,000 armed forces remaining on the Pakistan side of the cease-fire line and between 12,000 and 18,000 armed forces remaining on the India side of the cease-fire line, as suggested by the United Nations Representative in his proposals of 16 July 1952,[6] such specific numbers to be arrived at bearing in mind the principles or criteria contained in paragraph 7 of the United Nations Representative's proposal of 4 September 1952;[7]

5. *Records its gratitude* to the United Nations Representative for India and Pakistan for the great efforts which he has made to achieve a settlement and requests him to continue to make his services available to the Governments of India and Pakistan to this end;

6. *Requests* the Governments of India and Pakistan to report to the Security Council not later than thirty days from the date of the adoption of this resolution;

7. *Requests* the United Nations Representative for India and Pakistan to keep the Security Council informed of any progress.

Adopted at the 611th meeting by 9 votes to none, with 1 abstention (Union of Soviet Socialist Republics).[8]

[6] *Ibid.*, annex 3.
[7] *Ibid.*, annex 8.
[8] One member (Pakistan) did not participate in the voting.

1. *Approuve* les principes généraux sur la base desquels le représentant des Nations Unies s'est efforcé d'aboutir à un accord entre le Gouvernement de l'Inde et celui du Pakistan;

2. *Constate avec satisfaction* que le représentant des Nations Unies a fait savoir que les Gouvernements de l'Inde et du Pakistan avaient accepté l'ensemble de ses douze propositions[6] à l'exception de deux paragraphes seulement;

3. *Constate* que l'accord ne s'est pas fait sur un plan de démilitarisation de l'Etat de Jammu et Cachemire parce que les Gouvernements de l'Inde et du Pakistan n'avaient pas accepté l'ensemble du paragraphe 7 des douze propositions;

4. *Invite* les Gouvernements de l'Inde et du Pakistan à entamer immédiatement des négociations, sous les auspices du représentant des Nations Unies pour l'Inde et le Pakistan, afin d'aboutir à un accord sur les effectifs précis des forces armées à maintenir des deux côtés de la ligne de suspension d'armes à la fin de la période de démilitarisation, ces effectifs devant être de 3 000 à 6 000 hommes du côté pakistanais de la ligne de suspension d'armes et de 12 000 à 18 000 hommes du côté indien de la ligne de suspension d'armes, conformément à la proposition du représentant des Nations Unies en date du 16 juillet 1952[6]; en fixant ces effectifs, il conviendra de tenir compte des principes et des critères énoncés au paragraphe 7 de la proposition du représentant des Nations Unies en date du 4 septembre 1952[7]:

5. *Exprime sa reconnaissance* au représentant des Nations Unies pour l'Inde et le Pakistan pour les grands efforts qu'il a déployés afin d'aboutir à un règlement et l'invite à demeurer à la disposition des Gouvernements de l'Inde et du Pakistan à cet effet;

6. *Invite* les Gouvernements de l'Inde et du Pakistan à présenter un rapport au Conseil de sécurité dans un délai maximum de 30 jours à compter de la date d'adoption de la présente résolution;

7. *Charge* le représentant des Nations Unies pour l'Inde et le Pakistan de tenir le Conseil de sécurité au courant de l'évolution de la situation.

Adoptée à la 611e séance par 9 voix contre zéro, avec une abstention (Union des Républiques socialistes soviétiques)[8].

[6] *Ibid.*, annexe 3.
[7] *Ibid.*, annexe 8.
[8] Un des membres (Pakistan) n'a pas participé au vote

Annex IX - Pak-China Boundary Agreement of March 1963-1

THE BOUNDARY AGREEMENT BETWEEN CHINA AND PAKISTAN, 1963

The Government of the People's Republic of China and the Government of Pakistan;

Having agreed, with a view to ensuring to prevailing peace and tranquility on the border, to formally delimit and demarcate the boundary between China's Sinkiang and the contiguous areas the defence of which is under the actual control of Pakistan, in a spirit of fairness, reasonableness, mutual understanding and mutual accommodation, and on the basis of the ten principles as enunciated in the Bandung conference;

Being convinced that this would not only give full expression to the desire of the peoples of China and Pakistan for the development of good neighbourly and friendly relations, but also help safeguard Asian and world peace.

Have resolved for this purpose to conclude the present agreement and have appointed as their respective plenipotentiaries the following:

For the Government of the People's Republic of China; Chen Yi, Minister of Foreign Affairs;

For the Government of Pakistan; Mr. Zulfikar Ali Bhutto, Minister of External Affairs;

Who, having mutually examined their full powers and found them to be in good and due form, have agreed upon the following:

Article 1
In view of the fact that the boundary between China's Sinkiang and contiguous areas the defence of which is under the actual control of Pakistan has never been formally delimited, two parties agree to delimit it on the basis of the traditional customary boundary line including natural features and in a spirit of equality, mutual benefit and friendly co-operation.

Article 2
(One) In accordance with the principle expounded in Article 1 of the present agreement, the two parties have fixed, as follows the alignment of the entire boundary line between China's Sinkiang and the contiguous areas the defence of which is under the actual control of Pakistan:

(1) Commencing from its north-western extremity at height 5630 metres (a peak, the reference co-ordinates of which are approximately longitude 74 degrees 34 minutes east and latitude 37 degrees 03 minutes north), the boundary line runs generally eastward and then southeastward strictly along the main watershed between the tributaries of the Tashkurgan river of the Tarim river system on the one hand and tributaries of the Hunza river of the Indus river system on the other hand, passing through the Kalik Daban (Dawan), the Mintake Daban (pass), the Kharchanai Daban (named on the Chinese map only), the Mutsjilga Daban (named on the Chinese map only), and the Parpik Pass (named on the Pakistan map only), and reaches the Khunjerab (Yutr) Daban (Pass).

(2) After passing through the Khunjerab (Yutr) Daban (pass), the boundary line runs generally southward along the above mentioned main watershed up to a mountain-top south of this Daban (pass), where it leaves the main watershed to follow the crest of a spur lying generally in a southeasterly direction, which is the watershed between the Akijilga river (a nameless corresponding river on the Pakistan map) on the one hand, and the Taghumbash (Oprang) river and the Koliman Su (Oprang Jilga) on the other hand.

According to the map of the Chinese side, the boundary line, after leaving the southeastern extremity of this spur, runs along a small section of the middle line of the bed of the Keliman Su to reach its confluence with the Kelechin river. According to the map of the Pakistan side, the boundary line, after leaving the southeastern extremity of the spur, reaches the sharp bend of the Shaksgam or Muztagh River.

(3) From the aforesaid point, the boundary line runs up the Kelechin river (Shaksgam or Mistagh river) along the middle line of its bed to its confluence (reference co-ordinates approximately longitude 76 degrees 02 minutes east and latitude 36 degrees 26 minutes north) with the Snorbulak Daria (shimshal river or Braldu river).

(4) From the confluence of the aforesaid two rivers, the boundary line, according to the map of the Chinese side, ascends the crest of a spur and runs along it to join the Karokoram range main watershed at a mountain-top (reference co-ordinates approximately longitude 75 degrees 54 minutes east and latitude 36 degrees 15 minutes north) which on this map is shown as belonging to the Shorgulak mountain. According to the map of the Pakistan side, the boundary line from the confluence of the above-mentioned two rivers ascends the crest of a corresponding spur and runs along it, passing through height 6520 metres (21,390 feet) till it joins the Karakoram range

main watershed at a peak (reference co-ordinates approximately longitude 75 degrees 57 minutes east and latitude 36 degrees 03 minutes north).

(5) Thence, the boundary line, running generally southward and then eastward, strictly follows the Karakoram range main watershed which separates the Tarim river drainage system from the Indus river drainage system, passing through the east Mustagh pass (Mustagh pass), the top of the Chogri peak (K-2), the top of the broad peak, the top of the Gasherbrum mountain 8068, the Indirakoli pass (names on the Chinese maps only) and the top of the Teram Kankri peak, and reaches its southeastern extremity at the Karakoram pass.

(Two) The alignment of the entire boundary line as described in section one of this article, has been drawn on the one million scale map of the Chinese side in Chinese and the one million scale map of the Pakistan side in English which are signed and attached to the present agreement. (Not attached in this book)

(Three) In view of the fact that the maps of the two sides are not fully identical in their representation of the topographical features the two parties have agreed that the actual features on the ground shall prevail, so far as the location and alignment of the boundary described in Section one is concerned, and that they will be determined as far as possible by joint survey on the ground.

Article 3
The two parties have agreed that:
Wherever the boundary follows a river, the middle line of the river, the middle line of the river bed shall be the boundary line; and that
Wherever the boundary passes through Daban (pass), the water-parting line thereof shall be the boundary line.

Article 4

I. The two parties have agreed to set up, as soon as possible, a joint boundary demarcation commission. Each side will appoint a chairman, one or more members and a certain number of advisers and technical staff. The joint boundary demarcation commission is charged with the responsibility, in accordance with the provisions of the present agreement, to hold concrete discussions on and carry out the following tasks jointly:

(1) To conduct necessary surveys of the boundary area on the ground, as stated in Article 2 of the present agreement, so as to set up boundary markers at places considered to the appropriate by the two parties and to delineate the boundary line of the jointly prepared accurate maps.

(2) To draft a protocol setting forth in detail the alignment of the entire boundary line and the location of all the boundary markers and prepare and get printed detailed maps, to be attached to the protocol, with the boundary line and the location of the boundary markers shown on them.

II. The aforesaid protocol, upon being signed by the representatives of the Government of the two countries, shall become an annex to the present agreement, and the detailed maps shall replace the maps attached to the present agreement.

III. Upon the conclusion of the above-mentioned protocol, the tasks of the joint boundary demarcation commission shall be terminated.

Article 5
The two Parties have agreed that any dispute concerning the boundary, which may arise after the delimitation of the boundary line actually existing between the two countries shall be settled peacefully by the two parties through friendly consultations.

Article 6
The two Parties have agreed that after the settlement of the Kashmir dispute between Pakistan and India, the sovereign authority concerned will reopen negotiations with the Government of the People's Republic of China, on the boundary as described in Article Two of the present Agreement, so as to sign a formal Boundary Treaty to replace the present agreement:

Provided that in the event of that sovereign authority being Pakistan, the provisions of this agreement and the aforesaid Protocol shall be maintained in the formal Boundary Treaty to be signed between the Peoples Republic of China and Pakistan.

Ariticle 7
The present agreement shall come into force on the date of its signature.

Done in duplicate in Peking on the second day of March, 1963, in the Chinese and English language, both texts being eqully authentic.

Marshal Chen Yi,
Plenipotentiary of the
Government of the

Zulfikar Ali Bhutoo,
Plenipotentiary of the
Government of Pakistan

People's Republic of China

Annex X - UNSC Resolution of 6 June 1998

UNITED NATIONS

S

Security Council

Distr.
GENERAL

S/RES/1172 (1998)
6 June 1998

RESOLUTION 1172 (1998)

Adopted by the Security Council at its 3890th meeting, on 6 June 1998

The Security Council,

Reaffirming the statements of its President of 14 May 1998 (S/PRST/1998/12) and of 29 May 1998 (S/PRST/1998/17),

Reiterating the statement of its President of 31 January 1992 (S/23500), which stated, inter alia, that the proliferation of all weapons of mass destruction constitutes a threat to international peace and security,

Gravely concerned at the challenge that the nuclear tests conducted by India and then by Pakistan constitute to international efforts aimed at strengthening the global regime of non-proliferation of nuclear weapons, and also gravely concerned at the danger to peace and stability in the region,

Deeply concerned at the risk of a nuclear arms race in South Asia, and determined to prevent such a race,

Reaffirming the crucial importance of the Treaty on the Non-Proliferation of Nuclear Weapons and the Comprehensive Nuclear Test Ban Treaty for global efforts towards nuclear non-proliferation and nuclear disarmament,

Recalling the Principles and Objectives for Nuclear Non-Proliferation and Disarmament adopted by the 1995 Review and Extension Conference of the Parties to the Treaty on the Non-Proliferation of Nuclear Weapons, and the successful outcome of that Conference,

Affirming the need to continue to move with determination towards the full realization and effective implementation of all the provisions of the Treaty on the Non-Proliferation of Nuclear Weapons, and welcoming the determination of the five nuclear-weapon States to fulfil their commitments relating to nuclear disarmament under Article VI of that Treaty,

Mindful of its primary responsibility under the Charter of the United Nations for the maintenance of international peace and security,

S/RES/1172 (1998)
Page 2

1. Condemns the nuclear tests conducted by India on 11 and 13 May 1998 and by Pakistan on 28 and 30 May 1998;

2. Endorses the Joint Communique issued by the Foreign Ministers of China, France, the Russian Federation, the United Kingdom of Great Britain and Northern Ireland and the United States of America at their meeting in Geneva on 4 June 1998 (S/1998/473);

3. Demands that India and Pakistan refrain from further nuclear tests and in this context calls upon all States not to carry out any nuclear weapon test explosion or any other nuclear explosion in accordance with the provisions of the Comprehensive Nuclear Test Ban Treaty;

4. Urges India and Pakistan to exercise maximum restraint and to avoid threatening military movements, cross-border violations, or other provocations in order to prevent an aggravation of the situation;

5. Urges India and Pakistan to resume the dialogue between them on all outstanding issues, particularly on all matters pertaining to peace and security, in order to remove the tensions between them, and encourages them to find mutually acceptable solutions that address the root causes of those tensions, including Kashmir;

6. Welcomes the efforts of the Secretary-General to encourage India and Pakistan to enter into dialogue;

7. Calls upon India and Pakistan immediately to stop their nuclear weapon development programmes, to refrain from weaponization or from the deployment of nuclear weapons, to cease development of ballistic missiles capable of delivering nuclear weapons and any further production of fissile material for nuclear weapons, to confirm their policies not to export equipment, materials or technology that could contribute to weapons of mass destruction or missiles capable of delivering them and to undertake appropriate commitments in that regard;

8. Encourages all States to prevent the export of equipment, materials or technology that could in any way assist programmes in India or Pakistan for nuclear weapons or for ballistic missiles capable of delivering such weapons, and welcomes national policies adopted and declared in this respect;

9. Expresses its grave concern at the negative effect of the nuclear tests conducted by India and Pakistan on peace and stability in South Asia and beyond;

10. Reaffirms its full commitment to and the crucial importance of the Treaty on the Non-Proliferation of Nuclear Weapons and the Comprehensive Nuclear Test Ban Treaty as the cornerstones of the international regime on the non-proliferation of nuclear weapons and as essential foundations for the pursuit of nuclear disarmament;

11. Expresses its firm conviction that the international regime on the non-proliferation of nuclear weapons should be maintained and consolidated and

S/RES/1172 (1998)
Page 3

recalls that in accordance with the Treaty on the Non-Proliferation of Nuclear Weapons India or Pakistan cannot have the status of a nuclear-weapon State;

12. Recognizes that the tests conducted by India and Pakistan constitute a serious threat to global efforts towards nuclear non-proliferation and disarmament;

13. Urges India and Pakistan, and all other States that have not yet done so, to become Parties to the Treaty on the Non-Proliferation of Nuclear Weapons and to the Comprehensive Nuclear Test Ban Treaty without delay and without conditions;

14. Urges India and Pakistan to participate, in a positive spirit and on the basis of the agreed mandate, in negotiations at the Conference on Disarmament in Geneva on a treaty banning the production of fissile material for nuclear weapons or other nuclear explosive devices, with a view to reaching early agreement;

15. Requests the Secretary-General to report urgently to the Council on the steps taken by India and Pakistan to implement the present resolution;

16. Expresses its readiness to consider further how best to ensure the implementation of the present resolution;

17. Decides to remain actively seized of the matter.

Suggested Bibliography

Aiyar, Mani Shankar, Confessions Of A Secular Fundamentalist (New Delhi: Penguin Books, 2004).

Ali, Rao Farman, History of Armed Struggle in Kashmir (New Delhi: Jay Kay Books Kashmir, 2017).

Amin, Shahid M., Reminiscences of a Pakistani Diplomat (Karachi: Council on Foreign Relations, 2009).

Bazaz, Prem Nath, Truth about Kashmir (The Kashmir Democratic Union, 1950).

Burke, S.M., Pakistan's Foreign Policy: An Historical Analysis (Karachi: Oxford University Press, 1973).

Butt, Abdul Ghani, Beyond Me, Weaving yesterday's wavering with fragile threads into tomorrow (Srinagar: Gulshan Books Kashmir, 2016).

Davidsson, Elias, The Betrayal of India: Revisiting the 26/11 Evidence (New Delhi: Pharos Media & Publishing Pvt Ltd., 2017).

Dulat, A. S., Kashmir: The Vajpayee Years (Noida: HarperCollins Publishers, 2015).

Dutt, Barkha, The Unquiet Land: Stories from India's Fault Lines (New Delhi: Aleph Book Company, 2016).

Korbel, Josef, Danger in Kashmir (Princeton: Princeton University Press, 1954).

Kasuri, Khurshid Mahmud, Neither a Hawk Nor a Dove (Karachi: Oxford University Press, 2015).

Khurshid, Salman, The Other Side of the Mountain (New Delhi: Hay House Publishers, 2016).

Lamb, Alastair, Kashmir: A Disputed Legacy 1846-1990 (Karachi: Oxford Union Press, 1992).

Menon, Shivshankar, Choices: Inside the Making of India's Foreign Policy (Gurgaon: Penguin Random House, 2014).

Naqvi, Saba, Shades of Saffron: From Vajpayee to Modi (Chennai: Westland Publications Private Limited, 2018).

Nawaz, Shuja, Crossed Swords: Pakistan, Its Army, and the Wars Within (Karachi: Oxford University Press, 2008).

Noorani, A. G., The Destruction of Hyderabad (New Delhi: Tulika Books, 2013).

-----------------The Kashmir Dispute:1947-2012, 2 vols (New Delhi: Tulika Books, 2013).

Roy, Arundhati, Broken Republic (Karachi: Ushba Publishing International, 2011).

Saran, Shyam, How India Sees the World: Kautilya to the 21st Century (New Delhi: Juggernaut Books, 2017).

Singh, Jaswant, India at Risk (New Delhi: Rupa Publications Pvt. Ltd., 2013).

Small, Andrew, The China Pakistan Axis: Asia's New Geopolitics (Gurgaon: Random House, 2015).

Whitehead, Andrew, A Mission in Kashmir (New Delhi: Penguin Books India Pvt. Ltd., 2007).

About the Author

Ambassador **Abdul Basit** joined the Foreign Service of Pakistan in 1982. During his thirty-five years of diplomatic career he served in several Pakistan missions abroad including in Moscow, New York, Sana'a, Geneva and London. He also remained a spokesperson of the Pakistan Foreign Office for over three years before leaving for Germany in 2012 to take over as Pakistan ambassador in Berlin. His last assignment was as Pakistan high commissioner to India from 2014–17.

He served as president of the Islamabad Policy Research Institute (IPRI) from 2017–18, and is presently heading the Pakistan Institute for Conflict and Security Studies (PICSS).